From The Coal Mines of Derbyshire to Buckingham Palace

Thank you to our daughter Gale for fulfilling a promise made to her dad to complete his book.

Joan
X

From The Coal Mines of Derbyshire to Buckingham Palace

DOUGLAS BRADBURY MBE FWCF

Text Douglas Bradbury MBE FWCF and Judy Brown,
on behalf of StoryTerrace
Design Grade Design and Adeline Media, London
Copyright © Gale Walters

CONTENTS

PREFACE — 7

1. THE LONG ROWS — 11

2. DOWN THE PIT — 35

3. JOAN AND ME — 77

4. CHILDREN AND PIT PONIES — 113

5. A DERBYSHIRE FARRIER — 157

6. APPRENTICES — 207

7. FELLOW OF THE WORSHIPFUL COMPANY OF FARRIERS — 257

8. LECTURES AND LIVERY — 319

9. SILVER SHOES AND RACEHORSES — 389

10. ORTHOPAEDICS AND HONOURS — 459

EPILOGUE — 493

PREFACE

When Longfellow wrote the line, 'a smith, a mighty man is he', he could have been writing about Doug Bradbury. Doug's forge was not to be found, 'under a spreading chestnut tree', but in the centre of Clay Cross, a mining town in north Derbyshire.

Doug suffered life-changing injuries when he was 21 years old. It would have been easy for him to assume his disabilities meant he could not continue his career as a farrier. However, failure was not a word in his vocabulary, and he looked for ways to overcome adversity. Doug became a world-renowned farrier and a fine ambassador for his chosen profession. In the New Year Honours list of 31st December 2017, he was awarded an MBE in recognition of the outstanding contribution he made to farriery.

His wife Joan was always there to support and work with him on anything he decided to do. Their marriage was a true partnership that stood the test of time. His family meant everything to him and he was so proud of the achievements of his children and grandchildren. The birth of his first great-grandchild earlier this year gave him great joy.

Although Doug seemed easy-going, he had a keen sense of justice and did not suffer fools gladly. If he felt someone was wrong or not doing something they ought to be doing, he would say so in no uncertain terms.

Many people have the ability to laugh at others, but Doug was one of the few who are also able to laugh at themselves. When retirement beckoned, he began giving talks to local community groups about his life and work. The bookings snowballed, and he and Joan were soon fulfilling up to three engagements a week and raising thousands of pounds for local charities through their efforts. He expanded his Museum of Farriery and Local History, and the headline in the Derbyshire Times, 'Treasure-trove Derbyshire museum attracts world-wide interest', confirmed the high standard of the collection.

Clay Cross was Doug's lifelong home, but he and Joan loved to travel. Retirement gave them the opportunity to go further afield. They travelled the world, mainly on cruise ships. It was on one of these voyages that Doug became interested in painting. With his usual infectious enthusiasm, he was soon having his work published. Having more time meant he could also develop his skills in ornamental ironwork. His signature piece was a ram's head, a county emblem acknowledging his Derbyshire heritage. This design enhanced numerous pokers, chairs and wine carriers. Roses made of copper were also produced in large numbers, although each recipient was told it was an original design! Those of us fortunate enough to have some of these items have a lasting memory of a fine craftsman.

Doug was a charming, entertaining companion at any social occasion, and everyone felt better for having been in his company. He was a man who loved life and lived it to the full but always had time to help others along the way. Now you have the chance to go on a journey with a man who began his working life in the mines of Derbyshire and, by his own courage, conviction and hard work, achieved so much against all the odds.

It has been a great pleasure and privilege to write this introduction to Doug's autobiography. When the memories of those who knew him have faded, his life story will live on through these pages. Joan said that when she first read the manuscript it was like having Doug sitting next to her, and now he is waiting to share his remarkable story with you.

Edwena Bird JP
June 2020

1

THE LONG ROWS

I was born on 1st July 1937 at 37 Top Long Row, Clay Cross, Chesterfield, Derbyshire. I was the third surviving child of John Charles and Caroline Bradbury. My brother Charlie was 15 when I was born, my sister Annie was 12, and two other children had died at birth, so I was the baby of the family. My mother told me that one day while I was a baby in arms, a gypsy woman called at our house selling lace and lucky charms and also telling fortunes. She tried to sell Mum some lace for a shilling. Mum, who was very good at giving people the hard luck story, told the gypsy that she was finding it difficult to keep a home going and had no money for food, let alone lace. The gypsy said good morning and wished mum well, but before she left, she took a peep at the baby in her arms. I had blond curly hair, and for a short time in my life I must have looked quite a cherub. The gypsy said, "What a lovely baby," kissed a silver threepenny bit, placed it in my hand and promised, "This boy will never be short of money as long as he lives." Mum told me this story on many occasions. I am writing this account of my life in my 83rd year and I can honestly say that the gypsy was right. There have been times when my wife and I have been very short of money, but we have never been without it.

Top Long Row 1922

Bottom Long Row numbers 75 to 119

Street games

Mum, Dad and me with my cousin Ernest Maskill from Sunderland

Conkers in the school playground

Lining up after breaktime

The Long Rows, as they were known, were two terraces with 44 houses in each. The Clay Cross Company had built them in 1840 for its workforce after coal was discovered nearby in abundance. That was when Clay Cross started to become industrialised. Each house on the Long Rows had two rooms downstairs and two upstairs. They had gas lights in each of the two rooms downstairs: one in the kitchen area and one in the main room. Although the houses were only two-up two-down, they were home to very large families. And I mean large, with as many as 13 in one house (11 children plus the mum and dad). All the kids slept in one room in one bed. Nobody had an indoor toilet as the toilet blocks were across the yard. So the inevitable happened, and this meant that the smaller kids could swim before they could walk.

I had a friend along our row who was one of eleven children. The rest of us reckoned the reason there were so many of them was that their mum was a bit deaf. At bedtime their dad would say, "Shall I put the light out or what?" and their mum would say, "What?". At holiday times when the grandparents came to visit, Mum and Dad would get in bed with the children, and if Dad was a bit randy the kids had to link arms to stop them all falling out of bed. The doctor told their mum that if she did not stop having children it would kill her. So, their mum started to sleep downstairs and their dad upstairs. This went on for about a month until one night they met on the stairs. Their dad said, "Where are you going?" Mum replied, "Upstairs to die." Dad said, "That's funny, I was just on my way downstairs to kill you."

Every household paid rent of six shillings a week. When the rent man came to the first house in the row, the people inside would knock on the party wall. The walls were thin so the neighbours instantly got the message that they must lock the door, knock on the next wall and pretend they were not in. As the bolts went across one after another along the Long Rows, it was like a battery of guns going off.

In between the two rows of houses were the toilets and ash pits (dustbin holes). Each enclosure held six or more dustbins and we used them for goal posts, cricket stumps and any other games we could think of. On either side of these bin holes were three cubicles. These were the toilets, built as blocks of three with the number of your house on the toilet door. They didn't flush individually – the flush went automatically from one end to the other.

My friends from the Long Rows were Earnest Spencer (Bronco); brothers Raymond, George and Roy (Spooky) Fox; Ray, Peter, Colin and Ron (Sweetie) Greenfield; Joey Dye; Albert and Jimmy Cross; Roy and Denis (Spanner) Watson; Roy Whileman; Eric Morgan (Cobbler) and his brother George; Billy Tooley; Keith Bexston; George Bradbury; George Palfreyman; Dennis Cook; Ray Lunn; Jimmy Raywood; John (Chuck) Hawkins; Jimmy Bray; Norman Franks; and Charlie Kirman – though Charlie lived in a house on Eldon Street facing the Long Rows. Some of the girls that lived on the Long Rows and used to hang about with us were Kath and Clara Bradbury; Mary Parker; Lilley Bexton (Lulu); Freda Shaw; Jean and Pam Briden; Beryl Bexton; Edie and Freda Holmes; Dorothy Dye; Margaret Hudson; Brenda and Pat Franks; Joan and Barbara Smith; Faye Hawkins; and Edna Robinson.

There was a house in the middle of the bottom row where a lady called Mrs Mellor ran a small shop in her kitchen. She had only one leg and walked with a crutch so, if she were upstairs or out the back, it took her a long time to come through to the kitchen. When a gang of us lads went in, we'd have filled our pockets with sweets before she got there. She'd ask, "What do you lot want?" and most often it would be, "A penny candle, miss," because the candles were on the top shelf and she would have to go back out for the steps.

School

I don't need to tell you about my primary school as I wasn't there much. All us kids attended Clay Cross Secondary Modern in the town until we were 15. The teachers I remember from my last years in the senior boys included Mrs F. Clegg, D. Jones, R. Briggs, C. Milner, R. Gibbons, F. Owen and Miss Greaves, and a woodwork teacher by the name of Jerry. The headmaster was Mr Protherow. The school was run like a military camp. First whistle: stop, face front and stand at ease. Second whistle: spring to attention. Third whistle: move to your class lines and form a straight line. Fourth whistle: move off by the left foot and march to your classroom. When you got there you had to stand at ease at the back of your desk, wait for the command to sit, and then sit up straight. It was the same in reverse when you left the class to enter the playground or go home: wait for the command, stand up straight, turn to your right, and march out left foot first.

Not many of us boys attended school on a regular basis. We often played truant, although sometimes we ended up at school anyway when the school bobby caught us. He was a long thin fellow with only one arm and went by the name of Bobby Lester. When he caught you, he would seize you by the ear and bellow into it, "And why are you not in school?" I well remember being caught at the top of Holmgate Road on Mr Short's milk float. Milk was sold direct from the churn and was served out using a copper ladle in quarter-pint, half-pint and pint measures. We boys were there to give Mr Short a helping hand as well as to get a ride on the cart. On another occasion, Bobby Lester caught us when we had been potato picking on Bert Parr's farm at Stretton Hall. We were paid 12/6d (12 shillings and sixpence – that's 62 new pence) for four days' work on potatoes. Bobby Lester informed us he was going to see our parents and then prosecute us. He duly showed up at our front door and demanded to know what had been done with the money I had earned. Now, my mum Caroline was a big woman and afraid of nobody. She pointed to my feet and roared straight back: "New boots on his f... feet, so now you know. So, f... off and don't bother me. I have work to do."

If you had a day off school, you were meant to take a letter from your parents stating why you had not attended. That was me almost every week. You had to stay behind after assembly to explain yourself. The ones with notes went first.

"Where's your note, Bradbury?"

"Mother says if you want a note you will have to go and fetch it from her."

"Stand to the side, Bradbury." Next was Bronco Spencer. Same answer and he stood aside. Ray Spooky Fox, same again. The rest of them could carry on to their classes. Not producing a note earned you three strokes of the cane on each hand. I can assure you that used to warm your hands for a while.

This matter of attendance helps to explain why we were all in B classes.

I remember one teacher, Mr David Jones (Dedge is what we used to call him), who was a Welshman and rather small in stature. When he caned you, he would blow out his cheeks and bend the cane almost into a circle before snapping it down on your hand. One day he called Albert Cross out to the front for three on each hand. Albert was a well-made lad. He said, "You are not going to cane me." Dedge grabbed Albert's wrist and turned it palm up. In the same moment Albert spun round, put the schoolmaster's arm up his back and the schoolmaster on his arse. At this point Ralph Gibbons, the teacher from class 3A next door, heard the commotion and came in. He grabbed Albert and held him down whilst Dedge applied the cane.

The last class we were in was 4B and our form master was Frank Owen. One night some of the boys broke into railway property and stole some detonators. Lenny Whitmore held a detonator in his fingers and tried to light it with a cigarette. It blew off the end of one finger. We hurried him along to the doctor's surgery on High Street, where a lady who must have been the caretaker lived. It was late at night. She opened the door a crack and said, "What do you lot want?"

"Will you have a look at this, missis?"

By this time there was quite a lot of blood and she almost fainted. Lenny did get the attention he needed, but lost the end of his finger.

The problem the next day was how to dispose of the remaining detonator. The 4B classroom was in a separate building from the main school and was heated by a large black

Yorkshire range. It was cast iron and coal fired. We nominated Bronco Spencer to place the detonator on the fire. The plan was that when we all stood to attention at morning break, turned right and started to march out by the left foot, Bronco would be the last to leave. On his way past the Yorkshire range he would place the detonator on a piece of coal that had not yet caught fire.

It was a close thing. We had only just cleared the building when the Yorkshire range went off with a great 'BANG'. When the dust had settled, the big black grate was sat in the middle of the classroom floor. We were given the rest of the day off. The local colliery got the blame as it was decided there must have been a detonator that had not gone off and had been shovelled by mistake into the load of coal delivered to the school.

Fun and games

Out of school, we spent our time in and around the Long Rows. We had a range of artful hobbies. There was Bull Roaring, where you stuffed newspaper up a drainpipe and lit it. Also Window Tapping, where you tapped on windows from a long distance away using a small button tied to a bobbin of cotton. You fastened the bobbin to the frame by a drawing pin, pulled back the button then let it fly against the window pane. You could rely on this to wind up the people inside no end. Then we had the game of Cannon, which meant throwing a tennis ball from a distance of 10 or 12 yards at a set of nine-inch sticks arranged like cricket stumps. Another game was to balance a dustbin at an angle against someone's door at night, knock on the door and run for your life. Of course there was football, with as many as 15 to 20 a side. During the war we were all issued with gas masks, and lots of kids just turned these into footballs. For cricket we used the dustbins as wickets. When the ball happened to be hit over the rooftops into people's gardens, we found that somehow it always seemed to land in Jonnie Balls' gooseberry bushes or strawberry patch or whatever other fruit was in season at the time.

Other games included Rally Co and Up Stick a Bum, which was something that was done with frogs and cats, but I will pass on those two. In the summer we would go down to Kennings Park, where there used to be a paddling pool about halfway along the park for the smaller kids and then a stream running through the lower end of the park. Part of the stream had been made wider and dammed up with concrete, making a small waterfall and a pool about three feet deep at one end. We called this the dosher and you could take a swim in it if you were brave enough, along with the minnows and bullhead fish.

Swimming baths

If you could afford fourpence, you could visit the Miners Welfare ground and go in the swimming baths. The baths were run by Mr and Mrs Scothern in a large tin shed. It cost threepence to go in the baths and the penny left over was for an Oxo in the Miners Welfare. When you entered the shed, it was boys to the left and girls to the right. Most of us had swimming trunks which our mothers had knitted from wool, and when they were wet they would hang down to your knees. When you asked your mum for a towel for the baths, she would give you a square block of Fairy soap as well and tell you to get a wash whilst you were in the deep end. Now the problem was that the swimming pool rules forbade you to use the pool for washing yourself, but we had our mothers at us and could only do as we were told. What to do with the soap was a problem, as it was always a big chunk of Fairy. We solved it by putting the block in our trunks. That made the girls look. They must have thought the boys from the Long Rows were big lads. The method was to wash yourself in the four-foot end and then swim off to where it was more crowded so the suds got dispersed.

Bath night

At home we had a tin bath, which had to be filled from the copper in the kitchen and topped up from the one-gallon boiler on the Yorkshire range. The bath was placed in front of this range on bath nights and the whole family would take turns to use the same water; first Dad then the rest of us. On the Rows we were all poor, but there were some less fortunate than us who did not have a tin bath and would use a large second-hand beer barrel, which took a very long time to fill. They climbed into it from a chair and had to wash themselves standing up. A barrel was a difficult thing to store in a small house, and if it was not fastened down you would soon find it being used as a goal post or cricket stump.

Local cinemas

If you wanted to go to the pictures, you had a choice. There was the Parochial School on the left-hand side as you entered Clay Cross at the traffic lights on the A61. They always showed a main film and a weekly serial called The Clutching Hand. You should have heard the screams when the filmstrip broke and plunged the place into total darkness. It was always the girls in the audience who screamed – when the lads tried to grab something that they should not grab and found more than one hand where no hand should be.

The second picture house was the Ritz at Pilsley. Mr Hayward the projectionist had only one arm. It cost threepence to go in on a Saturday morning, and the show followed the same format as at the Parochial School, with one main film and a weekly serial. The main film was usually a Western starring Roy Rogers, Johnnie McBrown, Hopalong Cassidy or, of course, Gene Autry the Singing Cowboy. When the filmstrip broke, as it did quite often, there was total chaos in total darkness. Like at the Parochial School, girls would be screaming and a loud voice would shout out, "You bastards from Clay Cross, shut up and be quiet or you are going out." There was also a picture house we used to visit at Grassmoor. It was called the Roxie and stood next to the Boot and Shoe pub, at the junction where you come up from Hag Hill at Tupton.

Hopalong Cassidy

Roy Rogers

The billiard hall

In winter we used to visit the billiard and snooker hall on Broadleys, which had originally been a cinema. It was run by a small, very bow-legged man called Edgar. It was always warm in there, with big cast-iron pipes all the way around, fired by a large boiler in the cellar under the old stage. On the stage were two 6' x 3' tables for youngsters to play on. You paid threepence for half an hour. When the time was up, Edgar would flash the lights on and off several times and that meant you had to return the balls to his office. Getting down to the stage was a fair way for Edgar to come, as he had to hobble past eight full-size tables, four on each side, where the cinema seats would once have been. If a youngster climbed on the tables to reach a shot, everyone else would shout out, "He is riding the table, Edgar!" If you did not come off after the lights were flashed, Edgar would quietly come on the stage, not say a word, go down the stairs to the cellar and have a pee on the fire. The smell would come up through the floorboards and clear the stage in seconds.

The Clay Cross drill hall

During the war years there was a military camp for paratroopers at the drill hall, the one that sits beside the A61 just as you leave Clay Cross. We used to go along there collecting cap badges and anything we could lay our hands on. Just for fun, some of the troops would grab hold of us and toss us in a blanket. Half a dozen men would seize a blanket, put a kid in the middle and throw him up in the air, sometimes as high as a telegraph pole.

The miners' wives in the Long Rows would invite the troops to join them on a Sunday to share what food they had for Sunday lunch. This became a regular thing, and many a time the camp postman would bring out large joints of meat for the wives in the Long Rows to cook on Sundays. Thanks to the paratroopers, the people of the Rows did not go short of much.

After the troops were posted abroad, this camp was made into a prisoner of war camp. It housed German and Italian prisoners, who were allowed out to work on the land. They used to make all sorts of things for the local children round about Christmas time. One of the German prisoners got a local girl pregnant. When she gave him the news, he replied, "This is good. You must call the baby Herr Fritz in memory of the Fatherland." At this the girl told him what she thought of him. She added that the rash that would appear on his penis and balls in few days' time he could call German measles in memory of the Motherland.

The pawn shop

This was not a sex shop. Near the Long Rows on High Street was a pawnbroker's shop with its three brass balls hanging over the door. The owner of this property was Francis W. Campbell; at a later date it was sold to Kendrick Fieldsend. On Monday mornings our mum would look out anything she might take to Mr Campbell to get a loan on. I remember taking him sheets from the bedding and even mum's wedding ring. He would loan her six shillings to be paid back by Friday noon, and that was just to buy food.

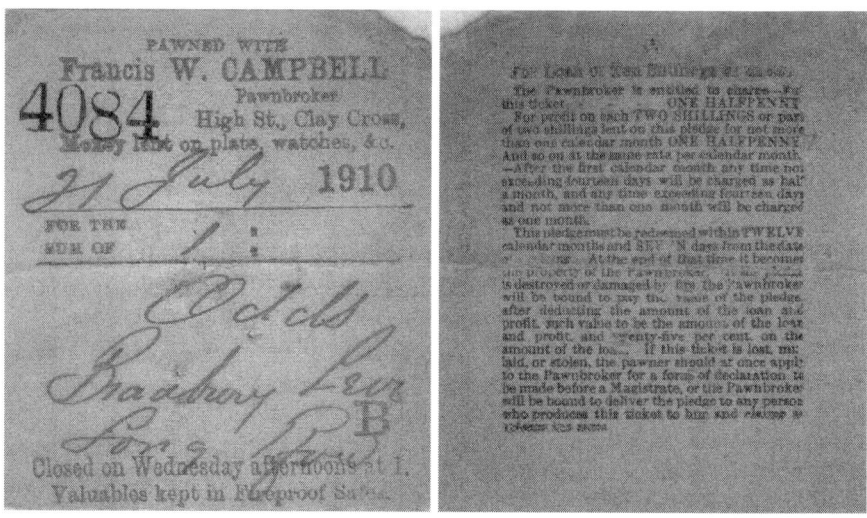

Pawn shop tickets

The army cadets at Clay Cross

In 1954, we heard that the local army cadets were going to a camp by the seaside at Mablethorpe for one week in the summer. They were to travel on army lorries and it was only five shillings for the week. At 14 years old we were very impressed and thought that must be a bargain. So we all joined the army cadets. When we turned up at the drill hall, we were given a uniform and taught rifle drill and how to fire a gun. We also learned marching in line, or 'foot slogging' as it was better known.

Earnest Spencer (Bronco) had a problem with his head. He could not stop it from shaking and therefore had difficulty in keeping his beret on.

It was not long before we were setting off to Mablethorpe in the lorries. On the first day you were given a cup, plate, knife and fork. They were all covered in thick grease and had to be dipped in boiling water to remove it. Then you got a sack to fill with straw for your bed.

Doug in his army cadet uniform

On day two we were to go on manoeuvres, but there was a shortage of rifles and that meant one gun and one bullet (blank) for every three lads. We made Bronco carry the gun because he was the smallest. He carried it for over three miles until we came to a stream. The rest of us jumped over, but Bronco fell in. He went right under so all you could see was his beret floating on the surface. We rescued him and carried on a further mile. Just when Bronco was about to have a chance to fire the gun he had been carrying, the marshal called, "All out! Return to camp." Bronco threw the gun on the floor, shouted "F.... you all!" and walked off.

Peeping Toms go piking

We were messing about one Sunday afternoon when we spotted a couple going for a walk. We decided to follow them at a distance. They had not gone very far when they got down in the grass at the back of a hedge. It was like being in the army cadets: a line of boys down on all fours and crawling up the hedgerow in Indian file to see what we could see. As we wriggled along, the person in the lead would reach back to touch the one behind, signalling "Hold and be quiet." Well, Bronco was behind me and as I reached back I must have put my hand in some dog shit. I did not realise until I touched Bronco on the forehead to hold back. He said, "Doug, there's a smell of shit." I looked back to see Bronco had a lump of it on his head. We all fell about laughing. At this point the people we were piking stood up and shouted, "Have you lot seen enough?" We jumped up and ran for our lives.

Please leave the church building

Us lads only ever wore hobnail boots or clogs on our feet out of school. Clogs were 2/6d a pair from Mr E. Cusson, master cobbler, in his shop on Lower High Street. None of the local youth clubs would allow us to join as they said our footwear would damage the dance floor. So we stayed out roaming the streets. That was until we met a lady by the name of Mrs Betty Belfield, whose father was the preacher at the local Baptist chapel. Mrs Belfield was small and very pretty. She suggested that we form a bible class in her father's church. This church had a stone floor so we could not damage it. I'm not sure that any of the bible stories stuck in our heads, but I got a signed book off the preacher which is still in my possession. There was always a cup of tea and a bun, and we rather liked going to this Sunday school.

Mrs Belfield started taking us to South Wingfield Baptist Church in her father's car, eight or nine of us in a Morris Minor. We thought this was great – we had never been in a car or to South Wingfield before, and for about a year we kept turning up for the rides. One Sunday in the bible class Mrs Belfield was sitting on a large stool reading to us. Her legs were crossed and the book was on her knee. Now from where we sat you could see her knickers, the bloomer type that go part way down the lady's thighs. You can imagine how a sight like that can affect a young lad. Funny things happen to his anatomy. This became obvious when I stood up.

"Douglas, what is the matter with you?" she asked.

"The devil is in me today, miss."

"Get out of the building now!"

You could say we were expelled from Sunday school – that must be a first.

Uncle Harry

My mother's brother Harry lived at Stonebroom and worked at the Clay Cross Gas Works. He used to catch his bus, the Blue Midland General, at the top of High Street opposite the Victoria Buildings to go back to his home in Stonebroom. He lived alone and never married, but he did father three children and was known as 'the Duke' in Stonebroom.

When Harry's mother (my grandmother) died, he burnt her will and claimed everything. My mother asked him about the will but he threw an inkwell at her, which cut her over the right eye and left a blue scar that remained the rest of her life. Nevertheless, during the winter months Mum used to cook him a dinner every night and take it up to the bus stop for him. One night she came back from the bus stop and told my dad that she felt sorry for Harry going home to a cold house. "Can't he come and live with us and share the back bedroom with our Doug?" Dad agreed and Uncle Harry moved in.

Harry's regular routine was to go up to the Red Lion pub every night for two pints and get back for 10 o'clock. We were never late to bed as Dad needed to be up for work at 4.30am every day. I had to share a double bed with my uncle. Every night when he came to bed he would rub my leg vigorously and say, "Are you warm enough?" I thought, *Bloody hell, what next?* I took to lying halfway up the wall and learned to sleep with one eye open. One day a parcel was delivered for Mum, and I saw it was wrapped in a thin strip of corrugated cardboard. I discreetly removed the cardboard and laid it under the bottom sheet of our bed on Harry's side. The next morning when my uncle woke up, he noticed red lines all the way down his back from his neck to his heel. He screamed for my mother. "Caroline, what's this on my back?" Mum said she didn't know but would send for Doctor Hanratty. The doctor did not know what it was either. I thought I ought to get rid of that piece of card as soon as possible. They never did find out about it, but I still continued to sleep with one eye open.

Dad gets injured underground

One day in 1945, I came home from school to hear the news that my dad had been buried down the coalmine. The man working next to him had taken out the wrong prop, and the roof fell in. Dad's friends dug him out from under tons of rock. His right arm was broken at the elbow joint but he was lucky to escape anything worse. The elbow was so swollen that the nurses at the hospital could not put it into a plaster cast and just gave him a collar and cuff bandage. They never washed his arm and it was still covered in coal dust. He was told the arm must remain in that position for at least two to three weeks. After a short time, it began to smell. I shall not go into detail, but it took a lot of sorting out.

Sadly, that was the end of my dad's underground working life, as the injury left the arm deformed and it would never go straight again. He was transferred to a job on the pit top and offered a small amount of compensation. He had the choice of taking the compensation either in a lump sum as a final settlement or as a payment of 12/6d (72.5p) a week for life.

He chose the 12/6d a week, and this turned out well for him as he lived to be 86 and the pension used to rise with the cost of living. Well done, Dad!

2

DOWN THE PIT

I leave school

When we left school, my mates and I each got a leaving certificate. The headmaster's parting words were, "Heaven help you, as none of you lot will amount to anything." I would have liked to join the army, possibly one of the Guards regiments, but at our school you didn't get a say in your choice of career. Boys from the Long Rows were born to be miners. When I asked why I couldn't try for the army instead of mining, Dad said "Why? We have kept you 15 years and now it's your turn to put some money back into this household. You are going down the pit, my lad."

So, off I went for an interview, along with my school mates from the Long Rows, to Park House Colliery, or Catty Pit as it was known. Why it had the name Catty Pit, I am told, was that one day a miner's wife was packing her husband's lunch box and did not know what to put in it as they were short of money. She did have a small tin of cat food in the larder, so she made his sandwiches with cat meat. Her husband ate and enjoyed the sandwiches but later broke his neck trying to lick his arse – and that, they said, was the reason for the name.

Parkhouse Colliery (Catty Pit) as seen from the top of the pit top, showing the blacksmith's shop next to the pond

Supplies arrive in the pit bottom

A pony pulling coal tubs to the pit bottom

Also, in line for the interview were A. Cross, E. Spencer, R. Greenfield, L. Harvey, D. Green, D. Burdett, R. Burdett, G. Cave, R. Fox, J. Dye and R. Watson. The training officer who interviewed us was Mr. H. Reeves, alongside Mr. R. Carter the mine manager, and they signed us all up. I really don't think they can have realised what a motley crew they were getting. We had to start by attending the new training centre at Grassmoor Colliery for a 16-week course. This was a brand-new facility, the old one at Williamthorpe Colliery having closed. The first day we arrived at Grassmoor, we were given a pair of safety boots, a boiler suit and a safety helmet. We wore the kit with a swagger – we were so proud now to be out of school and part of the British work force and the mining industry. We even travelled home on the bus in our new colliery rig-outs. We wanted to show the public we were working men and no longer kids.

Our head instructor was Philip Hickin. One of the first jobs we completed for Mr. Hickin at Grassmoor was to build a training gallery on the pit top. It stood on part of the old tip site and was made up of 10-foot steel arches at one yard apart, about the size of a typical tunnel bore, filled in with wooden boards and then back-filled with rubble. The purpose was to simulate underground conditions, and it meant a lot of shovel work. We would spend the morning making the tunnel and the afternoon in the classroom. When the first gallery was finished, it was fully equipped with a coal-cutting machine, rail tracks for the coal tubs to run on, and ponies. These training galleries we built remained standing right up until 2006, when they were dismantled.

At the end of the course we all had to sit an end-of-term

examination. I won a prize: a leather-cased shaving kit and an invitation to go on for further training in order to join the maintenance staff at the colliery. At school I had never won anything but stripes from the cane – maybe I wasn't as thick as they thought. But maintenance staff like fitters and electricians had to work longer hours for less money, and my father said, "No way. You're going underground, lad, and that's the end of the matter." Back at Catty Pit after this training course, we were met by Abel Jones, the safety officer. He showed us the baths and assigned us each a locker. I got the one directly above my father's.

Holiday pay

After the first week's work at the pit, we lined up for our wage packets. We couldn't believe what we found in them – almost £12. Just before we finished our initial training at Grassmoor Centre, the Park House Colliery had had its annual holiday. No one had told us we would be getting holiday pay, and my dad did not think it possible as we had only been there a week. He made me go back and enquire if it was correct before he and Mum would accept any of it for my board and lodging. The wages clerk said the money was ours to keep and do as we wished with. So, all us mates agreed to go to Blackpool for a week. This was to be our very first holiday by the sea, and we set off in style by train from Chesterfield, a brave band of young men out to have a good time.

Off to Blackpool 1952. Don Green, Doug, Roy Burdett, George Cave and Don Burdett

Don Green, Doug, Geoff Sims and the girls from Leeds

The first place we went to at Blackpool was the funfair. It didn't take long to meet some girls from Leeds queuing up for the rides. And not long after that, we were given to understand that we could all look forward to a bit of rumpy pumpy by the end of the week, providing we had protection. The next question was: who dare go into the chemist for the goods? We all went in twice and came out with toothbrushes. After a good deal of sweating and shuffling, we made it into the shop a third time, blurted out "One of them packets, please," and came out at top speed patting our pockets down. After all that, the girls never showed up. So, we were all left with a pack of three and our cherries still intact. We blew some of the goods up like balloons on the train on our way home.

The girls that never turned up, even though each of us had a toothbrush

'Not a plaything'

I had worn a dark green suit to go off on holiday, and Mum's first job next Monday morning was to do the washing and press the trousers. In the front of my trousers there was a small pocket and I had forgotten that I had left a little envelope in there. When I got up at 5.45am that morning for work – well, you can imagine the scene. Dad stood stiffly in front of the fire. In theatrical slow-motion Mum held the packet aloft, opened it and unrolled the contents.

"What do you think you are doing with this thing?"

"Just having a bit of fun, Mum."

"You do not have fun with these things. Your father and I have never used these things in all the years we have been married."

I said I was sorry, and that Don Green had put it in my pocket as joke. Dad said I was to go off to work and he would sort me out when I came home. I went for the bus thinking I had got out of that one very neatly, especially at that time of the morning.

I did not realise that Don Green was going to be on the afternoon shift after we returned from Blackpool. He arrived at 2.15pm and had to collect his pit check before he came down the shaft. I was waiting to come up the shaft and we had to pass in the pit bottom.

"Hey up, Doug, thee father's just had 'old of me on the pit top for putting a Durex in thee pocket. I told him that it was not me and we all had some. Tha can get ready when tha goes home. Ha ha, best of luck Brad, thaw'll need it."

The fallout was that all the money I earned was to be handed over to Mum and she would give me ten shillings (50p) a week spending money. That limited my activities somewhat.

Early bird

Dad was a very early riser as he was on the regular day shift. Although he did not start until 7am, he was always up at 4.30am every day and Mum got up with him. He would catch the 5.45am bus to Danesmoor, but not before he had made sure that I was out of bed. I took the opposite approach: I loved my bed. I would get up to keep him happy and after he had gone I used to have a bit longer on the sofa. Most mornings I would miss the bus and have to get my bike out. That was not bad as it was all downhill on the way. But, coming back was a different matter and I think that's why they call them push bikes.

Dad worked on the pit surface at the shaft entrance. His first job of the day was to collect the pit checks (a small brass disc with your number on it). The miners would have two of these checks, one to be handed in on the way down and one on the way out. It was a safety rule to make sure no one was left in the mine after their shift.

After all the men had descended the shaft, Dad worked as a banksman. He would push the empty tubs onto the cage and they in turn would push the full ones off the cage and send them rolling along to the tippler machine. The tippler would spin the tubs up and over, emptying the coal down a chute to be screened, sorted and tipped into wagons.

Down the mine

The first time we apprentices went down the shaft was a day I shall remember the rest of my life. It was a 600-yard drop down a 12-foot diameter shaft. The winder would ease the cage off the blocks and pull a lever to set it off. The cage travelled so fast that you felt it left your stomach behind. This was a working mine, remember, and that was an everyday working speed. Stepping out at the pit bottom, we were told to make our way to the men stood waiting on the right-hand side further on. These were the deputies and overmen in charge of the different districts (geographical sections of the mine). If you looked an average sort of boy, you were usually given jobs in and around the pit bottom. If you looked big and strong, the deputies would pick you to work out in the districts, under supervision of course. A tall man beckoned me towards him. He was a deputy by the name of Bud Hamilton and he was in charge of the Tupton coal seam in the 3Cs district. The seam was some 4' 6' thick and the coal face was about two miles walk from the pit bottom.

My first job was in the tailgate (the return passage from the coalface end). They told me to fetch a pony from the underground stables, get its tub loaded up with supplies and drive it along to the end of the coalface conveyor belt, a distance of about two miles. The job I had was not a pleasant one as the tailgate was the return airway carrying gases and stale air from the coalface, and it filled with smoke and dust every time a shot was fired on the face. There was no time to pause and you learned right from the start to work fast; the supplies had to be there and ready the moment they were needed. They included steel props measuring 4' 6', steel W bars for holding up the roof, and wooden chock nogs 2' long and 6' by 6' square. The W bars were rods 6-8-inch-wide and about 4 feet long – long enough to reach over two men working side by side. The chock nogs were for building the packs to support the tunnel as the coal face moved forward. There were also wooden lids called dominoes, measuring 6 x 6 x 2 inches, which went on top of the steel props to stop the props and W bars from slipping. The ponies would set off down the low narrow passage, pulling their tubs on rails and guided from behind by their driver. They kept their heads down and pushed open the ventilation doors as they came to them. The driver couldn't stand upright but walked bent double, and the only light came from his headlamp. The passages twisted and turned so it was impossible to run a conveyor belt along their length effectively; that was why they used ponies to pull the tubs. It was the downhill stretches that caused the worst problems for the ponies. The loaded tubs, sometimes coupled in a train of four or five together, would push the pony forward. Its speed would increase, its head would come up and, if it crashed into the rock wall at a bend, the injuries could be disastrous.

Boys were not allowed on the coalface until they were 18 years old. But in many cases curiosity got the better of us and we went to look anyway as we wanted to see what was going on. The coalface was where the money was made and where we planned to end up. To think that only weeks ago we were sitting in school and were now hundreds of feet underground, watching men dig black diamonds (as the coal was called). We saw the coal-cutting machine in action: coming down the face, which was 4'6' high, cutting under the coal for about six feet and leaving a gap of some six to eight inches. This machine was a Samson, made by Jeffrey Diamond Ltd of Wakefield. A miner would put wooden wedges under the coal to support it. Another would drill holes in the coal face and pack them with dynamite linked to the detonator by wires. He would then retreat and fire the detonator. Six to eight yards would be blasted at a time, and the job of digging out those eight yards would be one man's stint for the day. Often working on hands and knees, he would shovel the coal onto the conveyor belt and then put up props and W bars to support the roof. The bars were shaped for maximum strength, but even so would twist under the weight of the tunnel roof. The miners would fit replacements and send the bent bars back on the conveyor belt to be straightened. This was to be my next job.

50 H.P. ELECTRIC CHAIN COAL CUTTER

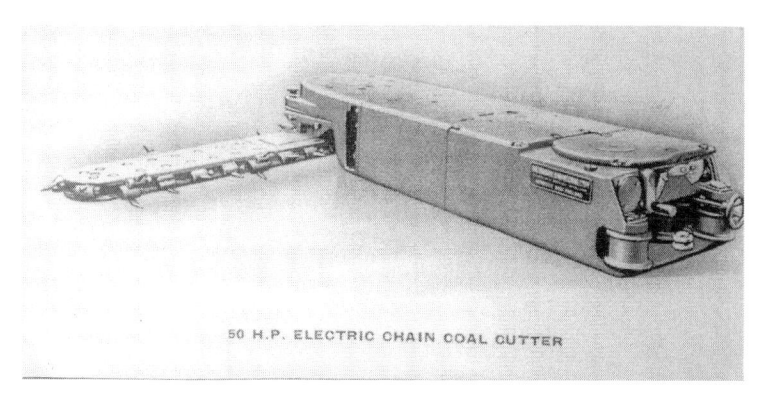

A coal-cutting machine in action

In the main gate

After several months in the tail gate I was sent to the top of the main gate quite near to the coal face. I was to work on the hydraulic bar press, straightening as best I could all the steel W roof bars and props that had bent under the weight of the tunnel roof. The main gate conveyor carried the coal from the two face conveyors, one from the left and one from the right. The man who operated the switch for all three conveyors was Mr. Earnest Elvin and we were to become the best of friends. Earnest was the belt repair man as well. When there was no trouble with the belt, he would give me a hand to get all the bars ready to be returned to the face. If too many came together, they would stick fast and Earn would have to stop the conveyors. Stopping the belt would madden the deputies and the overman so they would bark at us, "Hurry up! You are holding up production."

Get them off!

Now, there was an easy way of getting the props from the conveyor. There were three rollers under the rubber conveyor belts at intervals of about four feet. When a prop was midway over the roller, if you pressed on the back end you could flick it off quite easily.

One day the props were coming off the coalface thick and fast. Normally I would pull the two wires above my head to stop the conveyor very briefly whilst I got them all off, or if Earn saw that I was in trouble he would stop the belt for me. On this particular morning, the overman Dick Nutall stood by my side. He was a pain in the arse, always screaming and shouting, "Get that one and that one and don't stop the f... belt! Come on, move yourself faster."

As I said, there was a knack in how to get the props off the belt: a quick flick and the prop was on the floor. Unfortunately, on this day one of the larger props came off the face and along the conveyor, and the quick flick accidentally landed it across Mr. Nuttall's foot on the part that was not covered by the steel protector. Well, he jumped and did a dance, screaming and shouting "F... hell, it's broken my foot!" He called me and Earn all the names under the sun and finally "F... you all, I am going home." Dick Nuttall, overman for the 3Cs district, was off work after that for several weeks and all fell peaceful at the hydraulic bar press.

Earn used to stop behind after the shift had finished to do any belt repairs that were needed before the afternoon shift started, and he would also carry on with repairs on Sunday mornings until 12 noon. Sundays were paid as double time, so when he asked me if I would help him, I jumped at the chance. We soon became very close friends and he was like a father to me.

Roof bars being sent from the coalface to be straightened

Hold too tight – Earn goes white

On Friday nights a few of us used to go to the drill hall at Ashgate in Chesterfield to watch the wrestling. It cost two shillings and six pence (2/6d) and a shilling each way on the bus. When I got to work on the Saturday morning Earn would ask what sort of a night it had been and then, after the deputy had done his rounds, would say, "Show me the holds." One Saturday we were going through some of the holds, like the Boston Crab, the Half Nelson and then the Scissors. "What's the Scissors?" said Earn.

I said, "That's where you put your legs around your opponent's waist and cross your feet and squeeze, and hopefully your opponent will submit."

Earn asked me to give a demonstration. I squeezed my legs hard round his waist. Earn said "Gooooooood Hooooooood" and fell to the floor looking very pale. Two days later we found he had two broken ribs. After that we gave up the demonstrations and just used to talk about our night out at the drill hall.

Part-time job

My mum always did her shopping at the Star Tea Company on the High Street, Clay Cross, where Arthur Johnson was the manager. I used to get back home from the pit at around 3.30pm, and one day Mum informed me that Mr. Johnson wanted a delivery boy two evenings a week on Thursday and Friday and also Saturday afternoon. She informed me, "I have told him that you will do the job. He will pay you twelve shillings and sixpence a week, bike and clips provided, and you start this Thursday afternoon at 4.30pm."

My brother, sister and I were brought up not to answer back, and if you saw the size of our mother Caroline you would understand why. Tall and well overweight at about 14 stone, she was a big woman. Dad was not much smaller, so you see why we did as we were told.

When I arrived at the Star Tea Company on Thursday I was taken to see the transport. It was standing on the pavement outside the shop to advertise the company's services. Well, this delivery bike was as old as me and twice as heavy. It was the sort of bicycle you sometimes find these days in antique shops, the type with a small front wheel and a big wicker basket on the front. On the bar between the seat and handlebars was a steel plate with the shop's name and phone number, all adding to the weight. Shifting that bike took a lot of legwork. I would hang around the shop until the customers finished choosing their groceries and asked for a home delivery. At that point I would spring into action.

The type of bicycle I used

Mr. Johnson told me I was meant to do local deliveries only, and it was not too bad a job as long as it stayed local. One Saturday a customer came in, bought one bottle of Bulmer's cider, and asked could she have it delivered. This woman lived at Ashover Road, Tupton. I thought, *Bloody hell, that's a long way with one bottle in this big basket.* The route was down Holmgate Road to North Street, which in those days was just a country lane with a stream running alongside it all the way. It was a beautiful Saturday afternoon, so I thought I would take a rest by the stream. Feeling a bit thirsty, I carefully opened the bottle by wetting the label to peel it off and then unscrewing the cap. I drank my fill, topped up the bottle from the stream and carried on to Tupton. This woman did not tip and even gave me an empty to take back for her. However, that was the last home delivery she asked for, and my area became that bit smaller.

One Saturday Mrs. Froggatt came to the store and bought a small cream sandwich cake, value one shilling (10p). She asked for it to be delivered to her house. I was round the back when a voice called out: "Doug, got a delivery for you on the Mickley housing estate." Now, this estate is on the way to Alfreton on the A6 out of Clay Cross, about three-and-a-half miles from the shop. The road runs along the top of Stretton and past Ogston reservoir. The wind along there really blows and you could find yourself pedalling hard and not getting anywhere. Recalling how big and heavy the delivery bike was, I thought it would be a good idea if I were to take the order on my own bike, which was a racing model with drop handlebars. I asked the manager Mr. Johnson if that would be OK and he agreed. He said I might even get a cup of tea off the lady for delivering her cake. He did not know, and I did not tell him, that my bike had no pannier or basket to put the cream cake in. I improvised by tying it under the seat, and really did take great care of that cake as I made my way to Mickley through the wind and rain. When I arrived, there was no one in. That meant there was no cup of tea and no tip and there was also nowhere to leave the cake. So I gently folded it in half, careful to remove the luscious excess cream that was coming from the sides, and then inserted it in the letter box – just to be sure that the lady got her order.

Needless to say, I was not asked to do any more deliveries to Mickley. My delivery area was getting smaller every week. My plan was to get it down to the three streets around the Star Tea Company. I reckoned three streets was plenty for a wage of 12/6d a week, especially as Caroline held out her hand for that as well as my wage from the pit.

A new shop girl

Now that the delivery rounds were over a more reasonable area, I had a little more time to chat to the girls who worked in the shop. These were Mary Finch, Janet Revel, Joan Row and a new girl from Lower Pilsley, a lovely-looking 15-year-old with beautiful auburn hair. She was very shy, and her name was Joan Whitworth. I could not take my eyes off her. Mary Finch noticed, and I had to admit to her that Joan Whitworth was a bit of all right. Before long the rest of the girls were egging us on to go on a date. We had one date, then another, and soon Joan and I were an item. That girl was later to become my lovely wife, and you could say that we met over the bacon slicer.

My girlfriend Joan Whitworth

The Star Tea Company was Joan's first job after leaving school. When she turned 18, Mr. Johnson the manager gave her notice to quit. She was very upset when she came to tell me about this, so I went to see Mr. Johnson to ask why he had sacked her. He told me that when any member of staff reached the age of 18 he would have to start paying their national insurance stamps and it was better for the company accounts if he just employed school leavers to avoid paying this levy. Now, I was an 18-year-old full of life, and it did not take much to fire me up in those days. I blew my top, told him to stick his grocery orders up his arse and threw my bike clips on the desk.

He said, "What about your deliveries this weekend?"

I repeated what I already told him but a little stronger, and walked out of the Star Tea Company with my girl.

Soon after that, Joan got a job on the Christmas-card counter at Woolworths. Our courting was going strong now. One night I found Joan crying and, when I enquired why, she told me that every time one of the floor walkers went past he would get on at her to keep tidying the cards on the counter. I said he must not be allowed to throw his weight around like that and I would sort him out. I went down the next day after work and did just that. I asked Joan to point him out, walked over to him and told him to stop bullying her and leave her alone. "If not, I will take you outside and give you a bloody good hiding."

He said, "You do not think that I am going outside brawling with you?"

"You will not have a say because I will drag you out."

It must have been love that made me do it. But the same day,

Joan was asked to resign because "We do not like boyfriends threatening the staff." After that she got a job at Robinsons, became one of their indispensable angels and remained there for many years.

Back to the pit

I continued to work at the pit but working in all that dust and smoke did not do me any good. I had been there two years when I began to suffer with my chest. I had had a couple of attacks of pneumonia when I was younger. I think that maybe the lack of vitamins during the war years had brought it on. The latest attack happened when I was 17 and it made me so ill that my mother called the doctor. The treatment in those days was a course of M&B tablets (which had been credited with curing Winston Churchill's pneumonia during World War 2). The doctor advised earnestly that I should leave off working underground and take a job in the fresh air, but first take a holiday abroad. He suggested the Isle of Wight.

"Totally out of the question!" said Mum Caroline. The only time I had been out of Derbyshire was when I and my mates went to Blackpool for a week.

I returned to work down the pit after my illness, but had to go for a further check-up on my chest a few weeks later. The week when this was done, I was on the afternoon shift, so I went to work after seeing the doctor in the morning. Dad was on the cage entrance collecting the pit checks. He asked me what the doctor had said.

"He said like before – that I ought to leave the mine."

"Right", he said, "leave it to me."

When I got home that night Dad was sat at the table. "Right, my lad," he announced. "You start in the blacksmith's shop on Sunday morning. Report to the engine-wright, Mr. Les Willows."

Blacksmithing with Albert

I reported for work that Sunday at 7am. There were no buses on Sundays so getting to work meant biking it or walking. The job I was on was to assist the colliery blacksmith Albert Cowlishaw to put a new cap – a cup-shaped metal socket – on the winding rope for the main shaft. I needed to look and learn as this was a very important job. The metal winding rope held the cage that carried all the men and equipment up and down the shaft, and people's lives depended on it.

Capping the winding rope

A winding rope lasted three years. Every six months it would be taken off to be checked and re-capped. The six-foot length of rope that passed over the top of the winding wheel was the section subject to greatest strain as it ran over the arch of the wheel each time the cage went up and down, which could be thousands of times a day. At its six-monthly check, this section would be cut off and more rope pulled forward from the dead laps (loops of spare rope) on the winding drum, so that a fresh length took the heaviest strain. The old cap and chains would be sent to Sheffield for annealing, a form of heat treatment to make the steel less brittle and more workable. The rope we were working on was a 2" lock coil made by the White Cross Wire Rope Company. Every strand in the rope was twisted and of a different shape, and they all interlocked for strength. Only the centre strand was straight.

The end view of a 2" lock coil winding rope

6" of the rope cut off at the carpel end

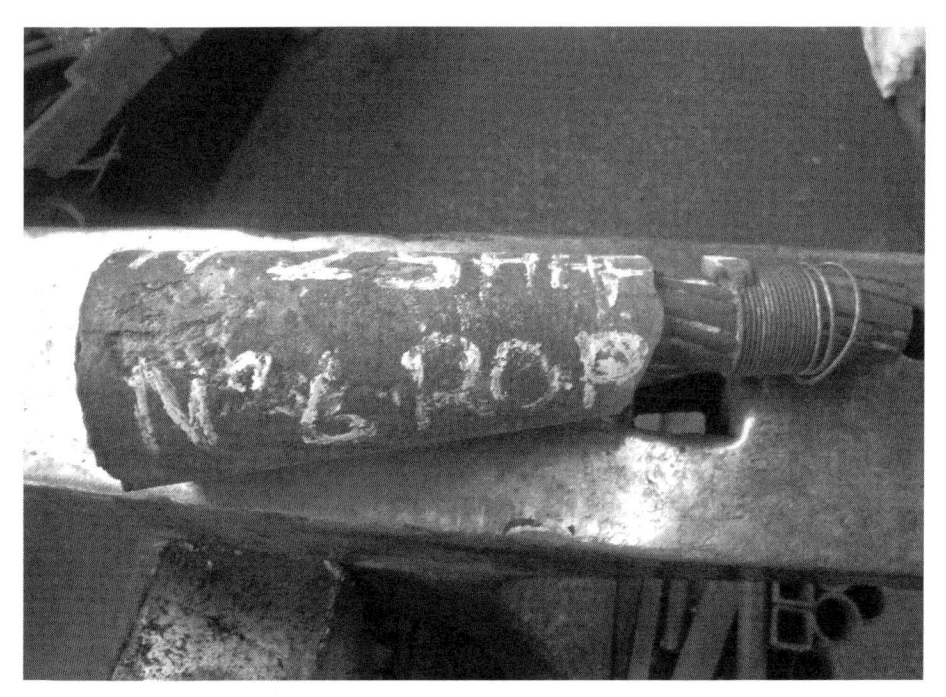

A piece of haulage rope capped in resin. Winding ropes use white metal

The detaching hook and chains from the cage are loaded ready to be sent for annealing to Sheffield. This is done every six months. This is not the King detaching hook but one designed by Edward Ormerod, which works in a similar way to the King hook

The newly capped rope would be fastened onto the detaching hook, then the hook would be coupled to the bull chains and they in turn to the cage, so that the hook supported the cage up in the head stocks. The King safety hook was invented in the village of Pinxton in Nottinghamshire in 1867 by John King. It had a copper rivet as thick as your thumb in the hook as a safety device – if the cage travelled too far into the headstock, the rivet would break and release a claw that would stop the cage where it was. There had been a case of an overwind at Markham pit, when the ascending cage failed to stop and the descending one fell to the bottom of the shaft. Several miners lost their lives and some were permanently disabled. In those days the engine and brakes were powered by steam, which was less easy to control than modern electric systems.

To test the rope after it had been capped, we would put four full tubs of waste on the cage and run it up and down the shaft. Two joiners wearing safety harness would ride on top of the cage to examine the shaft for any damage. This job had to be finished by the 12 o'Clock knock-off time. The team consisted of the joiners Jack Calladine and Lionel Swift, blacksmith Albert Cowlishaw and assistant engine-wright Clifford Hoburn.

New points

The first job on the Monday morning after capping the rope was for Albert to unwind every strand in the six-foot length he had cut off. Lock coil ropes look like a smooth bar of iron but, as I said, are made of layers of twisted steel strands. Albert would examine every strand and report to the engine-wright on any that were broken and which layer they came from. The centre one was straight, and when he got to that and found it to be sound, he would put it in his locker. I wondered why, and soon discovered the reason.

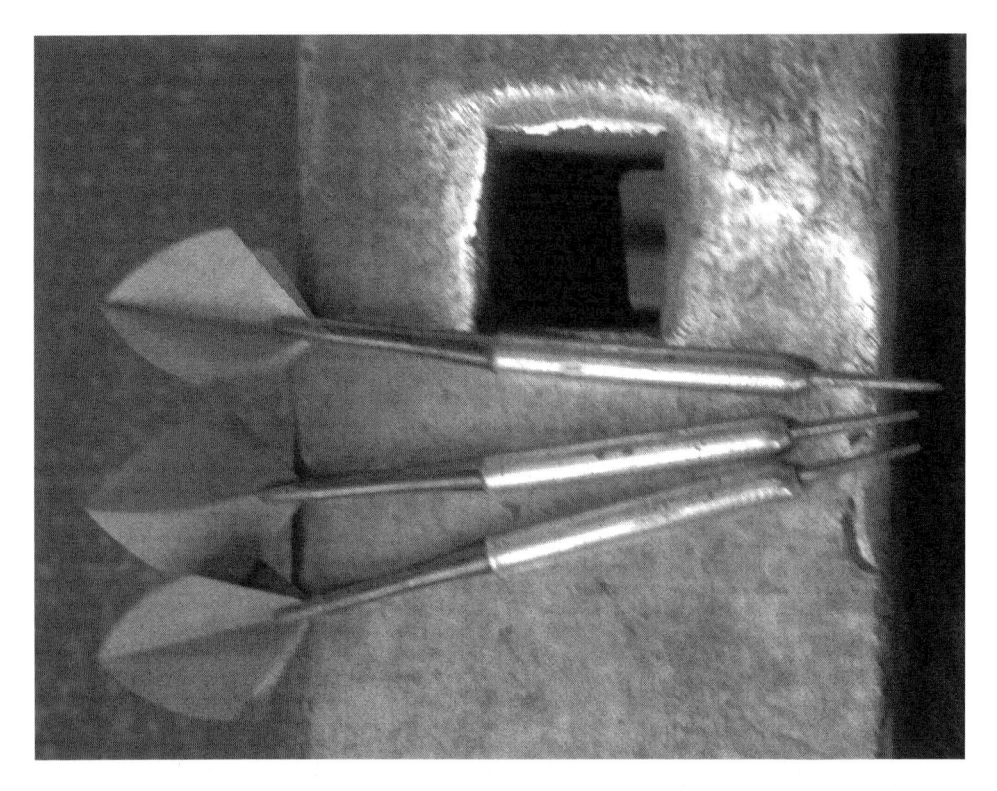

Darts

Most days, miners who arrived early for an afternoon shift would come into the forge and sit and talk until it was time for them to go down the shaft. One day I saw a miner give Albert a set of darts and ask if he would re-point them for him. Albert went to his locker and took out the centre strand piece from the winding rope we had worked on. He sweated out the old points from the darts, cut new points made from the centre strand of rope, and inserted these into the darts. The miner came the following day to collect the darts and gave Albert two shillings (10 new pence) for pointing them for him. I was curious as to why he would use that particular strand for this purpose. He told me it was because the centre strand was made of top-quality steel and did not go blunt easily when the dart fell onto the pub floor (most pubs had red tiles on the floor in the tap rooms at that time). This job was becoming more and more interesting as each day went on. Albert did not speak very much and I wondered if he felt awkward at having me in the forge with him, as he had never had a lad to train as a regular blacksmith's striker before. He would draw a line across the floor and cross it just once a day to toast his sandwiches on the fire with me. However, I soon found out that he suffered with a throat problem and it must have hurt him to speak. Having sorted that matter out, we became the very best of mates. It was Albert who taught me the art of blacksmithing. He was a first-class man.

Our duties

My job after I had clocked in at 7am was to make up the fire and check everything in the forge was well, then stand by for the engine-wright to do his rounds. All the craftsmen's shops were in a straight line at Park House. Starting from alongside the pit-head baths you came to: number one electrical shop, number two joiners, number three welders, number four hydraulic props repairs, number five blacksmiths and lastly number six was the fitting shop. The assistant engineer Cliff Hoburn would make his way through the shops, giving instructions on what would be required that day for the mine from each of them. Our shop was responsible for making and repairing all the hinges (door bands and hooks), all ventilation doors, all tub rail crossings, clamps for both shaft and underground pipes, and all types of brackets. We also did toolmaking and sharpening for all departments, including making lathe tools from 1½ inch manganese tool steel. I learned to use all sorts of metals and alloys. With brass, I learned it was best to work in a dim light, where you could judge whether you were using the right heat from the glow on the metal. We took the opportunity to make tools for ourselves, hammers and chisels and the like, as there would be plenty of metal around, especially up at the sidings where you could scrounge spare pieces of Sheffield steel that had been chucked out of the trucks. One day one of the men came up to me looking shifty. "Hey, Doug, I seen a water otter at the sidings. Get yourself up there if you want a look."

I searched high and low for the water otter. Only on the way back to the blacksmith's shop did I realise I'd been staring at an old kettle on top of a pile of scrap.

We worked in the shop until 2pm every day. Then Albert would send me for a spot lamp from the lamp room. He needed it for going down the shaft to the underground stables, where he would inspect the ponies' shoes and do what was necessary to their hooves. He would prepare the shoes on the surface and then fit them cold in the stables.

The colliery was cutting back on overtime in general, and if you got work on a Saturday or Sunday you were very lucky. A Saturday shift meant I would have about £11 in my wage packet that week. We always tried to make the jobs last and run over into the weekend, finishing them on a Sunday if we could. On Friday afternoon the assistant engine-wright would come through the shops telling each person whether they were needed or not for work at the weekend. He would come up to you and mutter in your ear "You come tomorrow but do not tell the others." Or it might be "Sorry, I have nothing for you this week." I did quite well for Saturday shifts, because whenever Albert had to go in on a Saturday morning, he would ask for me to come too. This was great for me as it meant overtime rates of pay. We would generally be needed to assist Charlie Hooper; he was a fitter on the screening plant and in charge of all the machines. Weekends were the only time when Charlie could get these repairs done. Some of the conveyors were made of steel plate and the hinges needed a lot of riveting. This type of conveyor carried coal that had been fed from the tubs through the tipplers and had to be screened and graded on its way to the pithead railway. Men would stand on each side of the belt picking off the lumps of rock and any waste that had found its way into the coal. After going past the pickers, the coal would carry on along to the railway wagons ready to be taken to the customers.

Coal pickers

A pit pony farrier

One day Albert said, "Would you like to learn how to shoe the ponies?"

I said I would, but had to add that going back underground could be a problem, as the reason I had been taken out of work in the gates was dust on my chest. I knew Albert stayed underground about two hours and came up in time for the 4pm bus. He didn't use the pit head baths as he preferred to bath at home. I also knew he suffered a bad back and wore a support corset.

He told me not to worry about coal dust as the ponies were stabled in the pit bottom near the shaft and it was only for two hours. It was my chance to become a farrier.

"Great, then, I'll come with you."

Albert said, "Thank the Lord, my back is killing me."

Hearing that, I wondered if I had done the right thing.

Albert was a top-class farrier as well as blacksmith. When I joined him there were only 14 ponies down in the Waterloo seam at Park House. The ponies were mostly of native Welsh or Scottish breed, quite stocky and up to around 13.2 hands in height. These small ponies worked quite as hard as any Draught horses used in haulage or on farms. They came from a supplier called Johnny and had only a couple of weeks' training before being sent down the pit. They were shod, groomed, fed and watered underground. It was not until the Coal Mines Act of 1911 that they started to be brought to the surface during the pit holidays once a year for a week. However, they would spend the week gorging on fresh grass, which upset their digestion and caused diarrhoea, making them too weak to work. So, their holiday was later extended to two weeks; the second week allowed their gut to adapt. Miners used to grow fond of the ponies and would take them a sprig of hawthorn or share an apple with them. You'd hear the pony drivers whistling or singing to them in the dark; they were good company and very hard workers. Here is a poem written by a miner from Doncaster a few years ago:

Spark the pit pony

When I was a pit pony driver
Just a boy all alone in the dark
In the dirt and the damp with a smoky oil lamp
My one grain of comfort was Spark.
There's something about that wee pony
On which I could depend,
Like a bond between shepherd and sheep dog
Or cowboy and four-legged friend.
I remember the first time that my lamp went out
The darkness was blacker than night.
I clung to Spark's tail knowing he would not fail
and he led me right back to the light.
When snap time came round, in my snap tin I found
That I hadn't got roast beef or ham;
Spark was such a pet he ate out of my hand
And got half my bread and jam.
At the end of the shift I came out of the pit
To wash off the dirt and the grime.
I hated to go, leaving Spark down below;
He stayed underground all the time.
One thing I liked, when we came out on strike
The ponies were brought out too.
It was a pit ponies' heaven, that colliery field
The only one they knew.
I shouted Spark's name. He came up to the gate
And looked at me through eyes rather dim
In his horse's way he was trying to say
It's lovely up here, Jim.

When the strike ended they went down again
to that dreary existence of hard work and pain
Where there was no difference between days and nights
And no chance of going on strike for their rights.
There are no ponies now in this mechanised age
But I've often thought, going down in the cage,
A machine never greets you with whinnies of joy
The way Spark greeted me when I was a pit boy.

by J R Green, Doncaster

The duties of the horse-keeper were clearly laid down by the Coal Mines Act 1911. They had to sign the record book every day and state the condition of all horses and ponies in their care. The record book had to be countersigned by the mine manager or under manager.

> This is a copy of a letter that was on show in the stables at Catty Pit:
>
> **PIT HORSES AND PONIES 12th MARCH 1928**
>
> Mr. Baxter, H.M Inspector of Horses, delivered a lecture at Leeds University on the care of pit ponies. These were his main points:
>
> 1. Best type of pony: Scotch and Welsh. From experience, the latter type are rather nervous.
> 2. Horse-keeper to see that ponies are equipped with properly fitting gear, as not only do they work better, but sores are prevented.

3. Feet to have proper attention (new shoes to be fitted every month).
4. Earthenware mangers, and peat moss or sawdust bedding.
5. To be fed on best bran and crushed oats. Ponies which are on very hard work should have a few beans. Normal quantity is 1lb per hand. A 12-hand pony would have 7lbs of oats, 2lbs of bran and 3lbs of chopped hay.
6. Ponies to be watered before feeding. Tanks or tubs in the stables to be kept full and at the same temperature as that of the mine.
7. On coming into the stables they will drink first and then eat greedily. By drinking first they will not get colic and indigestion.
8. Good grooming.
9. Sling gears [chains linking the pony's collar to the swingle tree] are preferred only where gradients are against the load. Some mechanical contrivance should be used for lowering and raising the tubs in steep gradients.
10. Attention was especially drawn to overloading as this accounted for a large number of accidents to ponies. For example, lads would be too late or inaccurate in slipping lockers (chocks of wood) between the spokes of tub wheels to act as brakes on downhill stretches – and the pony could consequently be run down by the tub and killed. Yorkshire pits had a 7% accident rate, as against 4% for the whole of England.
11. All purchase of ponies from dealers should be on a month's trial to ensure the ponies were suitable for underground work.
12. And finally, all stables must be well ventilated with intake air.

At Catty Pit, Bade Rowbottom was the horsekeeper on the day shift and John Short took over at night. John Short came from Newmarket – not the racing place in Suffolk but the one just down Clay Lane three miles from Catty Pit. There are two Newmarkets in Great Britain, and the one near the pit had a racecourse too up until the 1950s. Bade Rowbottom the horsekeeper used to work on the pit top, taking supplies to the shaft with the horse and cart. Albert told me that when the job of underground horse-keeper was advertised, Bade's son John, who also worked on the surface at Catty Pit, told his dad that he had applied for the job. His dad told him the job would not suit him and he was best staying where he was, so John withdrew his application. Little did John know that his father had applied for the job and they were the only two applicants. Bade was duly appointed the underground horsekeeper on the day shift.

Let me explain. When you go down the shaft you are on underground time and that means your shift is only seven-and-a-quarter hours. On the surface you do eight-and three-quarters hours for the same pay. So, working underground you get pay equivalent to one extra shift a week, plus an extra 2/6d a day if you are riding the rope (which means hitching, unhitching and riding on the tubs). Your overtime will start at 2.15pm and not 3.30pm.

Albert and I used to go down the pit at 2pm in between the shifts to inspect the shoes of the ponies that had come in from the morning shift and to check the feet of the ones going out on the afternoon shift. We made the horseshoes in the smithy and kept a stock of them in the stables with an anvil and our leather aprons. That meant we just had to carry our tools and nails to the stables underground.

When our work in the stables was completed, one of the perks of the job was to be allowed to go to the front of the queue in the pit bottom where all the miners were also waiting to go up the shaft after their shift. I suppose that I was lucky in one way with my training because Albert, as I said, suffered with his back and he would sit on his tool box and give me one-to-one instruction. His favourite saying was, 'I shall be glad when you do the job and can put the shoes on so I shall be able to stay on the pit top and leave this lot to you.' We worked together on the ponies for about two years, and as I became more proficient Albert would go to the feed area where all the bags of food for the ponies were kept. Here, he and Bade would sit and talk whilst I was left to do the shoeing. Unless I encountered a problem with the shoeing, I would join them afterwards and we would make a bit of overtime sat on our backsides.

Free nights out

I was by now well settled into this job of blacksmith's striker for Albert, and doing well for overtime. The only problem was that I still had to hand all my wages over to my mother Caroline, including anything I earned as errand boy for the Star Tea Company. She did not allow me to pay for my board but gave me 12 shillings and sixpence a week (12/6d, or 62.5 pence) and told me repeatedly what a lucky young man I was, having all my clothes bought for me as well as the 12/6d. I began to feel our house was getting a bit small.

My elder brother was a member of the local St John's

Ambulance Brigade and suggested that I might join, so I went along with him. It made an evening out of the house, for one thing. They met at Clay Cross Secondary Modern School on Tuesday evenings.

My brother John Charles Bradbury, 1952

Just plain Douglas Bradbury

Doug's first aid certificates

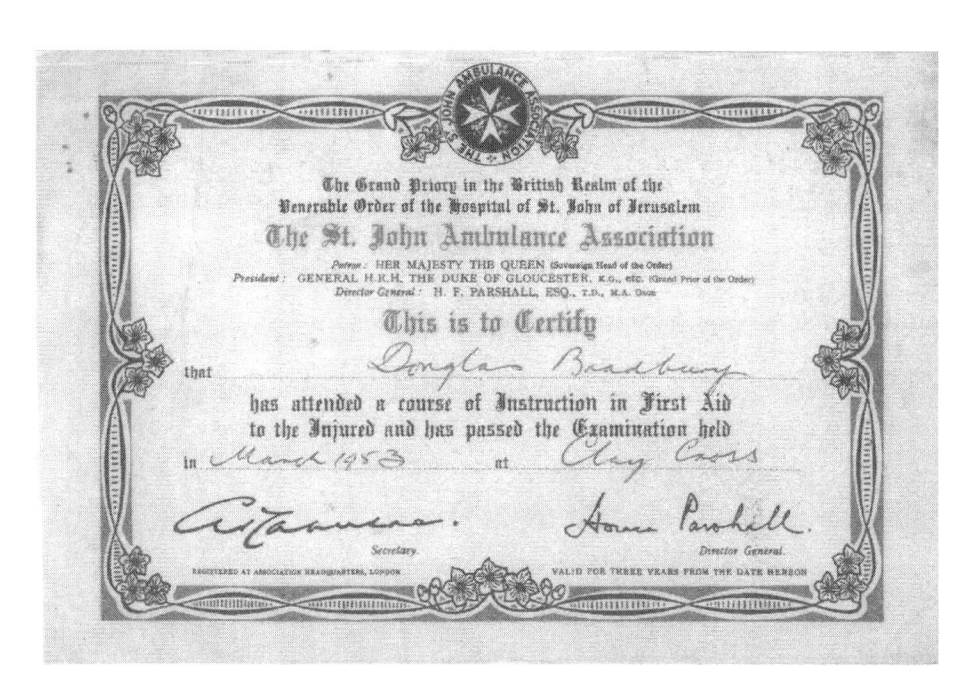

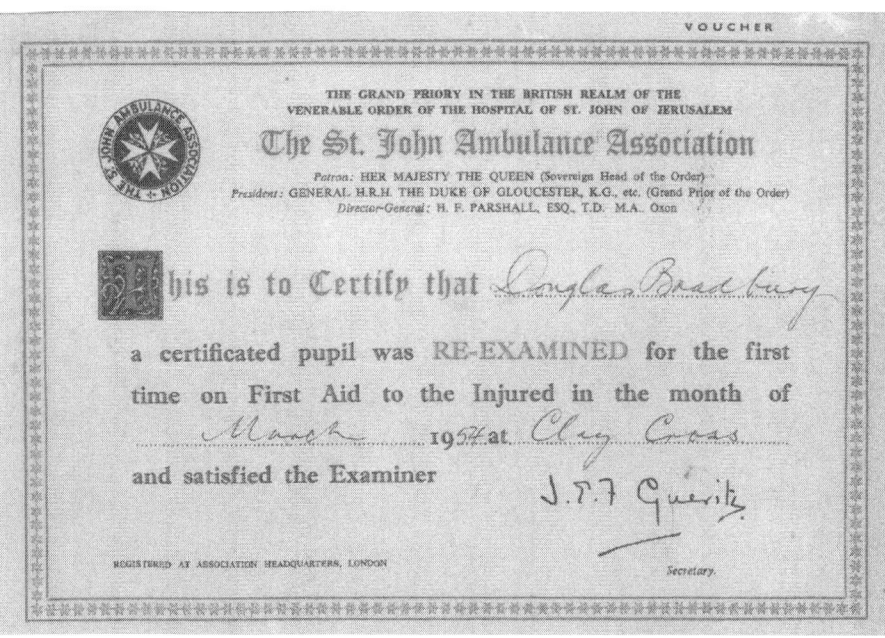

Each year you had to sit an examination. If you passed in years 1 and 2, you got a certificate. If you passed the third-year exam, you were given a bronze medallion. Every year after that, when you passed the exam there was a bronze label to clip onto the medallion. I did well with St John's, attaining two certificates, the medallion and two labels before I became too busy to attend.

One night at the meeting, the chief instructor said he had received a letter from the Chesterfield Hippodrome Theatre requesting one or two people to give their services by attending one evening performance a week in case of emergencies. The letter finished, 'Hoping you will accept, I enclose two free tickets.' My hand went up quick as a flash. So, the following week my girlfriend Joan and I went to the Hippodrome for free. One thing about a man in uniform is that he always looks smart and in my St John's Ambulance kit I was no exception. We were ushered through the door without any queuing or jostling. Safely inside, we made straight for the back row, where it was off with the hat and straight in with the snogging. It would have been just too bad if anyone had wanted first aid. Where else could you find a dark, warm, dry spot to do your courting all for free?

3

JOAN AND ME

Cinema cramp

Joan and I used to meet every night. On weekdays she always caught the 9.30pm bus home because we both had to be at work early the next day, but at weekends we could stay out much later. In Clay Cross we now had a new cinema called the Burn Cross, otherwise known as the Bug Hut. It was in the YMCA building and cost one shilling to go in. The projectionist's room was almost halfway down the hall, leaving two recesses on each side fitted with three rows of bus seats – double seats with no arm rests. That was where the courting couples went.

At the end of the show they always played 'God Save the King' and everybody stood to attention before they left. At this point the affliction known as cinema cramp became easy to recognise. In those days most young men wore a three-piece suit to go out in the evening. The suit consisted of jacket, trousers and waistcoat. When the National Anthem started, the boyfriends found that they could not stand up straight.

The reason was that their fly buttons were fastened to their waistcoat.

Joan and I had been courting for about two years now. Two of our best friends were Les Holmes and his girlfriend Joan Bowen, who was from Grassmoor. One day it was suggested that we might all go to Blackpool for a week during the pit annual holiday. Les said his relatives Bob and Mary Kimes would like to come too. They were a married couple, and Bob offered to take Les and his girl to Blackpool in their car. Joan and I said that we would go on the train. We booked a boarding house in Albert Road near the sea front for all six of us.

I found the best form of family planning did not come from the chemist's shop but from the words of my mother Caroline ringing in my ears: "Do not bring any trouble to this house. If you make your bed, you will lie on it." In other words, do not bring anything back you cannot sell. Not content with issuing advice, my mum and dad checked the bookings to make sure that we were not booked in as Mr. and Mrs. but that we had separate rooms. Not only that – both sets of parents turned up unannounced in Blackpool midweek, just to check up on us. They arrived in an Austin 7 belonging to Joan's dad – he used to have his own buses many years ago and had always had a car of some sort. I am pleased to report that we were not in each other's rooms at the time but at the pleasure park. By the time we returned to the boarding house, it was time for the mums and dads to go back home, having found everything shipshape. Afterwards Joan and I carried on having a fantastic week.

Mary and Bob Kimes, Joan and Doug, Joan Bowen and Les Holmes

On a roller coaster

No Penguin for you

Some months later we talked about getting engaged. We knew by then that we were meant for each other, and were thinking we might get married the following December on Joan's birthday. She said that I would have to ask her mum and dad. I used to go up to Joan's home once a week, usually on a Thursday, and return home on the 9.15pm bus. Her mum always made me a cup of tea and gave me a Penguin biscuit before I went home.

On the Thursday that I finally raised enough courage to ask Joan's mum for her daughter's hand in marriage, everything changed. She went ape shit. She jumped up and down and shouted that we were too young and did not know what we wanted. She became very awkward towards Joan and wouldn't speak to her. On Thursday nights when I visited, her mum still made me a cup of tea but stopped my Penguin and did not speak to me either. So, we both ignored her. Instead we carried on with our plans to marry and spend the rest of our lives together. One of the hit songs at that time was 'They tried to tell us we're too young' by Jimmy Young, and we adopted it as our theme tune. My mum reacted differently from Joan's: when I told Caroline that we would like to get married, straight away she increased my spending money from 12/6d to 24 shillings (£1.20) a week. *Whooooooo!*

Following a visit to Shipman's the jewellers at Holywell Cross, Chesterfield, we became officially engaged on 22nd December 1955, Joan's 18th birthday. We bought our wedding rings from the same shop the following year.

It was not until a couple of weeks before the wedding that

Joan told me her mother wanted to see me to discuss the wedding and future arrangements. She must have finally decided to accept the situation, and it proved to be the start of a lifelong friendship that grew and grew as the years went by. She would give me anything, and that goes for Joan's dad too – he was a man above all men.

We chose the New Inn in Market Street, Clay Cross, for our reception. When we went along to see the landlord, he told us not to waste money on expensive sherry for the toast as he had some cheap Tarragona at 2/6d a bottle. He said he would put it in some empty Harvey's Bristol Cream bottles. The guests would not know the difference and it would save us pounds.

Our wedding day

Joan and I were married on 22nd December 1956 at St Lawrence's Church, North Wingfield. The vicar was the Reverend Alex Frazer from Pilsley, who stood in at the last minute as the regular vicar was ill. This church dates back to the Norman era, and was recorded in the Domesday survey of 1086 as a church with a priest in the manor of North Wingfield, or Winnefelt as the parish was then known. Some of the fixtures are even older, being of Saxon origin. In Norman times, the manor of Winnefelt was in the possession of Walter De Ayncourt. The name eventually became shortened to Deincourt, a name used to this day by the village school and secondary school.

Having told you about the church, now back to our wedding. It was a cold dark day and we had fog, frost and snow all within the 24 hours. Joan was late arriving at the church. I knew lateness was to be expected, but this time it was taken to the extreme. We waited and waited. People began to look at me sideways. Only when the bride's car finally swerved into the kerb outside the church did we learn that a tree had fallen across the road in its path so it had had to detour. The day never really got light and it was not possible to take any photographs outside because of the poor light. However, some were taken in the church and at the reception in the New Inn.

St Lawrence's Church

St Lawrence's Church

Joan and her dad

Doug and his brother

Joan signs Bradbury for the first time. We are now Mr. and Mrs. Bradbury

My wife and I

We had a leaning tower too

Linda Roberts, Jean Booker, Monica Link, Ann Walvin, Jacqueline Bennett, Angela Bradbury

Everything is rosy

The photographer told us colour film was not available in Chesterfield. But he had a tip on how to save some money. "Carnations cost a lot less than roses, you know. You get your lady to carry a bunch of carnations, and I'll touch up the photo to make them look like roses."

By the time the wedding was upon us I had managed to save £90, one way and another. So, we decided to go to Blackpool for the honeymoon, and to travel in style instead of in a railway carriage. We went to see the taxi driver Mr. Fred Stoppard on High Street about hiring a car to Blackpool on the Sunday morning after the wedding. "Ah", he said, "I can do that job for you. It'll cost you £19, mind, what with having to make two double trips there and back to fetch and deliver you." Mr. Stoppard duly arrived on the Sunday morning. I was as rough as a bear's ass through drinking too much the night before. I could not fasten my shirt collar for fear of being sick. When we arrived in Blackpool the hotel manager greeted Joan like royalty but I think he had doubts about me; probably he thought I was her father. I did say that I looked rough.

The whip round

It was a very nice hotel but had no bar. The other guests sounded to us a bit upper class, and on Christmas Eve one of them suggested that we have a whip around so that two of the men could go out and buy some drinks and then we could party in the hotel. Everybody was in agreement and they started to collect the money. They were all putting £1 in the box. I thought, *Bloody hell, that's a bit steep*. I went along to the shop to see what they were going to buy. They came back with gin, whisky, brandy, rum and tonic. At 7.30pm one of these daft buggers stood up and said, "I do believe it's bedtime for our honeymoon couple."

I said, "Bollocks to that. We put in a pound the same as everybody else." I told Joan she could go upstairs if she wanted to but I was staying to have my money's worth.

Joan and I did go to the wrestling at the Tower one night just to see if there were any new moves we had not learnt.

Somewhere to stay

My parents said we could stay with them at number 37 Top Long Row until we found somewhere of our own to live. Caroline promised to get a single bed for Uncle Harry so he could move into their room and we could sleep in his. She charged us £6 a week board and lodging, though the board just meant the evening meals. We did not eat breakfast at home, but I took sandwiches to work and Joan had her dinner at Robinsons in Chesterfield, where she still worked. Also, we already had all our own bedding and a wardrobe. (In other words, Caroline was a tight old bastard.) As I worked at the pit I was allowed a ton of coal every four weeks. My dad had the same, even though it was the same address. Caroline used to sell some of ours on the quiet and keep the money.

New house

But to be fair, Caroline did her bit to help us get our first house. She would visit the council offices once or twice a week on our behalf to tell them how overcrowded we were at number 37. Overcrowding gave you a better chance of getting a new council house. I think in the end it was because they got so fed up with her that they gave her the key to no 54 Top Long Row.

Joan and Doug outside number 54

Doug returning from the outside loo

The council had been planning not to re-let the Long Row houses as they had been condemned. Number 54 had been boarded up for a while and all the windows, which were the 6" square type, were broken. Nevertheless, the houses were structurally sound, warm and dry; in fact, many were kept like palaces as the miners' wives were a proud lot. The doorsteps were always painted white or donkey stoned [scoured] front and back. Joan's dad put in about 20 new windowpanes for us. With what little they had, people helped each other in those days and all the neighbours pitched in.

Next on our list were furnishings, and like everybody else in Clay Cross we went along to Wigfalls and C. Jacobs for a bed and household goods, then to Parsons for a telly. Our first electric cooker was a small Baby Belling and it stood under the kitchen sink on a bracket that I had made. The goods all came on hire purchase, some for as little as one shilling a week. Joan and I had a tin money box with compartments for coins in it, one section for the gas and electric, one for the TV licence, another for clothes, and so on. We still have that very box now and our grandchildren use it for their coloured pencils. When they open it up, it brings back memories of those early days that Joan and I had to struggle through.

As I said, everybody would help one another. One night, Sarah Lowe came to see us. She lived at number 45 Top Long Row and suggested that as she finished work at 2pm (she worked at the Clay Cross Company factory) she could cook us a meal for when we arrived home in return for a bit of coal now and then. The coal was no problem; as I said, I was allowed one ton every four weeks, and with only one fire in the house we had a lot to spare. We did have to be very careful not to upset Caroline, as she could be very jealous. As it turned out though, Sarah did a very good job. Things were working out well and our home was in good shape.

Iron back

The small cooker was in an ideal spot just under the sink, but we had the odd spillage of fat on the floor around it, and it was tricky to clean as the floor was rather uneven. I thought if I might steal a piece of conveyor belt to use as a mat, it would be easier to keep clean. There happened to be a nice green roll of plastic-coated conveyor belting near the blacksmith's shop, waiting to go down the pit. Albert gave me a hand to cut off a strip about three feet long. The problem was: how was I going to get it out of the pit yard and home? Albert said "Tie it around your waist and put your big raincoat over the top. It will improve your posture and you'll walk straighter."

Well, that worked fine until I got on the bus to come home. When I sat down, I thought that my arms had been amputated as they shot up in the air. I had forgotten that the belting was 36" wide and the distance from my bottom to my arm pits was only 26". So, as I sat down my arms went up and it was impossible to lower them. I sat there stiff as a scarecrow. Luckily, I had my two pence bus fare to the Crown Pub in the High Street ready in my hand, as I could not have searched my pockets. After that, my nickname was 'Iron back'.

The water bosh in the forge

In the corner of the forge was a large water bosh used for quenching hot metal. There was a steel plate halfway across, covered with bits of metal off-cuts. The younger lads who were training to go on the maintenance staff had to serve four weeks in each department to give them an insight into the running of the pit. Now, we had a sledgehammer that weighed 25 pounds and Albert would set them on using it. When they rebelled, he and I would grab them and dunk them in the bosh. The water was never changed and did smell a bit, but it used to sort the lads out. One day, one of the boys was really misbehaving and he was clearly not afraid of us. After a while, enough was enough, and into the bosh he went, headfirst. As he came up, he hit his head on the steel plate and went back down with his mouth wide open. It did the trick and he was well-behaved after that. The same weekend, my wife and I were sitting having a beer in my regular pub, the Elm Tree, when a woman came up to me and started to bollock me for trying to drown her son at work. I told her that I was not trying to drown him but he did have to be taught not to answer back. Plenty of other lads were put in the bosh and never complained, including Russ Wilson, Cliff Williams and Archie Mather. These three still have a laugh about the big hammer, which they used to call the Monday hammer, and the dreaded bosh.

Albert

One morning Albert arrived at the time office to clock in, and collapsed. He died on the spot. The entire surface staff were left in shock, and not much work was done that day. Later that morning a new winding rope, a two-inch lock coil made by the White Cross Wire Rope Company, was delivered to the blacksmith's shop. It was due to be installed on the Sunday morning. Before this could happen, the sword end of the rope (the end that fitted on the winding Dr.um in the engine house) would need to be capped in the forge. The following morning, the engine-wright told me to do the capping. It would be the first time I had done this job alone, so he arranged for a White Cross representative to come and check it afterwards.

Well, I did the capping, and the inspector checked it. Next thing, Les Willows the chief engine-wright came to inform me that I was now the blacksmith in charge. My wages would be that of a craftsman and they would get someone to be my striker. Silently I thanked Albert for teaching me so well and giving me the confidence to do the job after such a short period of training. God bless him. Several other blacksmiths had come over from other pits when they heard there might be a job to apply for, so I felt very proud to think that I had been given the opportunity at the age of only 20.

A striker was appointed by the name of Joe Robinson from Ashover. He had been employed on the boring machines at the coal face, but was currently working on the surface after suffering from a nervous breakdown, partly caused I think by his wife playing around. Joe was a quiet man and we got on very well together.

After Albert's funeral I went to see Mrs. Cowlishaw, his widow, at their house on the new Addlingtons estate at Wingerworth. She told me, "Albert thought a lot of you," and gave me all his tools. I used to take her two bags of sticks every week for kindling; she had coal fires and they were of great help to her.

The one and only motorbike

A 1950's Matchless 350

The houses in our terrace had long gardens that ended at the main road, the A61. On this road and opposite where we lived was Brown's garage. They had motorbikes for sale, and one at £50 caught my eye. The model was a Matchless 350, a big heavy bike in good condition. I talked it over with Joan and decided to buy the bike. I did not have £50 to spend, but Mr. Brown said he would do a hire purchase deal at £4 pounds a month. I reckoned it was a good buy, considering how I would save on bus fares and time. I did not have a garage, so the bike stood outside our house. It was not long after I bought the bike that Albert died, and the bike panniers came in especially useful for supplying his wife with wood once a week.

The crash

One dark wet evening I was going through Tupton on the main A61 on a stretch of road in between two traffic islands. I had rounded the first island and was passing a small garage on the right-hand side, where some British Road Service lorries were parked up. The next thing I knew was a loud bang and I was on the ground with terrible pain blazing up my right leg. I tried to feel for the leg but couldn't find it; apparently it was bent up my back. I remember lying on the road with rain running quite fast by my head. This piece of road had no street lighting, and a lorry with no lights on had been coming the other way around a bend and hit me side on.

The first person to reach me was a lady called Mrs. Goodwin. She tried to comfort me and shelter me under her umbrella, but all I wanted was for her to tell me where my leg was as it was so painful. The next people were Jack Dennis the garage owner and his friend Eddie Shinwell. They ran and stopped a car and got the driver to shine its headlights on me to prevent me being run over. The BRS lorries all moved from the scene of the accident and parked further up the road. None of the drivers came near. Jack and Eddie said in court, "We would not have left a dog in the road the way those lorry drivers left that lad." The only other witness was the ambulance driver;

his name was McVickers and his wife was a district nurse. He said to the police, "The lad was never on the wrong side of the road. He was so far on his own side that he could have drowned in the gutter with the rain as it was that night."

I remember the trip in the ambulance, going round the corner at the crooked spire and entering the casualty department at the old Chesterfield hospital. I saw a porter I knew, and asked him if he would call my wife and tell her I had come off the bike. One of the nurses told me that my leg had been bent up my back for so long that I was lucky it was still on, as the blood flow had been reduced to my lower leg.

That was the last I remember. My arm was bleeding out of the leather cuffs on my coat and the nurses could not cut through it, so they tried to lift me. That's when I passed out. This was Wednesday and I did not regain consciousness until the Saturday afternoon. I learned later that my wife sat with me giving me two fluid ounces of water every four hours. I remember the consultant Mr. Stillman coming to see me after I woke up and listing my injuries: 1) a compound fracture of the right leg; 2) an extensive fracture of the pelvis; 3) a fracture of the right arm; 4) a burst bladder; and 5) a ruptured urethra. He told me that a machine was passing my water for me by a pump under the bed and I had a blood drip in my left arm. He added that whilst they were repairing my bladder they had removed my appendix. My wife told me that at that point I embarrassed her by blurting out to the doctor "Who the f... gave you permission to do that?" Mr. Stillman just looked at Joan and said, "If he is feeling like that, you can give him two ounces of ice cream as long as it is whipped up well." The nurses were continually wetting my lips with water on cotton wool because of my bladder problem.

After a few days my condition deteriorated, and I was rushed back to theatre. There had been an internal leak from the earlier operation. I was so ill that they sent for my wife. Over the next few weeks this happened again twice. At no time did I realise that I was so poorly. Mr. Stillman said that at that point I had only a 50/50 chance of making it to the end of the week. I did make it, but recovery was a slow job. I was in hospital for seven months and had nine operations in total on my injuries. I got to know Mr. Stillman well as I saw him on many other occasions, and we became very good friends.

A friend who was worse than me

In the bed directly opposite me on Murphy Ward was a man from Swadlincote near Burton upon Trent. We were both flat on our backs and could barely see each other around the metal frames over our legs, so we would pass notes across the ward. His name was George Jervis and he had been injured when he went to a scrapyard in Tibshelf to collect a pair of caterpillar tracks. While they were being lifted, the chain broke and fell on his legs. George lost one leg and the other was badly broken. His wife Ruby was heavily pregnant, and his employer paid for taxis every day for her to travel from Burton on Trent to the Chesterfield Royal. Ruby and Joan became lifelong friends.

Then things took a turn for the worse for me and I was transferred to Staveley Ward. This was the urology department. They told me that all the operations I had and would need in future meant I might not be able to father children. The ward was full of old men, mostly terminally ill, so there were not many people to talk to, but I kept in touch with George on Murphy Ward by letter.

When I eventually came home to our house in the Long Rows, I weighed nine stone and my wristwatch fit around my upper arm. The district nurse came every day to dress a large pressure sore at the bottom of my back, which I acquired whilst immobile in hospital on account of the fractured pelvis and the leakage from all the tubes inserted in my body. It left a scar that I shall carry for the rest of my life.

Joan carried on working at Robinsons as we most certainly needed the money. I was getting only £2 10s a week sick pay, and sat at home making woollen scarves on a loom that Joan's dad had made for her when she was at school. As well as weaving scarves, we would stitch two pieces of foam around a bar of soap to make an all-in-one sponge and soap pack. After dinner Joan would sit knitting slippers made from waste nylon sold on the market. She and her friends sold their produce at work; the slippers were 2/6d a pair. It was a minor sort of cottage industry, but everything helped in those times.

Berry Hill Rehabilitation Centre, Mansfield

When I became stronger, I was sent to Berry Hill near Mansfield. This was an NHS rehabilitation centre used by the Coal Board. Many of the miners sent there to recuperate had had cartilage operations. You stayed in the hospital from Monday to Friday in men-only dormitories. An ambulance would pick you up on Monday morning and drop you off again – in time to call at a pub on your way home – on Friday.

The food, physiotherapy and gymnasium at the centre were first class. We were free to do as we wished after 4.30pm each day. Supper was at 6pm and after that you could go to the snooker room, which was equipped with all types of games, or some would go into Mansfield to a pub. There was one just down the road called the Oak Tree. Most of these pubs would put on free sandwiches for the lads.

A few weeks after being admitted to Berry Hill, I was dropped off one Friday near the Rows. I was on my way across the yard to our house when I tripped and fell. I knew straight away that my leg had fractured again. The surgeon at Chesterfield Hospital said he was not surprised to see me again, but sending me home had been worth the chance. He told me that I needed a bone graft and he would do it the next morning. For me it meant a further setback: a stay in hospital and then back to Berry Hill for a further 12 weeks' treatment.

An orthopaedic surgeon used to visit Berry Hill once a month to check people's progress. I saw miners sitting on their bed the night before his visit and hitting their knee with a knot in a wet towel to make it swell. Then next morning the doctor would frown to see the swelling and would sign them off for another spell at Berry Hill. The reason for the wet towel was the industrial injuries benefit (compensation) they were getting all the time they were not at work. In my case I was only on sick pay of £2 10s a week and I needed to get back to work as soon as possible.

As a result of this accident my right leg was two inches shorter than the left and I needed to wear a raised shoe. On my left leg I had a caliper fitted in my shoe as the damage to my pelvis had caused drop foot, meaning my foot dragged on the ground when I walked. When it came to my turn to see Mr. Smith, the orthopaedic surgeon at Berry Hill, he asked me to run the length of the gym. It must have been quite a sight. When I had hobbled over the finish line, he laughed "Well, you remind me of Dr. Barbara Moore" (the lady who walked the length of Britain in 1959).

The doctor then asked about my right arm. This was the first time since the crash that anyone had ever asked me about this injury. He offered me his hand with two outstretched fingers to test my grip. I gripped, and Mr. Smith went white. He snatched his hand back and shook it. I was told later that I had broken one of his fingers, and that he has never offered anyone two fingers to squeeze since that day.

Back to work

After 13 months off work, I was discharged from medical care and started back at Catty Pit in April 1960. I sold the motorbike for scrap for the sum of £4, though I had still not paid back the HP, and went back to travelling by bus.

And after that whole saga of injury and rehabilitation, the police told me that they were going to prosecute me for driving without due care and attention. Two months before the court case, Mr. McVickers (the ambulance driver who picked me up and was a witness as to where on the road I was lying) fell off his motorbike on some ice on his way to work, fractured his skull and passed away. All the lorry drivers who had been in the vicinity worked for BRS, and so did the driver who hit me, Ronald Pritchard from Burton. I had been told I might expect a fair amount of compensation, but guess what – we were fighting a government agency. The judge found me guilty and fined me £50.

Our new house

The Long Rows had been condemned and in October 1960 Joan and I were offered a new council house on Wheatcroft Close, Penn Lane, Clay Cross, a brand-new estate. With the new house came new neighbours: on one side was Doris Bowen and on the other was Nan Fox. My parents were allocated to the same estate, eight houses further on along the avenue from ours. And, of course, Mum's brother Harry went with them.

We had been at Penn Lane about two years when Uncle Harry became ill. He kept asking, "Will our Doug take me a run in the car around Ogston Dam just one last time before I die?" This dam was still under construction at the time. So, I would put him in the car for a ride and he would say "Good lad, Doug, I shall make sure that you are OK when I go." Hearing that news, I would drive around the dam with all the windows wide open. But that had the opposite effect from the one I had in mind. The following day he would be fine and back to normal. This went on for about 18 months. Not only that, but my mum Caroline would say "Could you come and shave Uncle Harry as he can't manage it?" This was two or three times a week with new blades every time and all for no pay. In addition, my brother was coming down and giving him a bath once a week. It was a while before I realised the old bastard was not even going to pay for my new blades, and after that I lost interest. I did not stop doing the shaving but I did stop using new blades when I found I wasn't going to be refunded for them. Quite often the old blades would dig in and make him bleed. Harry would say "That razor is pulling a bit." He often looked as though he had been in a battle, with his face covered in bits of paper to stop the bleeding. Before he did eventually die, he and Caroline must have put their heads together, and Harry had the last laugh as I did not even get a mention in his will. I wonder why?

Ogston Dam

My first home workshop

I was given permission to put a shed in the back garden of our new council house. It measured 8' by 6' but had to be half glass. This was my first workshop. I managed to get a small portable forge and an anvil for it, plus a bench and a hand-operated bench drill. We had no electricity to the workshop and my wife spent many hours turning a handle to make stud holes in horseshoes. The workshop enabled me to finish off the jobs that I could not get done at the pit.

It was not long before I started to do a bit of shoeing for local customers as well as for the pit ponies. One day I was seeing to a horse for the daughter of Mr. Ephraim Cousins, a master cobbler from Lower High Street, Clay Cross. He noticed the awkward way I walked and asked if he could make me a pair of boots for work. I said, "Yes please, I would most definately appreciate that offer." The cobbler invited me to his shop and took all the measurements. He then showed me some leather hides and said I could choose the one I wanted. Well, I can tell you that the boots Mr. Cousins made for me were the most comfortable I have ever worn. They cost £8 and they made walking so much easier.

Doctors again

I carried on shoeing a few horses for people after work at the pit. But, my health was up and down. Things would be going fine one day, then next morning I would wake up sweating with a high temperature. The cause, I was eventually told, was that there were fragments of bone floating around in my body as a result of all the fractures I had suffered, and when a fragment got stuck somewhere it would cause an abscess to form.

One day I came home from work not feeling too good around my stomach. I guessed it was some infection and went to see the doctor. He was of the same opinion, gave me some antibiotics, told me to go home straight to bed and promised he would call and see me later on in the week. Well, after two or three days I was feeling much better but bored out of my mind at being stuck in bed. We had quite recently moved into our new council house at Wheatcroft Close, and Joan wanted a clothes stoop at the bottom of the garden to attach the clothesline to. So, on the Friday morning I planned to get out of bed and make one for her. I had a small welding machine at home, and reckoned to set it up outside the back door. I had a length of tubing and the cross pieces ready for welding so I knew the job would not take long. When my wife came upstairs after breakfast to clean and hoover, I told her that as I was feeling much better I would get up and do that job she wanted me to do.

At about 11am I was working away in the back porch when my wife heard a knock on the front door. Looking through the window she saw Dr. Proctor standing there. She shouted "Doug, the doctor's here. Get back in bed quick." I did just that, fully clothed, with a sweat from the welding all over my face. Only just in time – the doctor was following me upstairs. He took one look at me lying there, took my pulse and immediately phoned for an ambulance. When the ambulance men arrived they came upstairs with a chair to carry me down in. One of them turned to the other and said "He's a big one." Then to me: "Can you walk downstairs, mate?" I agreed I could and got myself into the ambulance, and we set off with the lights flashing.

I was taken to Staveley Ward and assigned to Dr. Stillman again. He thought I most likely had an abscess in my pelvis, so the first examination was a rectal one. Now, the doctor was a big man with hands like shovels and fingers like bananas. He said, "Lie on your side and pull your knees up to your chin." He then placed one of those banana-sized fingers right up my rectum. I can tell you that was one of the most painful experiences I have had and there is no chance of me ever becoming a homosexual. It was the Good Friday of Easter weekend when this took place, so there were no more examinations that weekend. I was just given antibiotics intravenously until after the bank holiday. But that was not the last of this type of examination. I was told that later that week I was to have a proctoscopy.

The dreaded proctoscope

When the time arrived Nurse Jennings, a nurse I had become friendly with over my long stays in hospital, came and told me she would be with me and we were to walk to the operating theatre as a proctoscopy was not a big job. At the theatre, the doctor told me to jump up onto the narrow table and lie face down. Nurse Jennings stood at the front end with the top of my head placed against her stomach whilst she held my shoulders. The doctor told me pull my knees up under my chin and lift my bottom up in the air. At this point it is difficult to express my feelings. Then came a shock: I glanced backwards and saw the doctor greasing what looked like an 18" length of chrome tubing with a light attached to the end. He did not have to tell me where that was going. As this apparatus entered my rectum, I uttered a great grunt and tried to shove forward into Nurse Jennings' stomach. I looked back and saw the doctor's cheek almost next to my scrotum. He said, "Have you ever had piles, Mr. Bradbury?"

As he withdrew the instrument I replied "Noooooow, sirrrrrrr."

"OK, all done. Off you go."

As you know, nurses walk very fast. Nurse Jennings was no exception. She set off from the theatre at quick march and I had to call to her to slow down as I was now only capable of walking like a penguin. It must have taken us almost an hour to get back to the ward, and was I glad to climb into bed that day. I was in hospital for a week.

The previous time I was in hospital, I had met a man from Clay Cross by the name of Joe Lynam. He had fractured his thigh underground at Catty Pit and as I was flat on my back, he got out of bed one day and shuffled down the ward on a tubular frame just to say hello. After I left hospital, he came to see me and take me to the Elm Tree pub on High Street for a drink. My wife was at work and it was easy to say yes. Now Joe was single and lived with his mother, and he was a drinking – and falling down – man of long standing. He and I palled up. We used to go to the Elm Tree every time, and it became a habit that almost broke up my marriage. Joe would call on a Sunday morning around 9.30am. We'd go in the pub by the back door while Spike, the landlord, was still in bed. He would call down, "Fill your own. I will see you in a bit." Some Sundays we could drink until 12 noon, wander out drunk and find men waiting to go into the pub at the official opening time, which was 12 noon until 2pm. Spike was a generous friend, and on a Saturday night when Joan and I would go in for a drink at the bar, he would save us a seat. I would order our drinks and pay with a £1 or 10/- note and he would give me the same amount back in change so other people would not know it was his treat. Spike was a very kind man who did a lot of good to a lot of people. But, these trips with Joe were not doing my wallet or my marriage any good. I decided it had to stop and it did.

4

CHILDREN AND PIT PONIES

Our first child

After a lot of trying and a lot of disappointments, Joan fell pregnant. The news came as a surprise to the doctors as they thought all the injuries I had suffered in the pelvic area would have made it impossible. Joan and I were so excited and looked forward eagerly to the birth. We had a problem in that I was due to have further surgery on my right foot as it was giving me a lot of pain and making me walk on the side of my foot. My consultant Mr. Smith told me I would need an operation called a triple arthrodesis, which involved fusing three joints in the foot and would put me out of action for several weeks. I told him we were expecting our first child, so we agreed to delay the operation until after Joan had given birth.

"Oh God no, it's my fifth"

Joan went into Scarsdale Hospital on 26th February 1961. Our daughter Gale arrived by breech birth at 12.50am on 3rd March.

The night before the birth, I sat at Joan's bedside in a two-bedded ward. There were screens around the lady in the next bed and in between sucks of gas and air she was continually screaming "Never ever, ever again, ever!" I was a nervous wreck listening to her. Her husband popped his head around the screens to say sorry.

I said "It's OK. Is it your first?"

"No, it's our fifth."

I thought: *Bloody hell, what have we done?*

The lady's husband asked would I like to go for a beer.

"Er, no thanks, mate." The nurse came to bustle me out of the way, so I kissed Joan goodnight and told her that I loved her and to be brave and I would ring her in the morning. There was no way I could have been allowed at the birth anyway; it was not possible in those days.

Joan was in hospital for ten days. The day she came out with our daughter was the day I was due in Chesterfield Royal Hospital for the operation on my foot. I was in Murphy Ward for six weeks, so I missed out on all those sleepless nights.

Our daughter Gale

The accident fund at the pit

About six months before I had the motorbike accident, the union at the pit had started a sickness and accident fund. Anyone that was off work for six weeks or more would be entitled to £12 from this fund. The rule was that you had to have paid sixpence (2½ new pence) a week for six weeks before you could Dr.aw any money, and I had been doing this regularly. Following the accident, I was off work for more than six weeks, so I was due the £12. Joe Lynam, whom I had met in hospital, was in the same situation. The union rep told us both there had been so many claims on the fund that "We are very sorry, but there is no money left for you two." That £12 would have made such a difference to our household, as all I was getting was £2 10s a week. When I started back to work after the accident, I found sixpence had been stopped from my first week's wages for the sickness and accident fund. I told the union man, Walter Hickin, that he must not stop me any more sixpences and, if I found it had happened again next week, he could go to hell.

Several months passed by and I was still attending the hospital as an outpatient. The orthopaedic surgeon told me that I needed a further operation to correct my foot and he would schedule it for about six weeks" time. Back at work I did not tell anyone what the surgeon had said. Instead I went to see Walter Hickin and told him that I had been reconsidering the sickness and accident fund and would like to rejoin, so he could stop me the sixpence again from this week.

"Good, I am pleased to have you back," he said.

My plan was that by the time the hospital sent for me I would just have paid my six weeks' qualifying contributions into this so-called benefit fund.

Everything went to plan, right to the day. I went into hospital knowing that I would be off work about 12 weeks. I put my claim in straight away and got paid my £12 this time, thanks very much. When I returned to the pit on the first day, I saw the union man and told him that he must not stop me any more money for the sickness and accident fund. I am not a person to bear a grudge but I did what I did because I'd found out more about that fund since being denied my pay-out last time. So now I was able to tell Mr. Hickin that a three-shilling investment pays £12, which is not a bad deal, and now you can f… your fund. You should have seen his face.

My first car

Within a year of coming to my senses, in other words having stopped going to the pub with Joe Lynam, I bought my first car for £375. It was an Austin A40 Farina, red with a black roof. The person who taught me to drive was Fred Wilson, who was a friend of mine and a driver for Greaves Furniture Company of Clay Cross. Fred refused to take any payment for the lessons or his time, and as he did not own a car, I let him use the Austin any time he wanted it. This worked well for both of us, and I passed my test in March 1962.

Catty to close

Times were really good and everything was fine, and then we heard that Park House Pit was on the list for closure. This came as a shock to the miners, as no one knew what was going to happen to us all or where we might be transferred. Some men started to look for a job as near to their home as possible. My friend Charlie Hooper, a fitter who worked on the screens at Catty and had worked with Albert and me on Saturdays, left almost as soon as he heard the news, and got a job at Shirland Pit. A few weeks later, Charlie came to see me and told me that the Shirland blacksmith Mr. Cyril Herod was retiring and they were desperate for someone to shoe the ponies. Cyril was not a farrier, so anyone who could shoe ponies as well as cap the winding rope would get the job as foreman blacksmith. I acted on Charlie's tip, went for the job and got it. I started at Shirland after serving my notice at Catty Pit. It proved almost as easy to get a lift to Shirland on the A61 towards Alfreton as going to Catty by bus.

Shirland Pit

Every pit had its characters and big Dave was one of Shirland's. Dave was their underground rope man (splicer). He had a car, in fact he had several, and he lived in Chesterfield. He would pick up Charlie Hooper and me on his way to work, and we never knew just what car he would turn up in as he would buy them at auctions for around £40–50 and run them until their engine gave out. He was convinced that this was the cheapest way of motoring, especially if he could make some cash out of charging his passengers some petrol money. He wanted 2/6d a week in return for the lift to work. We agreed to the plan, providing that he turned up before the latest possible bus went by, the last one that would get us to work in time for a 7am start. Some days Dave did not turn up, but when he did you could see him coming from miles away, just in front of a cloud of smoke. When you got in any of Dave's cars you had to be careful where you put your feet, as you could see the road through holes in the floor. If all else failed I had my pushbike, which I used anyway for getting to work at the weekends.

As you entered the pit yard, the canteen and the baths were on the left and the ponies were stabled on the right. This pit was now a Dr.ift mine but still had two shafts, which were maintained in working order in case of emergency. The time office was quite a way up the yard. After a few weeks I worked out that if I made a habit of checking the ponies' feet before clocking in, I could swing this in my favour even if I were late some mornings. I could wander up to the time office as late as 8am and say that I had spent an hour shoeing a pony. No problem, and my time was put in from 7am. In fact, at a later date I would work it that I got some extra overtime. The horsekeeper was Joe Wood from Stonebroom.

Shirland Pit. The blacksmiths' shop is the white building. The stables are on the far right and the entrance to the drift is in the foreground

My services are needed elsewhere

One day I was at work in the blacksmith's shop when the engine-wright Mr. Tom Mason sent for me to attend his office. He had had a request from the manager at B Winnings Pit, Mr. Peach, asking if it would be possible to have the services of the Shirland farrier to look after their ponies one full day a week as their own farrier, Mr. Sid Clay, had retired. None of the blacksmiths at B Winnings were trained to shoe horses and ponies, and the pit was in trouble about it from the mines inspector. Mr. Mason would not let me go for a full day but said that, if I agreed, I could go two days a week after 3.30pm when my shift at Shirland ended. I would be paid overtime and they would provide transport between the two pits. I agreed but on the understanding that some weeks I might need more than two visits a week. The engine-wright assented.

B Winnings Colliery was situated in the village of Hilcote, between Blackwell and Huthwaite in Nottinghamshire. A lorry was to be sent for me and my tools at 3.30pm on the Monday and again on the Thursday each week. That's when I first met the lorry driver Harold Bedford from South Normanton. His instructions were to fetch me at 3.30pm, wait until I was finished underground then take me back to Shirland. I did not leave B Winnings until about 6.30pm, so that meant by the time I had got back to Shirland and used the baths it was around 7.30pm. As there was no one in the time office at that time of night, next morning I had to tell the office staff the time that I finished the previous evening. So, it was quite easy to claim more time than the hours I had actually spent. (Would I do a thing like that?) The lorry driver was even more excited about this job than I was, as he would make more overtime than either me or the horsekeeper – he had to return the lorry to B Winnings after he had dropped me off at Shirland and, if he had to wait over three hours for me to do my job, he was allowed a meal in the pit canteen whilst he was waiting. He told me not to worry about keeping him waiting if the weather were bad as he would always have a warm coat and a flask in the cab, and if it were really bad he would come on his motorbike for me. I was not sure if he made this offer through dedicated loyalty or greed, but I do know he clocked up more overtime than anyone else.

Arthur Kirk the horsekeeper

Arthur was the underground horsekeeper at B Winnings. He lived at Water Lane, South Normanton. He was waiting for me when I arrived at the pit on my first visit, having told the manager that he needed to be there to show me the way and accompany me to the stables. The ponies at this pit worked two coal seams with a separate stable for each seam. At the first stop down the shaft there were six ponies working the Tupton seam. When the cage stopped, you had to stride across to the Tupton seam stable and do what work was required, and then get back on the cage and down to the shale, where 12 ponies were stabled. Arthur stayed with me all the time and it was a nice little earner for both of us. About a year later, the mine manager saw Arthur in the pit yard one day and said, "Hey up, Kirky, I see that you are still making overtime with the farrier. Does he not know the bloody way yet?"

Arthur replied that he was now my assistant as the job needed two of us.

To that the manager said, "OK, bugger off." The wage packets were looking good for us all.

Arthur Kirk winning the trophy

A bit of moonlighting

Arthur lived next door to his brothers Herbert and Walter. Herbert was self-employed and travelled around South Normanton with a horse and cart, doing shed removals and carrying a bit of coal. Walter worked at the granary in the A Winnings pit yard, which supplied the food for all the ponies in the No. 4 area. It was not long before Arthur asked me if I would make some shoes for his brother Herbert's horse, as the previous pit farrier used to do. He said he would bring me one of the horse's old shoes as a pattern, and I could go and fit them at his smallholding. He would pay me for the job. I think Arthur knew that I was up for doing a bit on the side, as it was called then. I agreed to his suggestion, and that was the start of a great life-long friendship.

Local horses and owners

I was aware there was quite a demand for farriery among traders and horse riders in our area. At this time there were still a few working horses in and around Clay Cross and the surrounding area. Local tradespeople used to take them to a blacksmith's forge at the back of the Queen's Head pub on Thanet Street. The forge belonged to Mr. George Martin, who lived in Market Street, Clay Cross. He was also the blacksmith at Morton Colliery and he worked nights regularly, so he had time to operate his forge on Thanet Street during the day.

George Martin's clients included Mr. Simon Holmes, a local trader, who had a two-wheeled cart and a 12.2hh pony to pull it. He dealt in household goods, bedding, tea towels and floor coverings. Most of his customers were not well off. He operated a scheme of weekly payments for them, but he used to hold their family allowance book as security. He would meet the young mothers outside the post office on a Monday morning and wait outside while they cashed their allowance to pay him.

Then there were Tommy and Sam Thorpe, who had a covered four-wheeled cart. They were fruit traders, selling all types of fruit and nuts. In later years, Sam and Tommy were to move out of their High Street shop and use one of my outbuildings as a store place for their goods. Tommy also had a donkey cart, and on Saturdays he would travel around the streets of Clay Cross, Pilsley, Grassmoor and Holmewood with it. Any kids that were willing to help were welcome to do so. There was no pay, but you could ride the donkeys back to the field at the end of the day.

A greengrocery dray

Another of George Martin's clients was Jimmy Stone the coal merchant. Part of Jimmy's job was to deliver miners' free coal allowance to their homes with his horse and cart. Each miner was allowed one ton every six weeks and Jimmy would tip it out loose outside their coal house. There's a tale of a coal merchant who delivered coal to a certain lady's house. She said, "I am sorry, but I have no money to pay you. Would you like to come upstairs to my bedroom for payment?" The coalman replied that his horse was the one who had pulled the heavy load from the pit top, so he should be the one to have a go. The lady said, "Very well, but put these pillows on his feet so the neighbours cannot hear him on the stairs."

There was Tommy Smith, who sold ice cream from a two-wheeled float pulled by a pony. And Teddy Collins, a funeral director who used a horse-drawn Shillibeer hearse – a type of all-in-one funeral carriage large enough to carry the mourners as well as the coffin – with beautifully engraved cut-glass sides. Teddy also used his horses in winter to clear the snow from the pavements with a small plough. In the summer he would take them to roll the cricket pitch and bowling greens on the Miners Welfare ground. The horses had to wear boots on their feet for this job to prevent damage to the turf.

George Martin shod all these horses at his forge behind the Queen's Head. When he retired, he sold his forge and other equipment for £20 to a man called Malcolm Gambling. Malcolm had once worked at Catty Pit but left to do his own thing. He had no idea how to run a business and was just messing about with the forge. He sold off bits of the blacksmithing kit just to live, as he did not like work and never used to turn up to do any shoeing. The tradespeople would not stand for that as they

Lawn sandals used on the horses' feet

needed their horses for work. So before long the forge closed and became a memory of the past. Malcolm Gambling went to live in Calverton in Nottinghamshire and got a job at the pit there.

All in all, I reckoned there would be quite a lot of trade for a new farrier to pick up.

Starbuck retires

There was a farrier in South Normanton known as Starbuck, who had a forge next to the Shoulder of Mutton pub. One of his customers was a man by the name of Joe Green, who worked at B Winnings Pit. When Mr. Starbuck retired, Joe said to me, "I want you to do my pony Peggy. You won't have to travel, because on Friday night after the manager has gone home I will bring Peggy to the pit and put her in the yard stables. You can do her shoes on the Saturday morning and I will fetch her about 8.30am before the manager or anyone that matters is about. I will leave the money and a dozen eggs in the stable."

Yes, on Saturday morning there was a £1 note, a dozen eggs and an extra pony in the stable. The same thing happened every six weeks when Peggy was due to have her new shoes. There is a saying that goes like this: "It's no good having cheek unless you have the face to carry it out."

Factory-made horseshoes

Arthur knew all the local horse owners, and this little job of ours was fast becoming big business. We were now shoeing the Scott's Ice Cream horses, which pulled floats around Sutton-in-Ashfield and Kirkby-in-Ashfield. Morris Brothers of Blackwell, who also sold ice cream from horse-drawn wagons, became regular customers too. To keep up with the demand for horseshoes, I located a company in Stamford that sold factory-made shoes. These were pretty rough and needed a lot of work putting in to them, but I used buy them and take them to the pit to finish off. They were the big flat roadster shoes with Mordax studs, four in each foot, which cost £1 10s a set plus studs. I got some comments at the pit about the size of the shoes I was making, but I had an excuse as we did have a horse on the pit top with big feet. We would just tell them that the shoes were for the pit yard horse, who was stabled in a large double stable at the top of the yard. It did not seem too unreasonable and no more was said.

False alarms

Early in 1964 I was still suffering with my right leg as it was one-and-a-half inches shorter than the other and twisted. I had never been officially discharged from the hospital as they said that I would need further treatment over the years, and they were right. In September 1964, the surgeon Mr. Smith suggested that I ought to have another operation to correct this problem. At this time, my wife Joan was pregnant with our second child. She had more than eight weeks to go before her due date, and the surgeon said not to worry as he would do the operation well before the birth. He planned to do a similar procedure as before and to put some staples in my foot.

After the operation I was sent to Morton Grange Hospital in Alfreton for ten days to recover. I left Morton Grange on crutches, but discovered I was able to drive my car if I put a small wooden box under the plaster cast on my lower right leg. I told Joan that whatever she did, she must not take ill in the night, as it would take me some time to get down the stairs and across the road for the car. However, once I was inside the car, I was able to push down on the accelerator pedal. So, I could drive but only at one speed – fast.

We made three trips to the Ashgate maternity hospital. All were in record time (nine minutes) and all were false alarms. Joan would rush into the hospital and I would follow on my crutches when I had sorted myself out. Eventually, on 24th November 1964, Joan gave birth to our son Neal.

Joan had to stay in hospital for a full ten days after the birth. The day before she came out, I had the plaster cast removed from my lower leg. I can tell you that when a cast comes off you are worse at walking than ever. But needs must and you find a way to DIY. In my case I needed to collect my wife from the hospital. I had Gale, our daughter, with me in the car and she wouldn't stop hanging onto my coat. We arrived at Ashgate to see Joan coming down the ward towards us, carrying our son and all her belongings. Gale ran to her mum and off they went to the car with me hobbling behind them.

Shirland to close

Things were going well. I had a growing family, a steady job with plenty of overtime and an increasing number of local customers to supplement the day job. Then in May 1965 the National Coal Board announced that Shirland was to close. As I was already working part time at B Winnings, the manager there snapped me up straight away. I was automatically transferred to B Winnings, but just before Shirland closed I was also asked to go to the Alfreton pit as the mines inspector had stopped the ponies from going to work until they had their feet attended to. I agreed to go on the Sunday morning as Sundays meant double time. Soon after that I was asked to visit Swanwick Pit as well, as they needed a farrier urgently. It was there I met Morris Brayley, the horsekeeper. He had been in charge for many years and his father before him had done the same job. Morris was another very interesting man and it was a pleasure to meet him.

Now I had started full time at B Winnings I had to use my own car, as it was difficult to get there by public transport for a 7am start. In the blacksmith's shop at this pit were two brothers, Knobby and Jack Clark. They were both blacksmiths but not farriers. Knobby retired soon after I started and that just left Jack and me. I was in charge, which did not go down well with Jack. So, we just did our own things. The horsekeeper Arthur and I had built up a small round of clients with horses by then, and we would go horseshoeing straight from work before I went home to my wife and dinner.

Great Yarmouth

Joan and I decided to take the children for a week's holiday at Great Yarmouth by car. We had just spent £675 on buying a brand-new Vauxhall Viva XL from Brocklehurst's in Chesterfield, and I looked forward to the drive. We phoned the AA for a route map (there were no Sat Navs back then) and had a good journey to the coast, arriving at the boarding house about midday on the Saturday. The weather was not bad and got better as the week went by.

On the Sunday we took our first-ever flight in an aeroplane. I recall it was £3 for a flight around Great Yarmouth in a single-engine monoplane. It had an open cockpit and two seats side by side plus one behind for the pilot. I do not think the pilot was Biggles but he wore a white silk scarf around his neck and looked just like him. This was the first time that Joan and I had ever been off the ground. We climbed into the cockpit and I took our daughter Gale on my knee while Joan had Neal on hers. I can tell you it was bloody cold up there. It was a short flight, but quite an experience for us and one we shall never forget. It was the first of many flights we were to take in later years to many other parts of the world.

The rest of the week went well, and it was soon Saturday

morning again and time to head back home. This time the traffic was horrendous: bumper to bumper from the moment we left our accommodation. We would move about three or four feet then stop. The roads were very narrow; there had been an accident; and there were also road works. It was a beautiful day and the sun was very hot, so we had all the windows open. Cars had no air conditioning back in those days. About halfway through the village of East Dereham, not very far from where we had set off, the car cut out and would not restart. We were blocking the road and traffic was building up behind us. There was a large house just where we were broken down so I went to the house to ask if I might push the car into their drive to let the traffic pass whilst I tried to start the engine. The lady of the house said that would be OK. I did not know anything about cars and because I kept trying to start the engine the car battery went flat. At this point the lady came out of the house and said, "Would you like me to phone my local mechanic for you?" I was so grateful and thanked her warmly. By this time, the kids were becoming restless and playing up. The lady must have heard them and she said, "Can I get you a sandwich whilst you're waiting?", adding in the very best upper-class tones, "I have loads of jam."

Before long, the mechanic arrived. The first thing he did was to remove the air filter and then disconnect the feed from the petrol tank to the carburettor. He told me to sit in the car and pump the accelerator pedal. Now, this car had been crawling along in the hot sun most of the morning, so the engine was red hot. There was a loud bang and the engine burst into flames. With fire licking up around the bonnet, I scrambled out and pulled a blanket from the boot to try and smother the flames. At that point, the lady ran from the house with a bucket of water and poured it straight over the bonnet. With the air filter gone, all the water went into the engine. It put out the fire most effectively. But until the engine dried out there was going to be no way to start the car and it looked like we'd be there for hours.

Eventually the mechanic got the engine going. He told us to drive very slowly and leave the air filter off. We dared not stop for fear of being unable to start the car again, and finally arrived home at 9pm. I took the car back to Brocklehurst in Chesterfield for them to sort out. We never did get an explanation as to what the problem was with the engine. It had been serviced just before we went away. Now all the paint had been burnt from under the bonnet. However, it was re-sprayed and came back as good as new.

As a footnote on cars: that Viva kept going for several years, until I realised that I needed more room for equipment as I was doing more shoeing. I traded it in for a new Datsun estate, which lasted until I took on my first apprentice. The Datsun was succeeded by different vans through the years. I eventually bought a car as well, as my work van stank so badly that I felt ashamed to go out anywhere in it at night.

Is this the big time?

Around this time, I was doing private work from Herbert Kirk's smallholding at the bottom of Water Lane in South Normanton. Arthur and I had a small forge here, which we used after work and at weekends. As I said before, miners were allowed one ton of coal every month. One day I had a delivery to my home and the delivery man noticed I had left some old horseshoes down by the dustbin. He asked my wife, "Who is the blacksmith?" She said it was me, and he asked if he could come and see me that night. He told her that he and his friends were desperate to get their horses shod following the death of their regular farrier, Teddy Marples of Toc H Yard, Chesterfield. They had over twenty pacing and trotting horses that were all in training and needed special handmade shoes. My wife said he had better come round the following night.

Next day at about 6.30pm, a big grey Jaguar pulled up outside my home. You can imagine the curtains twitching on all the neighbours' windows. Out stepped a well-dressed couple, who introduced themselves as Kate (a movie star) and Ron James of Matlock. Their main business was coal deliveries and ice cream vending. If I agreed to do their horses, they would take me around their friends' places that night to measure the horses' feet and would show me exactly what type of shoes they required. I said I would give it a go. The first call was to Ron's brother Derek, who lived at Dethick near Crich, and then to Cyril Swain's yard up at Riber, Matlock. Cyril Swain and his friend Jimmy Garthwight ran the small train and the boats in Matlock Park, but they also owned pacers. Next, we visited Clem Dodd at Sandy Lane, Matlock. Clem was a full-time horse trainer, who had thirteen horses all in work, most of them with shoes on. He trained for Bill Eyre, a market trader in Chesterfield. That was the final call of the day, and back home I went in that big beautiful Jaguar.

Next day at work I told my friend Arthur that this could be the big time for us. Having free use of the forge – provided we made sure that Arthur's brother's horse was always shod

– was a great help. By now we had a steady flow of customers from in and around Normanton, including cart horses, chilDr.en's ponies, show horses and donkeys, all visiting us at the forge on Saturday afternoons, Sunday mornings and evenings after work at the pit. Work on the harness racing circuit would give the business a big boost. But we would need some better equipment – currently we had only an old Hoover to blow the fire. Arthur, true to form, solved this by having a word with someone he knew with a bigger blower, who said we could borrow it for as long as we wanted it. So, we now started work for real, making special shoes for trotters and pacers.

Trotters and pacers

Every year there was a big race meeting for trotters at Appleby-in-Westmorland on the Tuesday of the Appleby Horse Fair, and another trotting derby at Musselburgh in Scotland. Clem Dodd had all his horses shod for these two events and it cost him £1 10s a set. Roping in all that cash made me think it would not be long before I could hand in my notice at the pit and go self-employed. However, it was a good job I didn't, as Clem came back from Appleby having sold all but two of the horses he took. That's just how it was with those owners: you never knew what horses you were going to see so you could not prepare shoes for them even one week in advance, let alone make long-term plans for your business. I gathered that many harness-racer owners were market traders, gypsies and wheeler dealers and were so bent that they could not lie in bed straight. Doping was common at the races. One man used to walk down the paddock with half an apple in his hand, pretending to take

Coal Star

A pacer in action

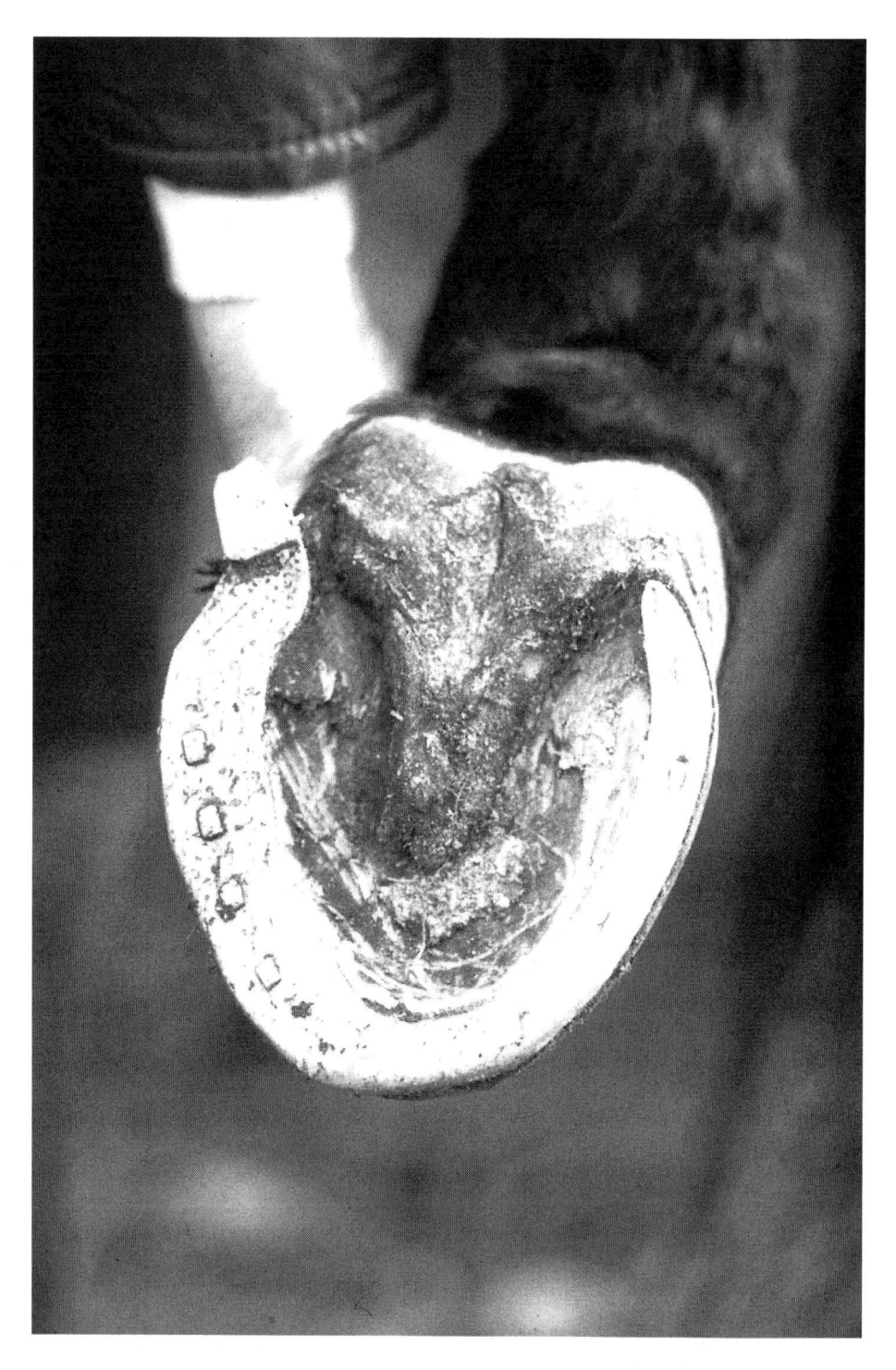

A hind hoof of a pacer fitted with a crossfire shoe

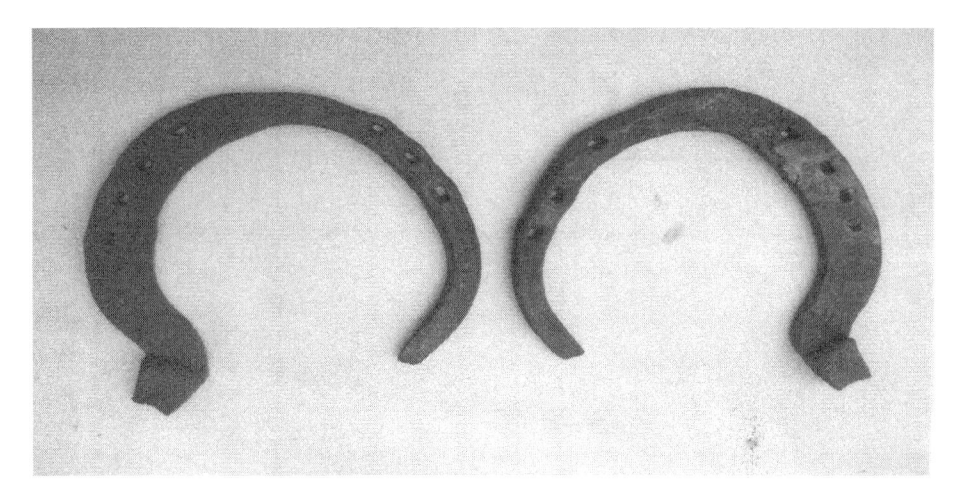

Crossfire shoes for pacing

Harness racing at Droylsden

a bite before sharing it with the horse he had entered. The centre would have been taken out and the apple filled with a go-faster drug. I even saw horses being injected before their race. None of this went on under Jockey Club rules of course. There was a big brand-new track at Prestatyn in North Wales which did operate under rules, but there were also lots of flapping (unlicensed) tracks around at that time. Organisers could hold a certain number of meetings a year without a licence.

Racetrack farrier

It was not long before Clem Dodd asked me if I would shoe the horses at the Droylsden track. This was the main official harness-racing track in the region. Races were held on a Monday night and the meetings were floodlit. This track was owned by Clem's cousin Edmund Dodd. Ted Marples from Chesterfield had been the regular farrier there until he died, turning up every week on his motorbike with his farriery kit in the sidecar. I agreed to take Ted's place. The racing started at 6.30pm with the last race at 9.30pm. It sounded like a good arrangement for me as I would stay for the racing and would be likely to pick up extra work when the horse boxes arrived. This did indeed prove to be a learning curve for me, as I had never been among so many wheeler dealers and crooks in my life.

Ron and Harry Ackers

The brothers Ron and Harry Ackers made their living by training other people's trotting and pacing horses, and would race them at Droylsden on Monday nights. I was working at the track one night when the brothers arrived. As they were unloading their horses, Harry called to Ron to come and look at one that had thrown a splint.

Ron said, "Bloody hell, he's in the third race." He put on a tight elastic bandage from the knee down to the fetlock and then to my surprise he hit the horse with a two-pound hammer directly on the swelling on the horse's leg. He told his brother it would disperse the splint. This horse was scratched from taking part in the third race as he was too lame.

A few weeks later there was a similar incident with one of the horses they unloaded. Harry called to Ron "The horse's lampas is down." (Lampas is a swelling in the gum, where the roof of the mouth fills with blood so the horse cannot graze properly.) Years ago, it was the job of the blacksmith to treat the condition. He would place a gag in the horse's mouth then take a piece of metal shaped to the inside of the teeth on a rod from the fire and burn the lampas back. The cost was two shillings. Not so in this case. Ron just pulled the horse's tongue to one side, opened his sheath knife and slit the roof of the horse's mouth. It was like flushing a toilet, the amount of blood that came from the mouth. Ron then chucked a handful of salt in the horse's mouth and began to harness it up for the first race.

I am sure it is practices like this, and all the doping that went on, and the type of people that it attracted, that explain why this sport has never really caught on in this country. The owners were among the most difficult people I have ever had to work for. Pacing and trotting are not natural gaits for horses to keep up over a long period, and the owners would demand all different types of fancy shoes for their animals. For pacers they always wanted crossfire shoes fitted on the back feet so that the inside of the hoof was lower than the outside. These shoes help prevent the hind hoof from clipping the heel or back of the foreleg when the horse is moving at speed. For the front feet they wanted light steel concave or aluminium shoes. For a trotting horse they would ask for toe weights on the shoes and sometimes weights that screwed on to the hoof capsule as well. On the hind feet the shoe had to be as light as possible. Not many farriers would bother with these people because they would continually ask for these fancy shoes but did not want to pay for the extra work involved in making them.

The ring of fire

I was working at Derek James' farm one day when he brought out a young horse he was training to pace. He had made a track around his house and through the wall into the next field, making a course about half a mile in circumference. This horse was harnessed up in the sulky (a two-wheel training cart) but would only go forward a few yards before it stopped and lay down on the track, still harnessed up. Derek cursed and bellowed and was getting madder by the minute. In the end he left the horse there, went to fetch a bale of straw and piled it all around the horse as close as he could get. Then he poured some petrol on the straw and lit it. It did not take the horse long to decide that was not the place to be, and he never got down on the track again.

Kaylifts Katie

Katie was a 16.2hh dark bay mare, a trotter and the property of Ron James (brother of Derek) of Crich in Derbyshire. Ron had several trotting horses, some of them from Germany, while Derek kept only pacers. They trained their horses at their home. I was at the farm one day when Ron came up and said, "What can you do for me with this horse? I am at my wits' end. She can go like the clappers and then suddenly she will brake, jump off her legs and pull up. I know there is nothing out there that can catch her if I can get her right. Her front feet are coming back and cutting her back legs. [This is known as scalping.] So come on, blacksmith, give me some idea of what you and I can do." He added with a laugh, "If you can stop her striking her back legs, there's a case of whisky in it for you. So, try and help me, please!"

I told him to bring the horse to the forge. When I saw her hind legs I saw straight away that the first job was to remove the metal that was causing the injuries. This meant the use of an open toe shoe. In other words, a reverse shoe on the front feet. I showed Ron what I meant, and he said, "What on earth are you doing? The shoe is back to front."

I told Ron not to worry. "Just think that the Lord Jesus wore open-toe sandals and look what they did for him."

The mare went back into training as soon as the cuts had healed, and won her next three races in succession. For the first race she was priced at 16 to one (not bad, hey!) The public were allowed in the paddock, and when people asked about the shoes Ron told them the farrier shod her late at night when he was Drunk. I did not get the whisky, because Ron's promises were like pie crusts; easily broken.

Ron James and his horse Kaylifts Katie

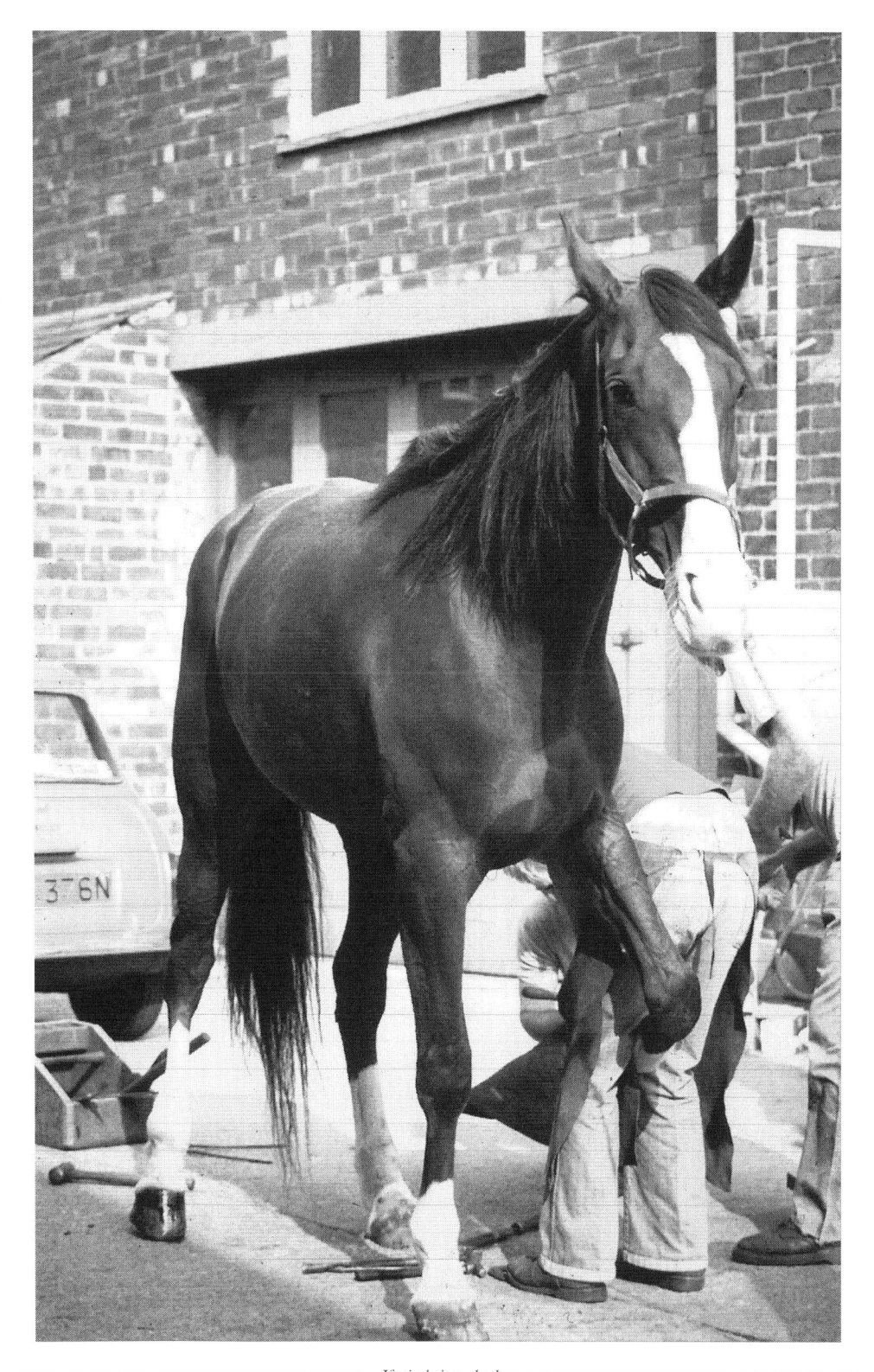

Katie being shod

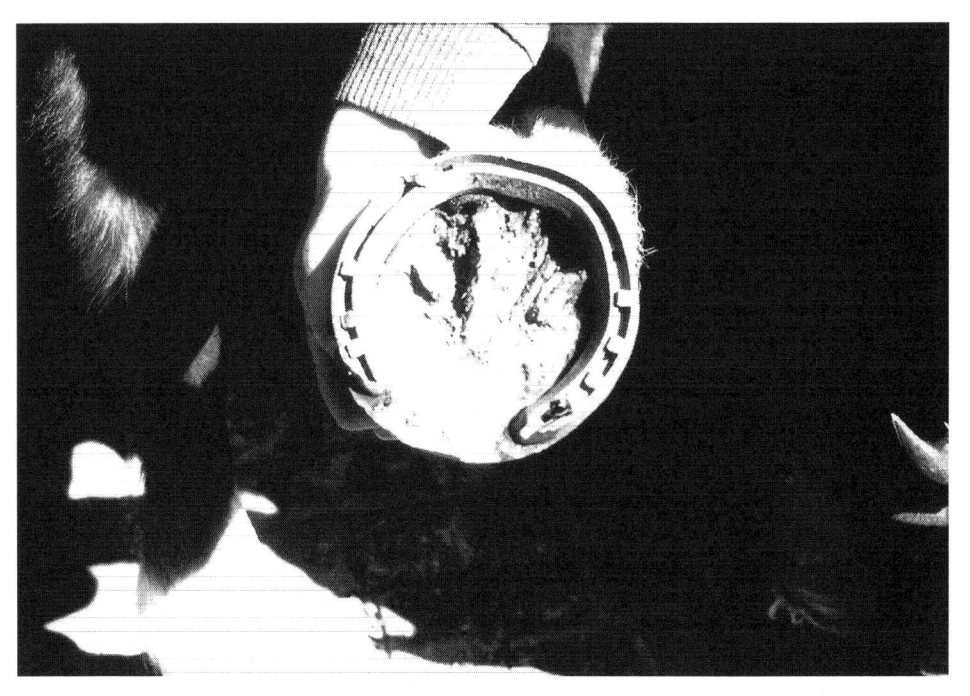

An open-toe shoe in place

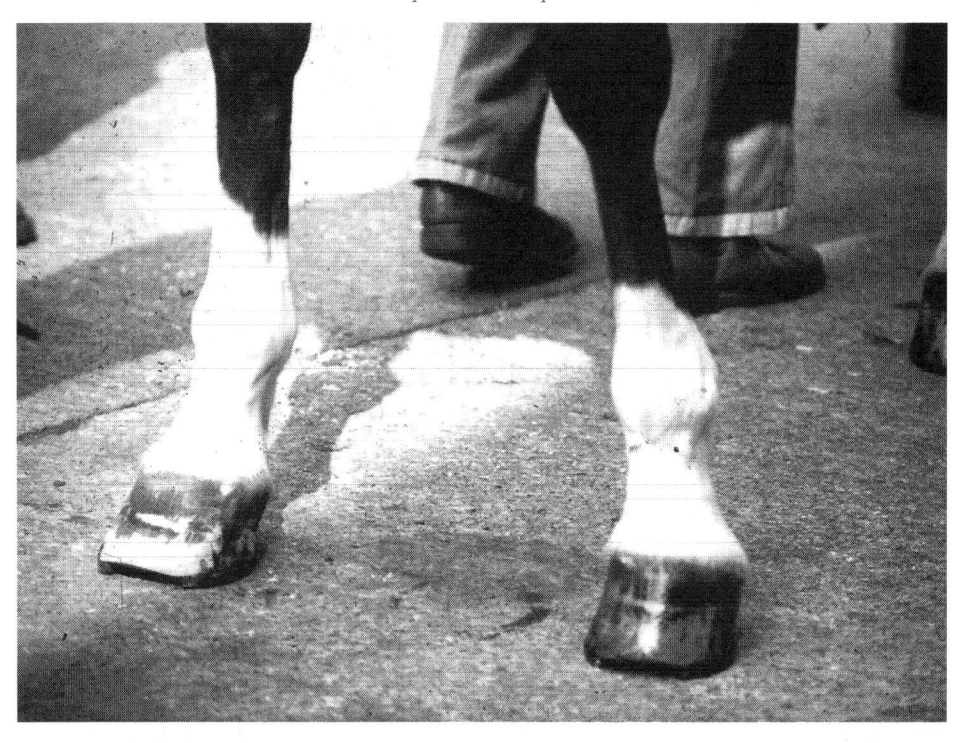

Newly shod forefeet

Arthur Kirk

Arthur sees the sea

Derek James arranged to race one of his horses, Blue John, at Prestatyn. This racecourse was near the sea in North Wales and was a new track, built in the American style. Derek said, "I think my horse can win on Tuesday night. You and Arthur can come in the lorry if you want to."

Arthur's eyes lit up as he had never seen the sea in his life. Up until the time he and I met, he had never even been outside of Nottinghamshire and his biggest trip had been to the Goose Fair at Nottingham. We both put in for a rest day from the pit and turned up at Derek's farm on the Tuesday lunchtime. Derek warned us it would be a long journey in the old lorry and, as his father-in-law was coming too, one of us would have to ride in the back with the horse. Straight away, Arthur volunteered to ride in the back.

It was a bright sunny day and that old lorry had a Perspex roof. When we took a break at a café outside Knutsford, Derek said he would drop the ramp and let the horse have a breather. As the ramp opened it was like a sauna – there was steam coming from the back and Arthur was as wet as the horse.

"That's f...ed it," said Derek. "I gave Blue John some dope just before we left. I shall have to give him some more at the track."

Arthur had a rub down and off we went again. He had been standing up all the way, looking over the back ramp, and was amazed at the hills and all the scenery. Derek said, "If he likes this now, wait till he sees the sea."

The heat had taken its toll on the horse by the time we arrived at the track. Derek said that if the horse had been all right, he would have asked Arthur and me to put money on him at the bookmakers, as they did not know us and the odds would be better. If he or his family were to go near a bookie, the odds would fall as they would guess what they were trying on. As there were only six horses in Blue John's race and he finished sixth, I reckoned Derek's plan was wishful thinking. So, the horse was loaded up again and we made our way back home. We arrived at Dethick at about 4am on the Wednesday morning. Arthur said that he had been stood on a bale of straw all the way there and back so he could see out the back, and he had never seen any scenery like that before. He was at the pit that morning at 6am to check the ponies before they went to work.

That was the first of many such adventures we had together. Arthur could not shoe horses but was a great help in every other way as we travelled around the area. He would agree that though he could do most of the work involved, knocking nails into a hoof was something he just could not manage. We were on the crest of a wave, Arthur and I.

Then we received the news that B Winnings was to close in November 1964. It seemed our luck had run out. With pits closing at such a rate, I could not help but wonder if the downturn might have been caused by people such as us two not pulling our weight. But, we were assured it was because there were no coal reserves left.

A Winnings colliery

Arthur and I were transferred to A Winnings, which was a bit nearer for me to travel from my home. It had a large forge with three other blacksmiths working there. None of them was a farrier, and they were not too pleased when I turned up because farriers were on underground time, with shifts of seven-and-a-quarter hours, while they were on eight-and-three-quarter hours. That did not go down well at all.

Checking the ponies' feet

My task was to go down the pit at 6.30am every day, spend two or three hours working on the ponies' feet and then put the world to rights with the horsekeeper, who was Arthur Kirk. Some days there were no ponies to shoe so Arthur and I would sit on the feed bags for two hours. I would come to the surface about 10.30am, go to the forge and have a bit of breakfast, and then make up the fire and make horseshoes – one set for the pit and two sets for me. No one was overworked at A Winnings, and we soon had the job sorted in our favour. I used to take a lot of my own shoes to finish making there. They were factory-made ones I had bought in, but they came without clips and needed one clip on the front and two on the back. No one asked any questions and you could do what you wished. As I said, my start time was 6.30am. The problem was that I was not very good at getting there on time. When I did arrive on time, I could finish at 2.15pm, and off Arthur and I would go on our local shoeing rounds. If I arrived a minute past 6.30am, the man in the time office would stop me half an hour's pay or tell me I had to make the time up at the end of the shift.

The all-important lift

One day when I had finished work, there was a terrible storm. As I drove by the time office, I saw Frank the maintenance man sheltering in a doorway. I stopped and asked if he wanted a lift. He was in the car almost before I could open the door. His was a job where you did not have many friends. He said thank you very much and would I drop him at the Blackwell Hotel. No problem. I used to do this every day, and it got that he would look out for me for the lift. Then one day it happened I was late to work, not arriving until about 7.10am, so I stopped later in the afternoon to make the time up. The next day as usual I picked up my friend. He said, "Where were you yesterday?"

"Sorry, Frank, but I was late to work and I stopped to make my time up."

He said. "Do not worry. Your time will be clocked as 6.30am every day from now on, no matter what time you arrive." Yes Arthur, we had cracked it.

The private work grew rapidly. We were now shoeing at local riding schools and doing more and more trotting horses. I hoped that one day there would be enough work to go self-employed doing the range of work that I enjoyed. During this period, I was going to Droylsden on a Monday morning and travelling around stables in that area, then making my way to the trotting track to see to the horses stabled there. I would stay on duty during the race meeting, which started at 6.30pm with the last race at 9.30pm, and arrive back home at about midnight.

I was then asked if I would do the track at Prestatyn and also see to some horses for a man by the name of Charlie Blissett, a Londoner who was renting stables at Larchmont Road in Rhyl. He had a large number of horses in training and his son was one of the many jockeys employed there. I spent a weekend at Rhyl sorting out his horses' feet, and was invited to stay a few days longer if I wished. That summer, Joan and I booked a holiday at the Miners Camp in Rhyl for us and the kids. Joan took the kids to the beach and I went up to the track to earn a few bob and then we would all go to the races at night. Later I carried on going down to Rhyl on Fridays after work on my own, coming back on the Sunday evening.

My wife Joan and I with our children Gale and Neal at the Miners Camp, Rhyl, 1965

Pit ponies to be phased out

Records show that in 1913 over 70,000 horses and ponies were employed in and around the pits, but over the years their numbers decreased quickly as the mining industry became more and more mechanised. In 1927 there were 56,000 and this reduced to 33,000 in 1937; 21,000 in 1947; 19,000 in 1949; 15,500 in 1951; 6,000 in 1962; 900 in 1967; 490 in 1972; 149 in 1978; and in 1984 only 55 ponies were left. The last of the ponies were employed at Ellington colliery in Northumberland and they were brought up from the pit when it closed in 1994. These were the last animals to work underground in England, although some horses and ponies remained at work in Wales in privately owned drift mines, or 'levels' as they were sometimes known. These animals were still protected by the Coal Mines Acts of 1911 and 1945. It was not rocket science for Arthur and I to realise that before long we would be out of a job in the mines.

At A Winnings there was a lot of jealousy from the blacksmiths because of the money I was making. They never knew the exact amount but could only guess. One man reported me to the management on more than one occasion but they never had any proof of any transactions. I had several other men at the pit doing jobs for me on the afternoon and night shifts, pressing out horseshoes on the hydraulic press, and I would pay them each week on Friday when they collected their NCB wages. They all looked forward to that little bit of extra cash. The management never did anything to stop me, but that did not prevent the other blacksmiths trying to bring me down.

While we were on holiday in Rhyl, a friend phoned to tell us that the place that used to be White's Corn Store at 40 Thanet

Street, with all its outbuildings, was coming up for sale. Back home, we enquired about the property and learned that the sale price was £3,750. That would mean taking a mortgage at payments of about £20 a month. In those days your wife's wages were not taken into account in mortgage applications and only the husband's wages were considered. All the same, I reckoned I could manage the payments and that the outbuildings could be just what I needed to set up a proper farriery business of my own.

So, Joan and I became the new owners of number 40 Thanet Street. There was plenty of room to put in a forge, and I began to look for equipment. As a start, I brought some of the stuff from Herbert Kirk's smallholding at Normanton. At the pit I noticed there was a spare two iron, not new but in very good condition. (A two iron is the tube that the fire is built around. It has water to protect the end and prevent it burning out.) So, one morning I put it on my shoulder, walked out of the pit yard and put it in my car. About a month later Big Jim, the foreman blacksmith and the man who was trying to cause the trouble, said "Brad, the two iron that was over there has gone missing. I know you have had it, but I can't prove it. I do not know how you got it past the security guards, but you have had it."

I laughed at him and said he didn't know what he was talking about. "Why would I need that two iron when I already have a forge at South Normanton?"

Not long after this, we were told that A Winnings was due to close, and so it did. It was looking more important than ever to prepare for the inevitable and become self-employed. For the time being, Arthur was transferred to Bentinck Colliery in Nottinghamshire and I was transferred to Pleasley Pit.

This is a spare two iron. They go through the wall at the back of the forge to the fire

The two iron in place

You need a cat

When I started at Pleasley, I was told there were no ponies at this pit and my job was in the forge on surface time of eight-and-three-quarter-hour shifts. I said I was a farrier not a blacksmith – I hoped I might be made redundant and draw a few pounds' compensation. No way; the manager remembered me from Catty Pit and knew I did blacksmithing as well as farriery.

I had only been there a week when the foreman blacksmith said, "I want you to go up there with the burring tackle." He pointed at the head stocks. I said he didn't need me but a bloody cat. He said that if I refused to do it, I would be on nights the next week.

"Really?" I said. "Nights are for burglars and bobbies. What shift would I be on the week after?"

He replied that it would be the day shift.

"Thanks very much. You will not see me next week or the week after, as that will be the second week of my notice. Good day." With that, I left the colliery for good.

When I first worked at Catty Pit with Albert Cowlishaw in the blacksmith's shop and started dealing with pit ponies, people had said I was wasting my time on horseshoeing. Times had changed, they said, and the horse job had had its day. How wrong they were. I owe big thanks to Albert for the time he spent with me, teaching me and giving me the chance to earn a very good living. I finished working for the National Coal Board in 1968 and set up on my own as a self-employed farrier.

5

A DERBYSHIRE FARRIER

I go self-employed

In those days horseshoeing was done hot if a client brought their horse to the forge, but it would be cold shoeing if the farrier travelled out to the client's yard and shod the animal there. I soon found myself driving all over Derbyshire to shoe horses. I often had company on these trips, as our children Gale and Neal, who were now aged about seven and four, would sooner come with me than go to school (not that they were given the option to miss school) and would also pester for a trip to the trotting track at Manchester. Whenever they were not at school and saw me setting off on a job, Neal would say "Can we come with you, Dad? Can we take a picnic?" They would pile into the car and Joan would hand out packs of sandwiches. Neal would have had eaten his before we were out of Clay Cross and would be wanting to call at the shops on the way for more food. One of their jobs on these trips was to collect the old horseshoes and put them in a bucket in the car. I told them they could have the money I got from the scrap man for the shoes. Winter and summer did not make much difference to either of them – they would still want to come. The fresh air most certainly did them a power of good as they very rarely caught a cold. When they did get a sniffle, their mum would give them a couple of tablets and pack them off to school just the same.

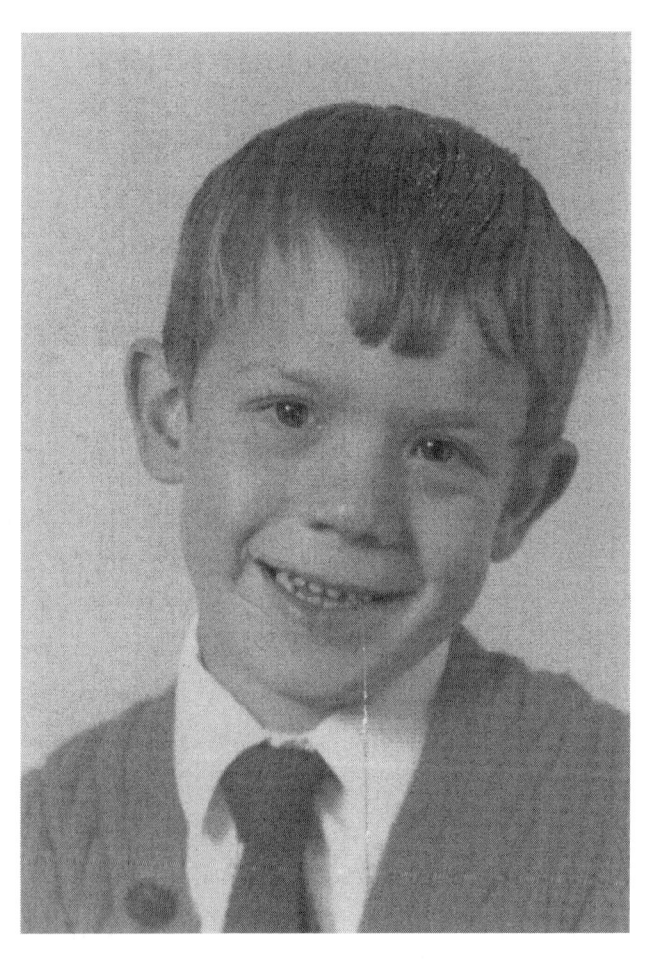

Our son Neal

Where is our son?

One day I was racing about Derbyshire from one client to another when Derek James phoned to say he wanted two horses shoeing urgently at his farm at Dethick near Crich. It was about 5.30pm when I got this message, so I said I would call before going home. I had Neal with me, and when we arrived we discovered it was the birthday of Derek's son Martin, who was the same age as Neal. Martin had been given a go-cart as a birthday present, and he took Neal to play with it on the rolled-stone track that was used to train the horses. This track went through two fields and the kids were blissfully happy playing there. After I'd finished the shoeing, Derek invited me in for a cuppa as usual – they were great tea drinkers – and a chat about what was happening in the trotting world. Derek paid me and I said good night. I arrived back home about 7.30pm and put the car away. As I walked in the house Joan was just putting the evening meal on the table. She asked, "Where's Neal?"

Shit. I'd left him at Derek's. I had never given him a thought. I phoned Derek quick, and he said Neal was still going round the track with Martin and had not missed me for a moment. Neal was about four then and he still laughs about it today.

Can we have a pony, Dad?

When I visited riding schools, the owners would offer the kids free rides. That was fine for a time, but before long they were asking if they could have a pony of their own to look after as they were getting bored with sitting on sluggish riding-school horses. First, I tried telling them we had nowhere to keep a pony. Then I told them I would look out for one on my rounds, but it would take some time as there were a lot of bad horses out there. And, I said, it was important that they have a perfect pony. Knowing it would be almost impossible to find such an animal, I managed to find something wrong with all the ponies we saw. It gave me time to think of some other excuse.

One day on my way home through Sheffield I passed Arthur Cottam & Company (Horseshoes) Ltd., which was then on Catley Road. Cottam & Co made all types of steel and aluminium horseshoes as well as the mouth bits and a new type of aluminium racing stirrups. They had given me one of the first pairs of these stirrups they had made. That gave me an idea. I called in at the shop and bought two pairs of stirrups with their leather straps – they gave me two for the price of one, so I was extra pleased. I did not tell the kids that I had something for them until the Saturday afternoon. I placed the stirrups over the arms of the settee and switched on the racing on the television. Then I sat Gale and Neal at either end of the settee with their feet in the stirrups and told them they were racing at Newmarket today. It was a far more economical solution than a pony – and easier to replace. They thought armchair racing was great, or so I was led to believe. Some years later I was telling one of my customers this story and laughing at the trick I had played. That was until the kids chimed in and said I was a tight old bastard – they knew perfectly well I had done it because it was cheaper to buy a new settee than keep a pony.

That's a lot of wind

My wife Joan decided to learn to drive. She had always said that one day she would, and having to use the local buses whilst I was in hospital convinced her she must gain her independence. Now she got down to it with determination, and duly passed her test. She was able to practise on the Morris Traveller I had recently bought in exchange for my pick-up van.

One day, Joan was on her way back from Matlock with our son Neal, who was aged about six at the time, and she called at Kennings Garage on Broadleys near to our home. She noticed one of the rear tyres was going down but wasn't sure what to do about it as she had never had to inflate a tyre before. Neal told her, "Dad does it by just putting that small end on and pressing the button on the side of the handle with his other hand." He did not tell his mum that you have to check the pressure gauge at the same time. I think you can guess what happened next. Joan left her finger on the button and very soon the needle on the pressure gauge had passed the point of no return. With an almighty bang, the tyre blew off the wheel. The lads in the garage fell about laughing, but were very good and changed the wheel for her. Finding that it had a slow puncture, they inflated it above the normal level and told her to just drive like hell to our yard at the end of the road before it went down again.

Joan becomes my assistant

Once both children were at school and I was out working all over the county, my wife was left at home alone for many long hours at a stretch. I suggested that she come with me on the rounds to get some fresh air and a change of scene. Joan was doubtful at first because she was rather afraid of horses, but she agreed to come and watch what went on. She became a real asset to the firm. One advantage was that she got to know the customers and where they lived, so she could work out the route from the map. That saved me a lot of time and petrol.

One day, I was shoeing a horse at home in the yard when it reared up. One of its front hooves caught me on the head and knocked me to the ground. The horse was about to come down on me when Joan saw what was happening and ran in between me and the animal. Her rapid action saved me from being trampled or worse. I think that incident gave her the confidence she needed. Afterwards she was happy to pull on her trousers and boots every morning and off we would go together. Her mum and dad used to come every day, meet the kids from school and stay until we got back. Then I would tidy up the house whilst Joan prepared dinner.

Joan carried on working with me until she reached retirement age.

My wife joins the rounds

A pony falls into the inspection pit

One morning our first call was at a large house on Old Hall Road in Chesterfield. It was a dismal morning, raining heavily, and when we arrived the lady who came to the door asked if we would like to do our shoeing in the coach house. This was a beautiful and spacious old building now used as a garage. The lady showed us the pony but disappeared straight back into the house, saying she was afraid of horses and her daughters could not help as they had gone off to school.

Entering the building, we saw a bench across the back wall. Placed on the bench to the left was a small rabbit hutch and in front of that was a set of wooden steps leading up to a hay loft. Working in a coach house felt like luxury; most of our customers had no such facilities and we usually did our shoeing in a field. We tied the pony to the steps in the corner. I took off one hind shoe and began taking off the other one. Joan, who was busy with the forge in the back of the van, called out "What size of shoes will you need? I'll put them in the forge for you."

Just at that moment there was a loud crash. The leg I was holding jerked out of my hands and I jumped aside. The pony was no longer there. He had fallen through the floor onto a ledge about three feet down. But, he was still tied to the steps and started to thrash about in panic. He scrambled back up into the coach house, pulling over the 13-step staircase, which in turn knocked over the rabbit hutch. The door flew open and the rabbit fell down the hole where the horse had been.

At this point the pony decided he must escape the disaster area. He bolted down the drive, dragging the set of steps, which banged about behind him. Luckily, Joan had run to cut off his escape route and by waving her arms managed to make him stop. She grabbed his headcollar and held on whilst I untied the rope. I managed to get a shoulder underneath the staircase and heave the whole thing back inside the coach house. I put the rabbit hutch back on the bench, and the next challenge was to get the rabbit out of the hole. What a job I had. He jumped out of the hole and shot to one end of the long bench. Each time I got near, he hopped to the other end. He did this several times – we were playing at silly buggers. Then I seized a brush stale and hit him on the head with it.

That stunned him for a moment, so I grabbed him and slung him in the hutch.

Whilst this was going on, Joan calmed the pony and brought him back to the coach house. At this point the lady came out of the house and said, "Did I hear a noise?"

I said "Mrs., you are so lucky that it was not your car that fell through the floor as you may never have got it back."

"Oh dear", she said, "has the horse hurt himself? I can see some blood on his leg. I will get some hot water and Dettol so you can bathe his leg for me." Not a word about whether Joan and I were all right. We left this appointment at 12 noon having spent the whole morning earning the price of one set of shoes: £4 10s (£4.50). All in a day's work. It turned out that at some time in the past the owner had dug an inspection pit in the coach house for their car. The pit had been covered with railway sleepers but these had rotted all the way through.

The rabbit recovered well.

Shoeing demonstrations were another part of the job. Here I am demonstrating how to put shoes on Silver at Inkersall School, Staveley 1970

"We turn the horses out at night"

During that same week, Joan and I attended a pony in South Wingfield. This pony was extremely overweight and clearly a candidate for laminitis (a hoof problem that can be fatal if it is not treated by the veterinary surgeon and a competent farrier). Farriers are not allowed to diagnose but may give advice to customers. My advice to this owner was that she must stop giving the pony extra food on top of all the grass it was eating. I told her that, if she didn't stop feeding the animal, she might kill it. Overfeeding a pony, whether from kindness or neglect, is just as bad as not feeding it. I thought I had got my message across – until the customer phoned me a week later to say they had sorted the problem with the over-feeding by turning the pony out at night so it couldn't see the grass!

"I want new gate posts"

Sunday was always a working day for me and, as I said before, Neal and Gale would usually come along too. They were never forced to come, but were in the car as fast as I was. On this occasion my first call was in the town of Heanor in Nottinghamshire at a large house on a hill behind the church. At this time I was driving a Renault 4, which had the handbrake on the dashboard. The car had four seats and a large boot, where I put all my tools and horseshoes plus all the different sizes of nails in 2lb boxes. I always carried a big stock of everything and had learnt to leave ample time in between calls, because people would often ask me to do their other horses whilst I was there.

The young owner went to fetch the horse and I started the job. Gale and Neal were running around as they usually did. The lady of the house came out shouting at the kids not to touch this and not to touch that as the gates had only been painted that last week. I put the horse's foot down, went across to the kids and made them sit in the car. They were happy to do as they were told and pretended to be going to Blackpool.

I had just started back on the horse's hoof when I noticed the Renault moving backwards and gathering momentum. I ran over and tried to open the door, but the kids had locked it and sat there laughing. The hatch to the boot was open wide but I could not scramble inside in time to stop the car smashing into the gate halfway down the drive – the gate that had only been painted last week. There were horseshoes, tools and boxes of nails down the road almost as far as Langley Mill. The lady came out screeching "Look at my gate!" I told her not to worry and I would have it put right. I pulled Neal out and slapped his legs and he said, "You made me wet my pants."

The damage to the car came to £150. Later that day I was doing some work for a master joiner and told him what had happened that morning. He promised to put the gate right for me, went to inspect it and said he could do the job for £5. When he turned up to do so, the lady told him not to bother, as she wanted new gates and posts off me. She later phoned to inform me of her requirements, so I told her to go to hell. We never heard any more about the matter.

Help from Big Joe and the NCB

Over the next few years my business expanded, and I found myself working a seven-day week. Luckily, there were factory-made horseshoes you could buy. One of the manufacturers was Bakers of Stourbridge. This company was over 100 years old and made shoes in over 80 different sizes for shipment around the world. They sold the shoes through their stockist, and their main agent at this time was Chas Grey & Co of Stamford. A.J. Pledger, also of Stamford, manufactured their own shoes and you could buy direct from them. They had their own lorries and made weekly deliveries. Then there was Arthur Cottam & Company of Sheffield, who also made shoes and sold them direct. Factory-made shoes were very basic and often the nail holes were not fully stamped through; in fact, they were lengths of concave iron just bent into the shape of the horse's foot. None of these companies put clips on their horseshoes and all heels were left blank. Having said that, the factory shoes came in very handy when you were too busy to make your own.

Just by chance I met a man by the name of Big Joe Davis with his wife Doris. Their son Nigel had suffered brain damage at birth. Joe was a blacksmith from Poolsbrook and a giant of a man. He worked for the National Coal Board at the local pit, doing day and afternoon shifts on alternate weeks. He suggested he could help me by clipping some ready-made factory shoes for me while he was on the afternoon shift, as he had a lot of spare time. This seemed to me a heaven-sent offer, which would certainly take a lot of pressure off me. So, I took him a large bag of factory-made shoes to clip. He told me to pick them up again from his house on the following Friday night. When I collected them I could see they were perfect. "What do I owe you, Joe?" I said.

Joe said, "Just give me a couple of quid."

I gave him a bit more than the £2 he asked for, and left a further large bag. Big Joe's assistance was a big boost to my business, and I took to making a regular weekly visit to his place to fetch and deliver horseshoes. As time went on, I was fast needing more and more shoes, and Joe suggested that if I could provide him with a small portable forge he could make them for me. He knew of a shed he could use at the farm just up the road, as the farmer was his friend and would be sure to agree. During the weeks when he was on afternoon shifts at the pit, he could spend the mornings clipping shoes for me at the farm. So, I bought a portable forge with a hand-operated fan on the back. It lasted about two years. At that point Joe phoned to say the fan had packed up because it had worn out. I managed to get hold of a second-hand cylinder Hoover, which contained a fan of about the right size, and that enabled Joe to become mechanised and step up the production of clipped shoes. I made a deal with the farmer to pay for the electricity.

Arthur Fielding

One day in 1971, a man by the name of Arthur Fielding came to see me. He was from School Lane, Selston in Nottinghamshire, and was secretary to the Derbyshire branch of the National Association of Farriers, Blacksmiths and Agriculture Engineers (NAFBAE). He wanted to know if I might be interested in joining. The NAFBAE head office was at Lofthouse Gate in Leeds and the general secretary was Ruth Rowley. The

Arthur Fielding RSS of Selston

Arthur Fielding RSS of Selston

Derbyshire branch held three meetings a year in the Three Horseshoes pub at Ripley. He said if I were interested, he would send me a notice for the next meeting. I went along and signed up.

Arthur and his wife were very nice people and we became life-long friends. He remained as branch secretary for over 40 years until he died. The meetings were always on a Saturday afternoon. We were not allowed in until the bar shut to the public at 3pm and we had to be out by 7pm, when it re-opened. I used to pick up Arthur on the way and drop him off afterwards, as he did not have a car. He had a small portable forge in the workshop at the bottom of his garden, and on one of my visits to his home he gave me a pair of pull-off pincers he had made for me out of old shoeing rasps. As I have said, he was a very nice man and I thanked him warmly.

But, he was also a cunning old bugger. He suggested that I should stand to be member of the committee. I did, and was duly elected. It came to be time for the AGM, which was to be held at Pitlochry in Scotland. I was informed: "Now that you are on the committee, you and I both I get to go to Scotland as delegates. We can go in your car as that will be better than the train."

The day came and I picked up Arthur from his home. We headed north on the M1 motorway. Arthur sat very quiet, so I put the radio on. At this, Arthur spoke. "Ha, my lad, we don't want that noise on all day, do we?"

It was a long way to Scotland.

We had agreed to save money by sharing a hotel room. When we got there, I opened a window.

"Oh my god, what are you doing? It's too cold for that, my

lad. Please close it," said my roommate.

Well, when Arthur began to undress, I could not believe my eyes. He was wearing two of everything. He left one layer on and then added his pyjamas on top. It was so hot in our room that I slept without sheets on top of the bed.

Arthur talked of the days when he was an apprentice and the jobs he had to do. He still had the original test piece of work that he made when he finished his apprenticeship. He gave it to me in 1973; it is a tool for getting the hubs off carriage wheels when they were taken to the wheelwright to have new tyres put on. He had made the tool by hand; forged, fire welded, riveted, threaded 3/8 and assessed at each step by the master farrier as a condition of completing his apprenticeship. This and other gifts from Arthur were to become part of the collection I built up for my horseshoeing museum at Thanet Street.

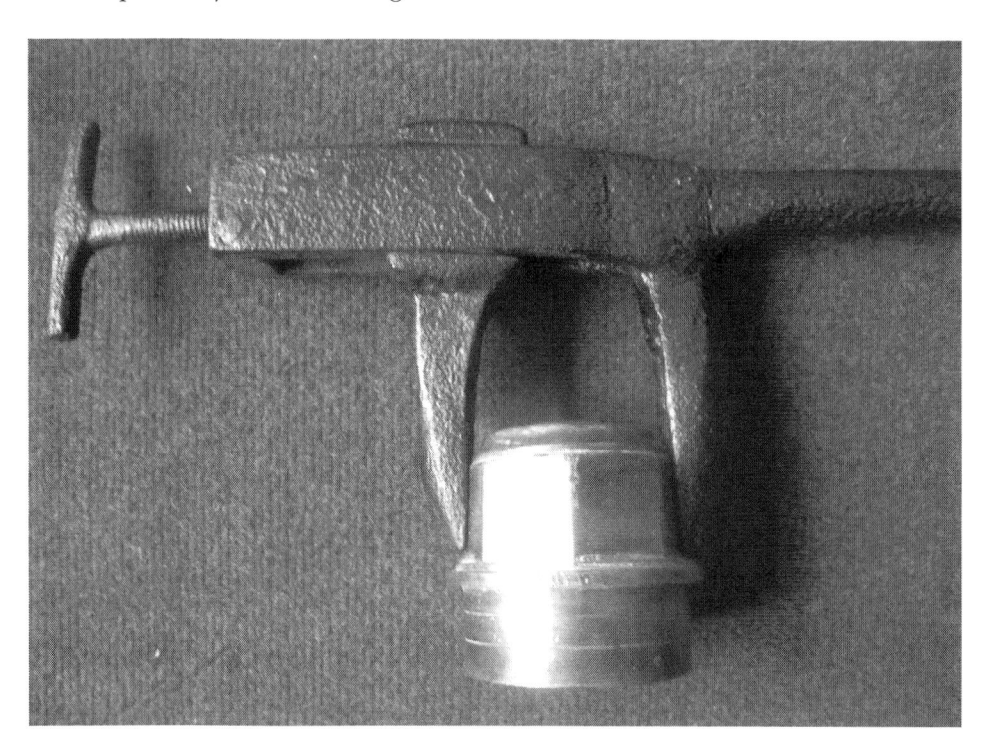

Test piece made by Arthur Fielding at the end of his apprenticeship

Mould supplied to the farriers making horseshoes for the MoD and army in the First World War

Lapel badge for war service in WW1 – farriers wore these to show they were doing legitimate war work rather than evading call-up

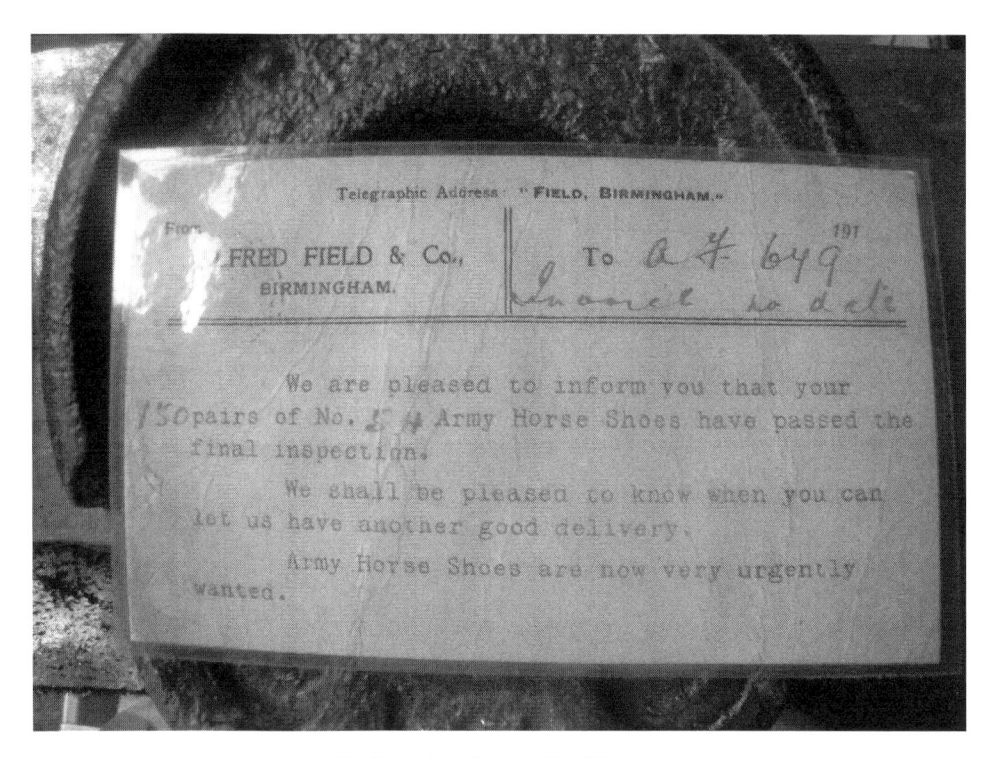

Send your horseshoes to this address

Arthur told me how, during and after the Second World War, the older farriers who were not called up for National Service were asked to make horseshoes for the army. If you agreed, you were given a mould of the shoe required and a size stamp. The shoes were to be sent to several depots around the country. One of these depots was a firm in Birmingham by the name of Alfred Field and Company.

Frederick Varnam

Thanks to Arthur Fielding and the NAFBAE, I got to know some great people. One of them, Fred Varnam from Leicestershire, was our branch chairman. He used to bring his wife Olive and daughter Edwena to our meetings. Fred was from a well-known family of farriers, who at one time operated three forges in the City of Leicester. One of these was open 24 hours a day. Fred was one of eleven children, three of whom became farriers. Fred had the letters AFCL after his name – Associate of the Farriers Company of London, which later became the Worshipful Company of Farriers – and he was a livery man of that company. He was also one of their most senior examiners and a highly respected man in our profession. He was among the first people to be awarded an Honorary Fellowship of the Worshipful Company of Farriers for his services to the farriery profession. This meant he could also use the letters FWCF after his name.

Fred and I became great friends and I think I am right in saying he was my first mentor. He would talk about his trips to London to attend the livery dinners. I was impressed, but the amount they cost in those days seemed to me a lot of money. Fred always said that one day he would introduce me to the livery company, but sadly he passed on before this happened. Under his guidance I did become very much involved with the NAFBAE, in due course taking over the chairmanship of the Derbyshire branch and later the East Midlands region and eventually being awarded a commendation for services to the association.

Fred Varnam working at his forge

Our first Saturday boy

One day in 1972 a lady approached me at work and said her son Martin was interested in becoming a farrier. As he wasn't due to leave school until the following year, she wondered if it might be possible for him to come on a Saturday and help me. I talked it over with Joan and we agreed to let the boy come to work part time, possibly with a view to taking him on as an apprentice when he left school, provided he proved keen and capable. From then on, Martin Bridge came to give me a hand every Saturday and also in the school holidays. We gave him spending money every week up until the day he left school. As we had hoped, in 1973 he became my first apprentice.

Apprenticeship involved a 13-week course at Hereford School of Farriery during the first year of training. The college provided accommodation for the students and taught them welding, wrought iron work, tractor work and general blacksmithing as well as horseshoeing. The course was run by the National Master Farriers' and Blacksmith's Association, and was in my opinion the best and most comprehensive course available. I told Martin that it would stand him in good stead in the future because, if he could not make a living shoeing horses, he would have the skills to find work as a blacksmith.

Martin Bridge

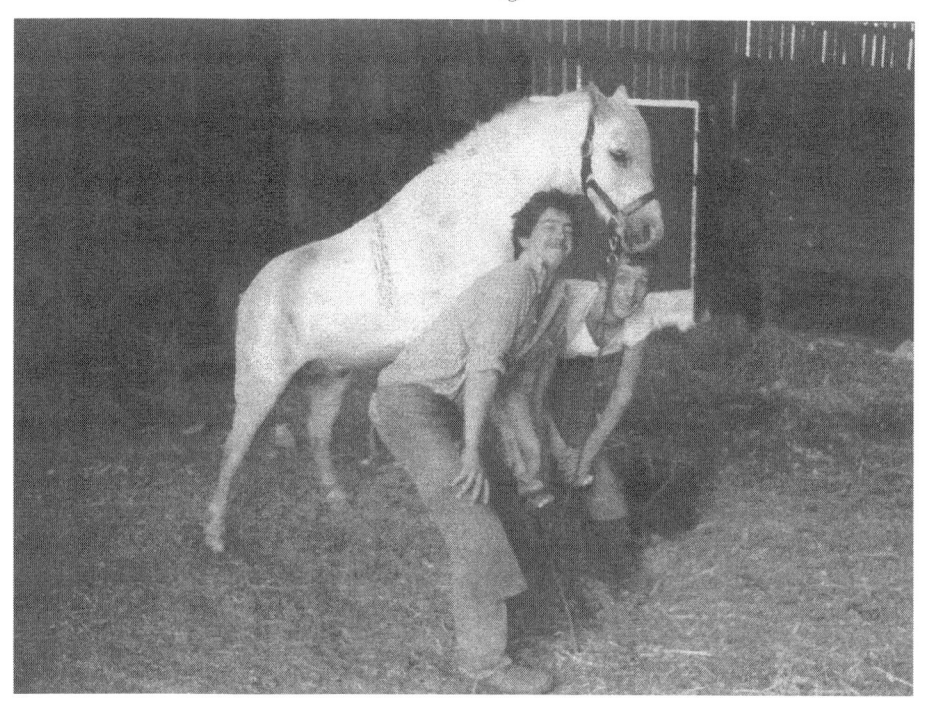

This pony had a knee problem so the apprentices raised both legs to clench up the nails

A note on training in farriery

Martin's apprenticeship meant he had to attend the college at Hereford each year for assessments and at the end of four years he had to take the examination known as the RSS (Registered Shoeing Smith) prescribed by the Worshipful Company of Farriers (WCF). This company, one of the livery companies of the City of London, was first formed in 1356 to improve the standards of horseshoeing in London, but later extended its scope to the rest of the country. It is responsible for farriery examinations to this day and holds examinations twice a year.

The Worshipful Company of Farriers offered qualifications in three stages. The first was the RSS: Registered Shoeing Smith. This grade tested basic farriery skills, knowledge of the anatomy of the horse's limb and foot, and a certain amount of the theory of remedial shoeing for common complaints. You took the exam at the end of your apprenticeship and if you passed, it meant the examiners considered you competent to practise basic farriery in a way that did no harm to horses. You could use the letters RSS after your name, which always gave the students something to aim for. In 1975 the RSS was renamed the DipWCF or WCF Diploma in Farriery.

The second examination in farriery is the AWCF (Associateship of the Worshipful Company of Farriers of London). Until 1990 it used to be called Associateship of the Farriers Company of London (AFCL). To achieve this grade you have to prove to the examiner's satisfaction that you have an extremely high standard of technical skills and are capable of remedial and therapeutic shoeing. You should have held the RSS or DipWCF for at least two years before taking the exam.

The third exam is the FWCF (Fellowship of the Worshipful Company of Farriers). This is the highest award possible. Not only must you prove you have maintained the technical standards you demonstrated in passing the AFCL or AWCF, but you must submit a thesis on farriery and be able to lecture on the subject. It is a difficult examination and only those at the very top of the profession can attain it. You must have been an associate for at least 12 months and must have had a full five years' practical experience since passing the RSS or DipWCF. There are currently fewer than 50 people worldwide holding the title of FWCF.

Qualified and practising registered farriers can also take a Diploma in Higher Education in Farriery and then top it up to degree level to gain BSc (Hons) Farriery. In the army you can take military farriers courses at an equivalent standard to the DipWCF and AWCF.

Time to get registered

In 1974 there was a private members bill going through Parliament to make it illegal for persons to shoe horses without being registered as farriers. This bill was in three parts. Part one was for farriers holding qualifications. Part two was for those who were not qualified but had been in business as farriers for more than two years and had account books to prove it. Part three was for those who were not making a living from farriery but were able to shoe their own horses and friends' horses without financial gain. I had not taken any farriery exams yet, though I had been learning on the job ever since being introduced to the pit ponies at Catty Pit. And throughout all those weeks lying in hospital after successive operations on my leg, I had been studying books on farriery, equine anatomy and the treatment of hoof and leg problems. With the Farriers Registration Bill looming, it seemed a good idea for me to get some paper qualifications and also top up my skills. I had already joined the National Association of Master Farriers, Blacksmiths and Agricultural Engineers at the request of the branch and district secretary Arthur Fielding from Selston. Now I arranged to spend a day with a WCF member called Graham Sutton at his forge at Osmaston near Ashbourne, and another with Fred Varnam, the branch chairman.

Fred Varnam, as I said earlier, was a Fellow of the Worshipful Company of Farriers and one of their chief examiners. He offered to help me prepare for my examination for the Registered Shoeing Smith (RSS) certificate. Fred invited me to his home on Wilberforce Road in Leicester, where he staged a mock examination of a written paper just to give an idea of what to expect on the day. I asked my friend Roger Price if he wished to come too, and he brought another friend, Fred Gibson (or Freddie Fish as we called him because in his spare time he sold fish from the back of a lorry in the Sheffield area). Mr. and Mrs. Varnam made us most welcome. We found the day a great help and it gave me the motivation to go all the way up the examination ladder.

At our next branch meeting I asked Roger if he might also be interested in going with me to the School of Farriery at Hereford on revision courses. Roger was keen and so was Freddie, so all three of us attended college courses in October 1974 and March 1975.

In October 1975 we took the RSS examination. There were

14 candidates, and everybody was very nervous. Roger Price was the first to go in for the theory test. He came out smiling and lit up a cigar. We asked him what the questions were. He said one of them was to describe the suspensory ligament and that his was the best description the examiners had ever heard. At the end of the day, we were to learn if we had passed or not. When the examiners came to tell us, they started by saying that there was only one disappointment today and that was a Mr. Price, who would have to sit the whole exam again. In fact, it took Roger five attempts in all to gain his RSS. During this time at college we all became friends, and some of us decided to carry on and try for the next exam, the associateship. Sadly, I was the only one from this area to do so. But Steven Langford from South Wales, Alan Worthington from Ormskirk, Tom Wright from South Wales and Alan Calvert from Cheshire joined me, and we are all still good friends and all have the letters AFCL (or AWCF as it later became known) after our name. I achieved mine in 1976. At that point, having added two sets of letters to my name, I sat back for a few years.

The firm

Meanwhile, throughout the mid-70s, everything was going well for me. My staff were Big Joe, who was still clipping shoes for me; Joan, who took the bookings and held the horses for me; and Martin Bridge as my apprentice. Between us we continued to build up our client base. Martin worked towards his RSS examination and passed first time. I tried to encourage him to go further and take his AFCL exam; in fact, I paid for him to go on a revision course at Hereford College. He did go on the first course but said it was too difficult and he was not bothered about carrying on with study anyway. True to his word, he never did. However, he went on working for me for 11 years and we never fell out once. He ran the firm whilst I was on holiday. We treated him like our own son. We bought him a used Volvo Estate and after that car broke down he took over one of the vans from the business in return for just paying the VAT of £100. Then one day he came to work and said that he was leaving to start up on his own. I had hoped he would stay on so that he and my son could have the business and I could back off, but that was not to be. Martin left and since then has never spoken to my wife or me to this day. We never knew the reason, and it was his loss.

Keith from Scotland

Keith did not start off in the farriery profession. He came from Invershin in Scotland, where his parents owned a large hotel. He came south during the 1970s to train as a riding instructor, and we met him while he was a working pupil under the supervision of Eric Burr BHSII at a riding school that we used to visit every week on the Hardstoft Road in Tibshelf. Keith was aiming to become an intermediate instructor, like Eric Burr, with the British Horse Society. Whenever we visited the yard he would hang around to watch the shoeing. One day he asked if I would teach him how to put a shoe on his own horse, as sometimes I would cast one while competing at shows and there was not always a duty farrier available to replace the shoe. I agreed to show him what to do on the understanding that he would practise on his own horse and, if anything went wrong, it was his baby. After some time, he became quite competent and could do a good job. This must have given him the urge to improve his skills as he then asked if he might possibly come to the forge at night for more tuition after finishing his shift at the stables.

After about a year Keith was doing well but needed more practice. He told me that his ambition, when he had qualified with the BHS, was to open a livery yard in the grounds of his parents' hotel. There was a shortage of farriers in Scotland, so he would want to be able to shoe his own horses. As the Farriers Registration Act did not yet cover the Highlands of Scotland, it was not strictly necessary for Keith to sit the farriery examination as we had to do in England and Wales. However, he decided it would stand him in good stead if he applied to go on the Register. The Farriers Registration Council had to send two senior farriers up to his home to see him do a forge test. The two experts selected were Mr. Eric Plant FWCF Hon. and Mr. E Martin FWCF. Keith's test piece was a caulk and wedge shoe (these are commonly used to increase traction on muddy or slippery ground). He made one in the old-fashioned way I had shown him: by holding the shoe at the heel with two pairs of tongs, putting in half a twist and forging the wedge for the inside of the shoe. The two examiners awarded a pass and asked him where he had learnt to do that.

Keith went on to build up his business combining show jumping with a horseshoeing round. In fact, he became so busy that he decided to attend the Hereford School of Farriery to gain his diploma. This enabled him to take on apprentices. After training six lads successfully, he came to see my wife and I to thank us for setting him on the right track. He arrived that night at the front door announcing he had brought us a bit of Highland venison and would just go and fetch it from the car. He reappeared grinning with a dead deer over his shoulder. He had hit it on the road on his way south – a gift from Scotland but one that wanted skinning and then having the tarmac cleaned off it.

Keith still keeps in touch and actually named one of his sons after me.

Keith with some donkey clients

Lady Godiva

One of our clients was Mrs. Brenda G., a doctor's wife from Wingerworth. They had two daughters and the mother was a bit of an eccentric, to say the least. The story starts when the family lived at Grassmoor. Mrs. G. had two horses; the one she rode most often was called Rudy, and he could be bolshie. One day Mrs. G. went out riding. As she passed a parked tipper lorry, the driver started to empty out the load of bricks. The horse reared in alarm. Mrs. G. fell off and hit her head. The injury left her quite ill for a while and she started acting oddly. Early one morning she left the house without getting dressed, saddled up Rudy and went for a ride in the nude, as unadorned as Lady Godiva.

Soon after that, the family moved house to Wingerworth, and this was where I met them. They asked me to do their regular shoeing. For the first appointment, Mrs. G. just booked in the one horse, Rudy. He was a complete bastard, pulling me all around the garage where we were working. I did not carry a mobile forge in those days, but Mrs. G. insisted the shoes must be burnt on. "Mrs. G., do not worry," I said. "I usually put them in my wife's Rayburn stove." That was a mistake – she took me at my word. She called her husband to put the shoes in their own cooker. It took ages for them to get warm. Meanwhile I carried on dressing Rudy's feet. He was already fed up, and got worse. Mrs. G. said, "Hold on a moment. I will get something for him."

There was me, imagining that as a doctor's wife she would be coming back with a shot of tranquilliser. So much for wishful thinking. She brought the horse two carrots.

One Monday Mrs. G. phoned to say that her horses were turned out to grass at Worksop and she wanted their shoes taken off. She added, "If I pick you up and take you in my car, I shall not have to pay you the 2/6d for travelling, will I?"

Mrs. G. duly arrived at my yard. I couldn't deny she was a good-looking woman. She was dressed in hot pants and a summer blouse with a coat slung around her shoulders. Steering with one hand and brushing her hair with the other, she drove us straight through Chesterfield and also through the red traffic lights in the town centre.

On the way back she announced that as a thank you she would buy me a drink in my local pub. My local was the Elm Tree, but I thought, *Shit, I had better not go in there as it will be full of all my mates.* I told her to stop at the Furnace Inn, so she parked right outside, breezed in and ordered, "A gin and tonic please, landlord, and whatever my friend wants." I had forgotten that the Death and Divide club met there on Mondays, meaning the Furnace too was full of my mates. When I got back home I mentioned to my wife that I had been for a drink with Mrs. G., and she said that she had already been told.

Mrs. G.'s stables were at the bottom of their garden in Wingerworth. One summer day when I arrived with Joan and an apprentice for an appointment, I found the front door open. I knocked and shouted "Hello? Blacksmith!"

I could see Mrs. G.'s husband Mack doing some hoovering and dressed only in a pair of Bermuda shorts.

"Hello, Mr. Bradbury," he said. "Brenda is not in, but our daughter is down at the stables. I will give her a call." He yelled across the garden "Ann, the farrier is here."

The reply came: "But Daddy, I have no clothes on."

I can tell you that everybody's eyes were on bird watch. Ann ran from the stables around the back of the house and returned wearing only a bra and a white silk underslip. I did say they were an odd family.

My wife was with me on one occasion when I paid a visit to Mrs. G.'s. The lady was on the sun lounger in the garden, scantily clothed, when we turned up. She said hello to my wife, started telling her some long story and didn't stop. I wasn't sure what it was about, but it must have been something of a medical nature as the next thing was that Mrs. G. dropped her pants to show my wife a scar in her groin. And then she called, "Mr. Bradbury, look – can you see what I mean?" There she was, pants around her knees, exposing herself. I just averted my eyes and carried on shoeing the horse.

Mountie Joe 1981

How do you fancy standing on your head on a pony's back, surrounded by flames? Doesn't appeal? Well, how about a sword dance on a horse's back? Of course, I am not suggesting you should try these things, quite the reverse in fact, but you must agree that doing them would demand a very special relationship between horse and rider.

Mountie Joe Roberts had such a relationship with his 10-year-old part-bred Arab mare, Lady Athena. The two had spent the last four years riding around the country raising funds for cancer research. Sponsorship was difficult to come by, and after 12,500 miles it became apparent that this method was not going to raise enough money. So, Joe broadened his repertoire to include a stage cabaret show where he would sing and do impersonations. In addition, he had an outside events display which he would perform wherever show organisers were willing to give him the opportunity. His 15-minute act incorporated music, gunfire and flames in a breathtaking show. By the time I met him, Joe's dedicated efforts had raised £14,500 pounds for Stoke Mandeville Hospital's cancer and heart disease wards. Plus, a further £2,065 to the University of Cambridge cancer treatment scheme. Apart from this, Joe was an extremely accomplished horseman, who had served in the Household Cavalry. His horse Lady Athena had been with him since she was six months old. He had broken and schooled her, building up a partnership based on complete trust – so essential during their exciting and dangerous show.

I first met this extraordinary man when he came into my forge and asked me if I would shoe his horse for him. He explained what he was doing and why he was dressed as a Canadian mounted policeman. He told me he was here as part of his attempt to ride the length of Britain to raise money for cancer charities. He had found that the roads in Scotland were the worst as regards wear on the horse's shoes. He was continually needing to replace the shoes, and he was wondering if I might consider sponsoring the ones he needed for that part of his journey. I said, "I will, Joe, and I will put you some welding in the area of greatest wear on Lady Athena's current set of shoes to make them last a bit longer. Also, I will give you a spare set to take with you to be ready for the next time you need to find a farrier." I wished him well and on his way he went, but not before giving us a demonstration of what he could do on his horse.

Our local Dick Turpin

The man in the mask dressed as Dick Turpin was a local farmer, Lawrence Naylor. In 1982 he decided to try to raise money for local charities and his plan was to follow the road that the original Dick Turpin took from London to York, not in record time but at a leisurely pace and collecting as much money as he could on the way. He came to my forge to get his horse shod for the ride and asked if we would sponsor the horseshoes. I agreed and off he went.

Dick Turpin

A visit to the Abbey

One day we were asked to shoe some hunters at Newstead Abbey in Nottinghamshire for a gentleman by the name of Jim Leverton. He provided livery for about ten horses, whose owners all followed the South Notts Hunt. Jim agreed to have the horses shod cold as we did not have a portable forge, so I arranged to go and see to them every Tuesday, the day after the hunt's regular meet. Before long, all Jim's mates had heard about our first-class service and wanted us to shoe their horses on the same day. They all treated us very well. One owner in particular, George Valance, instructed his groom to make sure there was always coffee and tea available in the gun room whenever we were there. To broaden the scope of our services, we got ourselves one of the new portable gas forges, made in France and sold by Cottam & Co at £50. These forges were very good but would easily go out if left unattended.

A newcomer installed his horse at the Abbey, a car dealer who knew everything. His hunter was not in the best of condition, and that was reflected in its feet. One Saturday the horse lost a shoe. The owner could not wait until the Tuesday morning, when we were due to call. Instead he engaged a man called M. Gamblin from Mansfield Woodhouse. This man was said to be able to shoe but had never taken any examinations. He reckoned he could gauge the clenches whilst the horse had his feet on the ground. He was as rough as a bear's arse in all aspects of the job. Anyway, this owner called him in to shoe his horse on the Sunday morning so he could hunt on Monday. The cost was £1.50. In the course of the hunt, three of the new shoes came off. The owner then had the cheek to put his horse on Jim Leverton's list – without asking or offering to pay – for us to see to. We sorted out the horse because we did not want to upset Jim Leverton, but it upset me to think people could do such things. It played on my mind and I could not stop mulling over the high-handed way this owner had treated me. I went to bed trying to think how to get the message over. About 2am I woke up with a verse in my head. I said to Joan, "Quick, write this down for me." It went something like this:

ON A RECENT VISIT TO THE ABBEY,
THEY HAD A HORSE WITH FEET ALL SHABBY
IT HAD BEEN SHOD A DAY BUT ONE
THE PHANTOM SMITH HAD KNOCKED THEM ON
HAMMER AND NAILS AT THE READY
HE ATTEMPTS TO SHOE THIS DARK BAY NEDDY
WHAT AN ADVERT FOR THE PARK
HE WOULD HAVE DONE BETTER IN THE DARK
THIS WRONG HAS BEEN PUT RIGHT AND THE PHANTOM SMITH IS NOT IN SIGHT
IF YOU'RE A MEMBER OF THE HUNT
BE SURE AND EMPLOY A QUALIFIED FARRIER AND NOT A C...

On our next visit I nailed this up in the tack room for all to see. It did a lot of good and from then on we were treated with much more respect. We continued to shoe the Newstead Abbey hunters for many years.

The next apprentice

We took on another apprentice, a boy from Doncaster by the name of Martin Elliott. One day, after teaching the lad how to put clips on shoes, I left him in the forge to do just that. On our return he greeted us with a big smile. "How about that, boss? I have done 92 shoes, fronts and backs."

I thought, *Bloody hell, that's a lot of shoes*. Let's have a look. Well, every single one had to go in the scrap bin. Martin got a right bollocking and the message that I would rather see a few properly clipped shoes than a load of spoilt ones. He had

Martin Elliott

to take his time and go for quality ahead of quantity. We had a similar problem with his anatomy studies – rushing through the issues without understanding them. But in the end, we got there and Martin eventually passed his RSS exam. After he left my employment, he went on to gain his AWCF, took on other apprentices and eventually took his son into business with him at his forge in Doncaster.

After the Farriers Registration Act came to fruition in 1975, Mike Cox had become the field officer for the Farriers Registration Council. The FRC had taken over administration of the farriery apprenticeship scheme from CoSIRA (Council for Small Industries in Rural Areas). Mike's job was to visit the forges that employed apprentices and to sort out any problems. He would now and then find a few boys not doing as they were asked or master farriers not teaching them properly. If the issues could not be resolved, the answer could be to transfer the boy to a different master. If the problem was thought to be the lad's fault, then he would be placed as far away from home as possible with a master who was willing and able to take him on. If the boy refused to go, the apprenticeship was terminated. I had met Mike Cox at the Hereford School of Farriery on an AFCL revision course. We had soon struck up a friendship, and Mike knew that I could handle lads. As field officer, he would often ring me to say he had a lad that needed sorting out and would I consider taking him on. I would reply, "Send him up for an interview and I will have a look at him." I think the problem was often that the master farrier had not given the lad a fair chance. All the apprentices I took turned out to be first-class craftsmen and all went on into full-time work after leaving me.

Mike Cox FWCF and his wife Gwyneth at the Mansion House, London

One day Mike Cox phoned to ask if Joan and I could look after a young man from Switzerland for two or three weeks. His name was Bernard Duvernay and he was fully qualified as a farrier at home but wanted to see the way we shod horses in England. His father ran a fleet of lorries that made weekly trips to the UK, so Bernard had no trouble in getting a lift to Derbyshire. He settled in straight away at our house and we soon found out that he had a good sense of humour. Bernard told me that his ambition in life was to travel the world and visit the poorer parts of each country to try and teach the local farriers better hoof care so they could look after their customers' horses and prevent the suffering caused through poor shoeing.

Bernard back home: the shoe must go on

Bernard at work in my forge

During Bernard's visit, our rounds took us to Somercotes. The customer had two horses plus some goats, ducks, chickens, rabbits and ferrets, and most of them lived in the house with her. She was not a pretty woman; she was about 18 stone in weight and had a beard. She always wore a beret on the side of her head, a long raincoat both in winter and summer and, of course, wellington boots. Besides Bernard, who knew nothing about this lady, I had two other boys in the van with me. When Bernard asked where we were heading for, I told him that the lady whose yard we were going to was not very good at paying. "What she does, Bernard, is run up a large bill and after a time she will say, 'One of you come in the house for some fun and we will call the bill settled.' Now Bernard, as you are our guest and it is time for her to pay the bill again, you can be the one who goes in the house."

Bernard's eyes lit up.

As we pulled up in the lady's yard, she came wobbling out of the barn. "Hello there, Doug," she boomed. "I will go and get the horses."

Bernard took one look and said in broken English, "Doug, thank you very much but I think I will stay in the van."

Bernard did achieve his life-long ambition of travelling the world. He still keeps in touch and sends us postcards from the different places he visits.

Steven Hardaker, apprentice

Steven was one of the apprentices I was telling you about, who Mike Cox had to relocate with a new master. This lad was from Keighley in West Yorkshire and had been working for a farrier in Scotland. The farrier could not afford to pay him so he was moved to a new master in Whitby. The man in Whitby took to sending him out on his own to shoe clients' horses. One day he lamed a horse by putting a nail in the wrong place. The horse belonged to the master of the local hunt so Steven was in big trouble. Besides that, the farrier could not pay his wages.

Steven's grandfather brought him to see me. He turned up wearing a flat cap, braces, and clogs. I said, "OK, we have room for one more. I'll give you a weeks' trial."

The grandad said "Do you mind if I use your phone to give the wife three bells? She will not pick up the phone, but if I just let it ring three times she will know it's me and I'm on my way back."

Steven Hardaker

Steven's birthday strippergram

This lad Steven stayed with me for five years. He became a first-class craftsman and won the vet's award at college for anatomy studies. However, shoes and horses weren't the only things he learned about while he was here. At 11.30am one Monday morning we drove into the yard at some hunt stables for our second call of the day. On top of the muck heap was a girl wielding a pitchfork. Steven's eyes went wide. He said that was the nicest thing he had ever seen on a muck heap. Moreover, he told the girl so (some chat-up line). This was the first girl he had ever asked out. Well, I knew this girl and I thought she was a bit hot for Steven, and unfortunately, he was due to take his diploma exam at college very soon, but what can you say?

They had been going out for a few weeks when he told me that on Saturday, he was taking the girl to meet his parents back home in Keighley. The following Monday morning he was back at work and we all wanted to know how the weekend had gone. Now, Steven was a bit old-fashioned in his ways. He had an old Rover car and dressed the part, down to the flat cap and gloves to drive in. He told us that on the Saturday he took the girl to lunch and bought her a cheese-and-onion sandwich and half a pint of beer. That night he drove her up on the hills to show her the beautiful sunsets you get up there in Bronte country. (Me and the other lads were riveted to his every word.) He said – and this is a true record of our conversation – "She looked at me and said, 'It is lovely up here.' Then she slowly turned towards me and started to unbutton her blouse. She said, 'What do you want now, Steven?'"

I told her "Half the petrol money, please."

On the weekend before Steven's final exam at college, I went out for Sunday lunch. When I came home, my wife said, "Go in the lounge and have a look at Steven." He was draped over the settee crying his eyes out.

"What is up with you, lad?"

"She's dumped me, boss."

What a blessing, I thought. I said "Not to worry, these things happen. You and Neal go and have a drink." I gave them a tenner to help them along. They returned at 4.30pm, both as drunk as lords.

Now, Steven used to go to college on Sunday night ready for classes to start on Monday morning. That Sunday, no way was he going to be able to get himself to Hereford in the state he was in. Joan and I sat with him giving him pots of coffee and he set off at 4.30am on Monday. At lunchtime Steven phoned my wife to tell her he had completed his theory paper and thought he had done all right, but Joan said he was still sobbing on the phone.

In fact, Steven did pass both parts of his exam. Afterwards he carried on working for us for about a year while building up a business of his own. At first, he worked with me five days a week and as he gained more customers, he would drop a day at a time, and this continued until he had enough work to make a living. I suggested he should go and introduce himself to the local vets and tell them that he was trained to do all types of remedial work if they needed him. This went down well with the vets; they thanked him and said he was the first person to do that and they would most certainly use his services in future.

When the time came for Steven to leave us, his mum and dad came over for the weekend. They took us out for a meal, and that's when Steven presented us with a silver-plated tray. He had had it engraved: TO DOUG AND JOAN THANKS FOR THE LAST 5 YEARS STEVEN. And then, as he left, he broke down crying.

6

APPRENTICES AT THE FORGE

Our son becomes an apprentice

Neal and Gale had been involved in our business since they were at school. When Neal approached school-leaving age, I must admit he wasn't allowed a very wide choice of career. Fortunately, he was as keen to stay in the family firm as I was keen to keep him there. As soon as he left school, we applied to the Joint Apprenticeship Council for him to become an apprentice with me. That was the only way to go about things at that time. Applicants' names went forward to the Council for Small Industries in Rural Areas (CoSIRA), which ran selection tests and offered grants to pay for the college-based part of the training.

Neal went to Salisbury to sit the tests. He was interviewed by a panel of 12 of this country's top farriers. He was one of 90 applicants for just 30 places. They did not award him a grant but told him he could go to college if his father paid for him privately. When Neal got back and reported this, I went ape shit. To think that my fellow farriers could say something

Neal with the shield he won as first prize in the apprenticeship class at the Leicester County Show

like that to a boy that had already got a job with me, in fact had been working with me for years, did not make sense. Neal knew what farriery was all about; he had no illusions about the difficult bits; and he had every wish and every incentive to stay in the job. Yet he had been turned down when every year there were trainees dropping out because they couldn't take the pressure or had no intention of sticking it. I was very actively involved in NAFBAE (the National Association of Farriers, Blacksmiths and Agricultural Engineers) and I let them know just what I thought of this system.

Neal enrolled at the Chesterfield Technical College on a welding course until he was able to reapply to CoSIRA for the next farriery intake. This time he was accepted and duly started his working life with me.

I would say at this point it is not always a good idea to train your own son, especially if you have other boys on the work force. The simple reason is that you always expect 110 per cent from one of your own. And when you do not get it, this creates problems with the wife. She tells you: "You are expecting too much from your son. He is with you 24/7 so ease up on him." Many times.

Boys do play you up and Neal was no exception. But I had an ace up my sleeve. I had met a Welsh farrier called Steven Langford whilst I was on an AFCL revision course at Hereford, and we became good friends. I was telling him about Neal one day and Steven said, "Why not send him down to me for a week? My dad's got a riding school and there are lots of horses to practise on."

So, the next time Neal played up I was ready for him. I told him he was going to Wales for a spell and drove him down to the Langfords' place. He spent the time travelling around with Steven's apprentice, a boy by the name of Grant Moon. They had an old post office van to use, with not a lot of floor left in it. (This boy Grant passed his diploma exam with honours and in subsequent years was to become six times world champion at the Calgary Stampede held in Alberta, Canada – but more about that later.)

Well, after a week in Wales it was time for Neal to return home. Much to our surprise, he did not want to come back. However, Grant offered to give him a lift back to Clay Cross at the weekend on the way to visit his parents, who had bought a small hotel in Narborough, Leicestershire. When the pair turned up, we found out why Neal had been reluctant to come back. Apparently, Mr. Langford had lots of young girls working with the horses at the riding school, plus one lad about 20 years old by the name of Barney. Neal told us that Barney carried a pocket-knife and would go around the girls, put his hand up their back, cut their bra straps and tell them to let it all hang out. We began to see why Neal did not want to come home; he had never seen anything like that in Derbyshire. He said thank you for sending him to paradise for a week.

Grant and Neal became lifelong friends. When Grant's dad sold his business in Leicestershire, he bought the Old Railway Hotel in Derby right opposite the Royal Infirmary. After that we saw even more of Grant, as he and Neal took to travelling around the country to farriery competitions, leaving me and the rest of the staff to carry the business. Nobody minded, as all the lads were given the chance to go to the shows and if they wanted to go my wife would sponsor them. Sometimes I would go along too and work the forge for any lad that needed an assistant for his test piece. All my apprentices did quite well in the shows. Yorkshire farriers used to put on quite a few competitions, often as part of agricultural shows such as those at Penistone, Otley, Londonderry, Spofforth and the Great Yorkshire, and Vaux Brewery in Sunderland.

Grant did not work full time as a farrier but had to help out in the hotel. He was good at that too, but his heart was with the horses. His brother Mark was totally into the hotel business and not really interested in horses, and when Grant was supposed to be at work in the hotel he would often ask Mark to cover for him while he went out for a drink with Neal. Some days he volunteered to come out shoeing with us, just for a change. He asked if he could use my forge from time to time to practise on, as he really wanted to aim for associateship (AWCF), which was the next level of qualification after the DipWCF. Knowing I had passed my associateship exam (known as the AFCL at the time) a few years earlier, he also suggested "Why you don't take your fellowship exam at the same time? We could practise together." That seemed a good idea to me, and we spent that winter practising with the intention of attempting the exams in the spring.

Mark Caudwell FWCF

I first met Mark while Grant Moon was practising for his AWCF examination. They were both at the School of Farriery at Hereford. At weekends they would travel around the country gaining knowledge from other farriers. Another of their mates was Robin Pape, who came from Scotland and was studying at Hereford for his DipWCF. They would all call at Clay Cross on their way to Grant's home, which at the time was his parents' hotel, The Gables, on London Road in Derby. The hotel was handy for night clubs, but clubbing was not the scene for Robin as he was much older and wiser. He asked if he might stay the weekend with me instead and do some work in return for his board and some tuition.

This was no problem for Joan and me. It proved the start of a lifelong friendship. Robin stayed with us on several occasions whenever he was down this way. He did have one fault: he smoked a pipe. That was OK, but the stink was out of this world. He would take only about six puffs and then put it down. When he lit up I would open all the doors and windows to get a through draught. Robin would just laugh and say, "Doug, are you trying to tell me something?" I did ask if it might be donkey shit that he had in his pipe.

Robin in London at the diploma presentations

Robin on honorary farrier duties at a Highland show

Mark, Grant and Robin all passed their exams at the first attempt. Soon after that, however, Mark hit a bad patch in his life up north where he was working. Grant suggested he ask if I could take him on as an assistant, so Mark came to talk it over with Joan and myself. He would want accommodation as well as a job as he had nowhere to stay. We also needed to discuss his wages. Mark suggested he could work on contract as he was now qualified to associate level, and that I should pay him £1.50 per horse on all phone bookings. Joan and I thought about this and agreed. At that time, it was a very good wage.

This was around 1980-81, and by now we had Martin Bridge, Steven Hardaker, our son Neal, Mark Caudwell and me all working for the firm, with two vans on the go. The arrangement started well and Mark got respect from the boys. Before the end of his first week with us, he had them making shoes at night after completing the day's appointments.

On the Thursday of his second week we were at a big riding school, a rather up-market establishment, in Holmesfield. When I first went there I was asked whether I wanted the horses presented in bridles or headcollars, and all the stable hands, both boys and girls, had to wear clean jodhpurs and shirts every day. Mark was there with our lads but I had an appointment elsewhere. One of the girls walked past. Mark grabbed her, hoisted her over his shoulder and told her, "You have a lovely arse. I am taking you home with me." The lads looked on in disgust and muttered about what Mr. Bradbury would say when he found out.

I did not get a chance to say much at the time, as the following day we had a booking just up the road from the forge at a riding centre owned by a young lady called Jane. Now

Jane could be difficult and not many people took to her, but at that time she was spending about £1,000 a year with me. When we arrived she told us just what she required. Mark got his tools ready while I took one of the horses into the loose box. I had started to shoe it when I heard this exchange:

"Could you please put a couple of nails in the small grey?"

Mark said it wanted a set of shoes.

Jane said "No, just two nails, please."

"I tell you it wants a set."

This went on for a while. Tempers rose. Finally, Mark burst out: "You make me sick! Fur coat and no knickers, that's your type." With no respect for the person or her property, he threw his tools in the van, strode off and lit a cigarette.

I went to see Jane and apologised for the outburst.

She shrugged. "He does not bother me. If he would have listened to me, I was about to explain that the pony is being turned out to grass tomorrow as the owner's children are back at school and won't need it again until half term. Just do not bring that man on my property again, please." That was the end of the matter for her.

It was also the end for me in regards to Mark. I told him it was not going to work out for him in our business and he must leave that day. He said he was sorry and agreed to go. Just before he left I did a spot check on his tool box. I found several sets of shoes the boys had made during the week. Also, a shoe-turning hammer my son had been given whilst he was in Canada, plus a tool and fuller block that belonged to me. It was just as well he was leaving.

That weekend we had a phone call from a finance company trying to trace a Mr. M. N. Caudwell as his hired van had not been paid for. I said we were sorry, but he had moved on. And then a lady phoned to ask when Mark was coming to fetch his dog now, he had found somewhere to live. She was given the same answer: he had moved on. He had never mentioned a dog to me, but if he had asked to keep one at our place, the answer would have been no. I had a German Shepherd of my own, and no way would that dog have accepted another on her patch.

Despite all that, Mark and I parted as friends and have remained so to this day. Mark has done well for himself and is now the senior tutor in farriery at Myerscough College in Lancashire. Robin, our friend from Scotland, remained a Diploma farrier for a few years but intends to take his AWCF in the not-too-distant future.

World champions

Grant passed his AWCF exam first time. Sadly, I did not gain my fellowship on this occasion, but more on that later. That same year, Grant said he wanted to enter a shoeing competition in Texas. A man by the name of John Marino had sent him a photo of the shoes he had to make for it. Grant was so talented that he did not need to practise for long before he figured out exactly how to make them. He did very well in the competition and came back full of himself. The big plan was to go and live in Texas, where he and John Marino were to open a school of farriery. Whilst he was in Texas he had applied to enter the world championships in Canada next year (1982) and now he asked my son Neal: "Are you coming?"

So, we had "Dad, can I go with Grant next year?"

His mother and I agreed on the condition that he got stuck in at his studies and at work.

Before long, the time came around for the shoeing championships at the Calgary Stampede. Neal was not eligible to enter the live shoeing trial as he was still an apprentice, but he could enter the shoe-making contest. We reckoned the experience would do him good. They were joined by two more of Grant's friends, Carl Bettison and Billy Crothers, who had been at college with him and had also passed their diploma exam with honours. Carl travelled with Neal and Grant on the plane, but Billy said he could do it more cheaply by going as a groom with a friend's horses to New York and then hitch-hiking up to Canada. He arrived at the lads' room in Calgary in the early hours with a plea for Grant, Carl and Neal to budge up and let him get a kip. Neal and Grant went in for the pairs carthorse shoe-making class and won 600 dollars. I believe a good time was had by all.

G. Moon, B. Crothers, D. Ducket, N. Bradbury and C. Bettison at Calgary

Neal was no sooner home than he was asking "Can I go again next year, Dad?"

I said, "Just wait and see."

Grant had an idea. "Why don't you and Joan come too?"

A couple of months later we were shoeing a horse for a young woman who worked for Wardair as a chief stewardess and sales coordinator. When I told her, we were thinking about a trip to Calgary, she said, "Let me do the bookings for you. I can get you a very good discount."

For us it was a heaven-sent offer. She gave us first-class service and it turned out to be the trip of a lifetime. When we got on the plane, the captain even took the trouble to wish the lads well in the competition.

The organisers met us on arrival and took us to our hotels. Joan and I stayed at the Hilton and the lads at the Stampede Hotel, but we were invited round to the Stampede for the pre-show talks. These included a pot-luck class, which I was asked to judge along with Bob Marshall Senior. For this class, every entrant had to bring a present from their country, so each of them, prizewinner or not, got a gift. Neal took a Crown Derby plate, Grant took two mugs with a picture of the Prince of Wales on them, and a Swiss guy brought a large alpine horn. You had to draw a slip of paper from a hat, telling you what sort of metal to make something out of, and then you had 20 minutes to make it. Grant's slip said, "12 inches of barbed wire" while Neal drew a 12-inch nail, Pat Balfour had 12 inches of tubing, Vern Hornquest got a bar 2 x ½ x 12 inches, Lee Green a rod 12 inches x 1 inch diameter, and so on. Neal said, "What I can do with this nail, Dad?" I suggested he might make it into a snake by using two old rasps, but that I wouldn't be able to place him as I was one of the judges. I also gave Grant some ideas.

Everyone got stuck in, but with only a few minutes to go Grant found he was running out of options. Each time he put the barbed wire in the fire it just melted. He had about two inches left. Then squinting around the room he saw something in the corner. He ran across the floor, came back with a piece of orange bailer twine, fastened it to the wire and called it a fishhook. Now, the sponsors were the Mustad Horse Nail Company and the only things they made were horseshoe nails and fishhooks. Grant won first place for his innovative quick thinking. Neal came second and Pat Balfour was third with what he called a haggis charmer made from 12 x 1-inch tubing. Lee Green hit his metal rod just once and threw it on the floor. He said it was a dead fish and was put in 11th place. The TV reporter who was filming the event asked Pat to blow down the haggis charmer. Pat blew, but explained that nobody would have heard the noise it made because a haggis charmer's pitch was too high for the human ear.

"How do you use it, then?" asked the reporter.

Pat said, "We blow, and when the haggis pops its head up from the ground we shoot it."

That night there was a barbeque at the home of the chief organiser Bill Pratt. A bus was laid on to take us there as it was a large ranch a fair way out of town. All the items made in the potluck competition were to be sold by auction. Ollie Mustad arrived to represent the Mustad family, and he sat on the grass as drunk as he could be, just rocking to and fro. The auctioneer must have thought he was bidding as he seemed to be buying everything. I managed to secure the nail that Neal made into a snake, but it cost us 30 dollars.

The $30 snake

Competitors from around the world at the Calgary Stampede 1983

Ollie Mustad and Jay Sharp offering Grant their condolences

Neal and the new 1983 world champion, Shane Carter

On the day of the championship competition, Grant was doing brilliantly. He was leading Shane Carter by three points, and it looked like he could only lose if he were disqualified. And lo and behold, that is just what happened. He and Neal were in the carthorse shoe-making class and their fire was not going well as the brushes needed changing. There was a spare fire at the side of theirs and Grant said to me, "Start that fire for me, would you Doug?" I got the fire to the same heat as the one they were on and the lads just moved across and carried on working. They finished on time, only to be told that they had been disqualified for not asking permission to move. The title went to Shane Carter. I thought that was petty and a poor decision, but there you go. One thing about farriers is there is never any ill feeling. The competitors just wished each other well and said, "See you next time."

Joan and I had a wonderful five days in Calgary. Then we set off across the Rocky Mountains by bus, stopping at top-grade hotels on our way. The bus company was called Brewsters and we rightly complimented them on a first-class service. We stayed in Banff, Lake Louise, Jasper, Kamloops and Icefields Parkway and then went on to Vancouver and over to Vancouver Island. We flew back from Vancouver at the end of a tremendous tour, all arranged for us by the young lady from Wardair whose horse we had shod.

Grant carried on attending the world championships each year and has so far won the title no less than six times. He fulfilled his dream of going to live in Texas. The plan for a school of farriery did not come to fruition as John Marino's wife became terminally ill, so Grant did some local work for a while. Then the Mustad Nail Company took him on as a consultant, and he travelled the world on their behalf doing clinics. He told me one day that his air fares added up to over $50,000. Grant took out American citizenship and soon became a member of the US national farriery team. This meant that he came over to England for the international horseshoeing competition held at the Royal Show at Stoneleigh in Warwickshire each year. Guess where the team all came to practise and sleep – not at the Moons' hotel in Derby with 60 bedrooms, but to my wife and I at Clay Cross. They would work in the forge until Joan had made dinner for us all, and after dinner we would go over to the local pub. The lads would stay up until 2 or 3am then crowd into our three bedrooms, with some of them sleeping on the floor, and they thought it was great. Grant brought the team to stay with us several times, and they always got a good welcome from Joan and I. All good fun and fond memories.

After the American lads left, it was back to earning a living.

Grant 'Trazer' Moon, Jim Kelly, Bill Poor, Doug and Joan, Neal, Craig D., AnDr.ew F., Gordon H.

At 2am after the pub shut: Joan and Doug, Neal, Craig, AnDr.ew, Bob Pethic, Dave Ferguson, Shane Carter, Grant Moon, Jim Keife

One day's work for the USA team

Gordon, Bill Poor, Andrew, Craig, Scot Davison, Neal and Grant

Neal Bradbury DipWCF

One day Mike Cox called to see Joan and me to say he thought he ought to tell us that Neal was falling behind at college. Joan said it must be my fault for driving our son too hard. Straight after dinner every evening he would go out, and we felt he must be doing it to escape us. However, it turned out that Neal was struggling with college work because he was dyslexic. This had never been picked up throughout his eleven years at school. So, Joan and I set about looking for ways to deal with the issue. We eventually paid for Neal to see a psychiatrist in Derby, who took great trouble to explain to us how the brain works cross-laterally and how Neal had a normal IQ but saw his Bs and Ds back to front.

The psychiatrist gave us the address of the Friends Meeting House in Sheffield, where a tutor was offering one-to-one help with dyslexia. Neal started going twice a week and the result was a huge improvement in his reading and writing. He settled down to studying for his diploma at Hereford School of Farriery and sat the exam in 1985. His teacher in Sheffield gave him a letter about the dyslexia to hand to Tom Williams, the senior tutor at Hereford. Mr. Williams, however, did not believe in excuses and never opened the letter. All he said was, "These lads try it on." I am pleased to say that times have now changed, and any student who struggles with dyslexia is allowed extra time in their examinations. Neal missed an honours grade in his exam because of his writing, but he scored A+ in the practical part and his final mark was B+. The presentation ceremony took place as part of the Hereford Old Boys reunion dinner, where David Height, the secretary of the NAFBAE, gave out the awards.

David Height, secretary of NAFBAE, presenting Neal with his diploma at the School of Farriery reunion dinner, 1985

Tom Williams, tutor at the School of Farriery, with Joan and Neal at the presentation in 1985

Reunion dinners were held at the Moat House in Hereford and always had a good turnout. There would be about 150 to 200 people dancing until the early hours of the morning and then carrying on partying in the rooms. It was Grant Moon and Mark Caudwell who turned the dinner into a regular black-tie event.

Neal was to go on to gain his AWCF and train his own apprentices. And one of the achievements that made me especially proud of him was when he won the Varnam trophy in 1990. This was an award instituted by Frederick Varnam RSS AFCL FWCF (Hon), who was my friend and mentor and one of the farriers I most respected throughout my career. The prize was to be awarded to the farrier gaining the most points for the best specimen shoe made each year during the AWCF examination. The trophy was a silver salver, which was presented to the Worshipful Company of Farriers in memory of Fred's late father William Varnam RSS. Herbert (Bert) Varnam, one of Fred's brothers, was a carpenter and he made a most beautiful case for this silver salver. The case was made of thirteen different types of wood, all inlaid. Fred said the case was worth more than the silver inside it. Sadly, Fred passed away in 1987 and it was Bert who presented the trophy to Arnold Scott, then master of the WCF, in 1988.

The first person to win this prestigious award was David Wilson AWFC from Scotland. The picture shows David Wilson being presented with this trophy by the Master of the Worshipful Company. It was 1990, as I said, when my son Neal won it, the first English farrier to gain this award. It was not presented the following year (1991), when none of the entries reached a high enough standard. In 1992 it was presented to

The master of the WCF Mr. Arnold Scott receiving the gift from Mr. and Mrs. Herbert (Bert) Varnam in 1988

There are 13 different types of wood in this case

a farrier from Lincolnshire, M.D. Hawes AWCF. The format of the examination was changed in 1993 after the fourth person had won it. The trophy was put in the Company's safe for a number of years and was reintroduced in 1999, when it was won by J.C. Ravenscroft AWCF. Subsequent winners have been S.A. Armstrong AWCF, F.W. Youngson AWCF, and D.J. Varnini AWCF. In 2003 it was not awarded, then in 2005 it went to S. Bean AWCF and C.A. Wiggins. Well done, boys.

1988 Master John Alford presenting the Varnam trophy to David Wilson AWCF at the court dinner

1989 Master Derrick Taverner presenting the V.T. to Rory Robb AWCF

1990 Master Tim Milligan presenting the V.T. to Neal Bradbury AWCF

1993 Master Sir Gordon Shattock presenting the V.T. to Matthew Hawes AWCF

This is the shoe Neal made in the exam. It was chrome plated by the WCF and presented back to Neal at the court dinner in London in 1991

Keith Dodsworth

Back to the 1980s... our next apprentice was a lad from Braintree in Essex, whose initial apprenticeship had not worked out well. He had been working in Wales, and it was another case of the master using the lad as cheap labour and not paying the right wages. Keith was a good-looking lad with ginger hair, but the first time he came to see us we couldn't help remarking on a sharp medicinal smell rising off him. He admitted he had been using ointment on a muscle injury in his back; he had had the tube in his coat pocket, and it had burst.

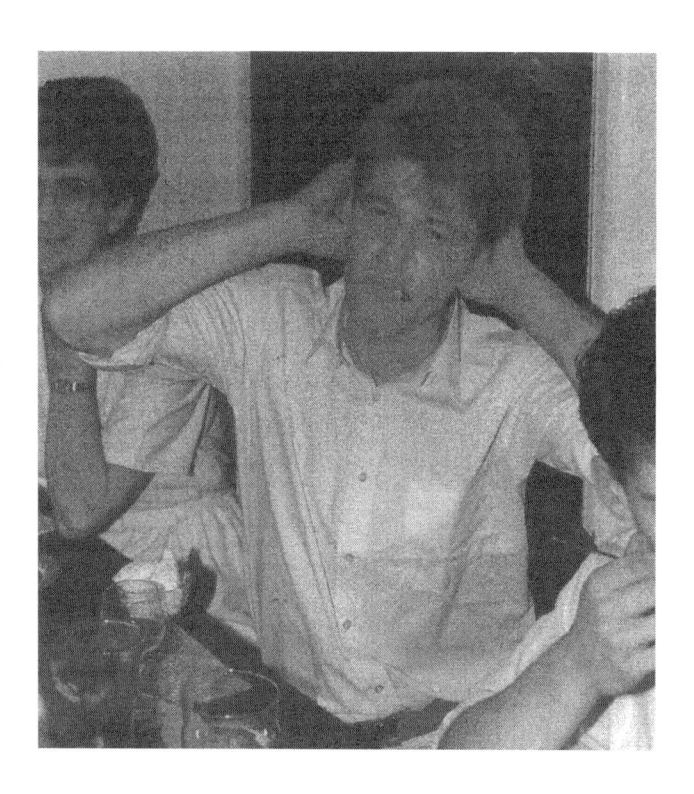

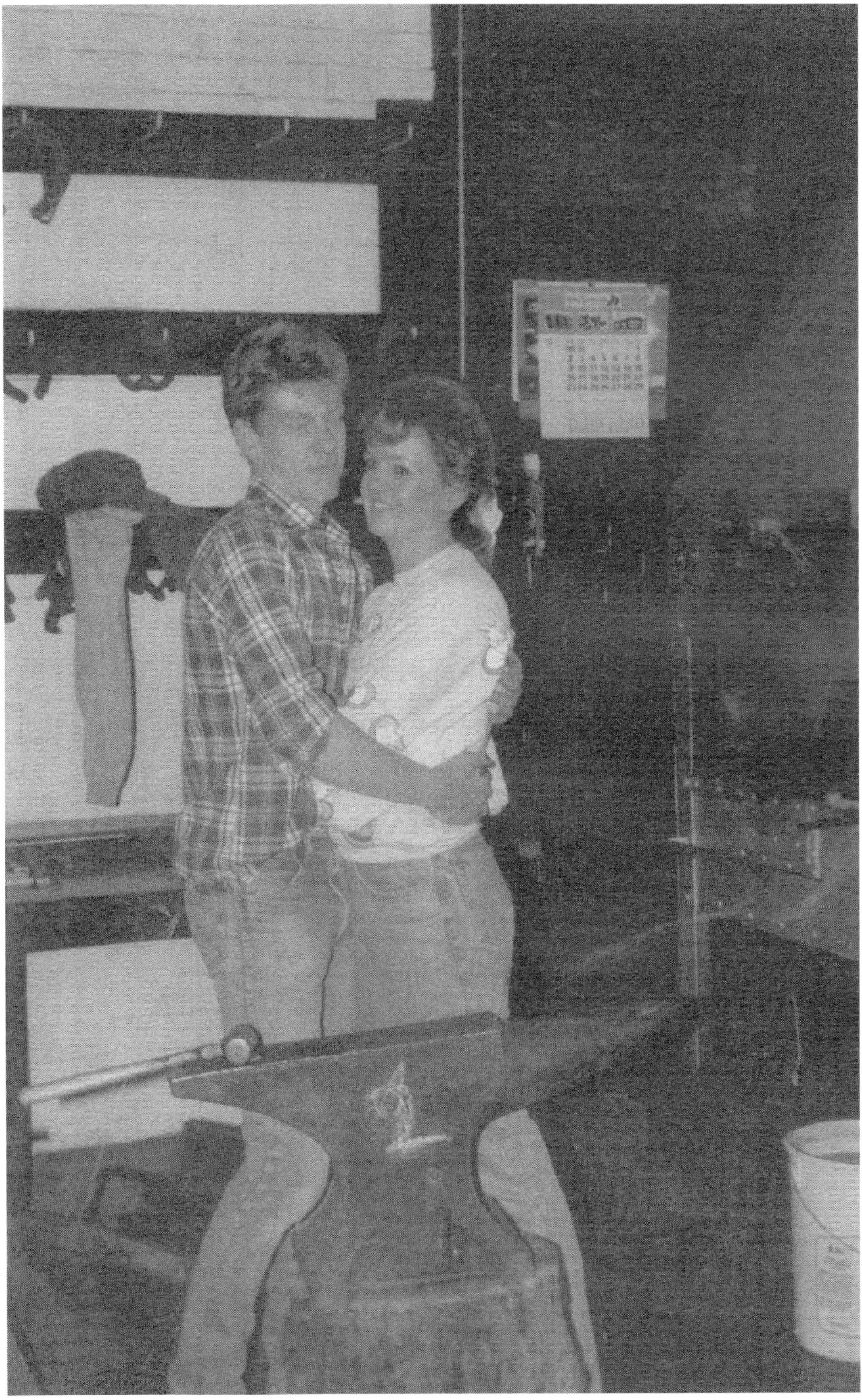

Keith lived in the house with us and proved to be a good lad. Our only concern was with the way he would smoke roll-ups in his bedroom, open the window and blow the smoke out. Joan found a tin when she was cleaning his room and in it was a substance that looked like weed. Now, the tutor at the camera club I went to at that time was a photographer for the Derbyshire police forensic section. I asked him if he could get a sample from Keith's tin analysed for me. Luckily for Keith, the results came back clear.

Keith was with us for just over three years, including the college-based block-release training periods at Hereford. When apprentices attended the School of Farriery in Hereford for the first time, Mike Cox was always present to inspect the tool kit they had been given by the WCF. The lads would all line up for the inspection. When he got to Keith, Mike asked, "Why are you different to all the other boys?"

"Don't know, sir."

"You are the only one with dirty boots. Fall out and clean them before you start work in the forge." Keith soon got into step with the regime, as it was a rule in our company that all the lads must clean their boots at least once a week.

On his second stint at college, Keith and his mate fell asleep in the classroom one day. They mumbled some excuse, which their senior tutor Tom Williams did not believe. He sent them to the hospital for a check-up just to cover the college's liability on health and safety grounds. When the report came back, his secretary opened it but, preferring not to read it out loud, she handed it over for Mr. Williams to see for himself. It said the boys were sexually exhausted. Apparently, Keith and his mate had rented a small cottage in Hereford and had brought their girlfriends to live with them.

This was not the only such issue that came up with Keith. While he was working at our forge, we had to go to some effort to keep the girls away. On his return from college in the second year, he decided to buy a small terraced house at Hepthorn Lane, North Wingfield, about three miles from the forge. We thought it a hasty decision, but he said he wanted to buy now because the house was cheap and it meant he would have something to sell when he finished his apprenticeship in a year's time.

Every Friday we used to visit a big livery yard. The owner's wife would ring up with the list of horses that needed new shoes. Now these people at the livery yard had a daughter, and she and Keith started to go out together. After a few months I said to my wife, "Do you think what I think about that girl that Keith is with?"

"What makes you think that, Doug?"

"Well, she stands holding the horses with her hand on her side, and the wax coat she wears is getting tighter."

Keith duly passed his exams and left my employment to work with his stepfather back home. Soon after he had left, the lady at the livery yard phoned to give Joan the shoeing list for the following day. Then she went on "Mrs. Bradbury, tell the lads not to laugh, but our daughter had a baby in the night. She did not know she was having one and nor did we. She needed to go to the toilet and that's where he was born. He bumped his little head and we had to have two ambulances."

I said to my wife "I bet they call him Louie."

When I saw the girl's father next day, he said "That bloody lad of yours."

"Just a minute! I only teach them to shoe horses and nothing else."

Keith and the girl never married. The son they had is now in his 30s.

Youth exchange scheme

Every year the National Association of Farriers, Blacksmiths and Agricultural Engineers run an exchange scheme. They arrange for two newly qualified farriers from the UK to go to America or Europe for three months, all expenses paid, and in return we in this country host two farriers from either of these continents. The cost is borne by NAFBAE and the Worshipful Company of Farriers, and a team of NAFBAE members volunteer to host the boys and girls from abroad for a fortnight each. My wife and I were part of that team, I am pleased to say, and the agreement was that we had the student for two weeks and then delivered them to the next person in the chain. Whilst they were in your care, they would receive free board and lodgings and you would do their washing and give them £25 spending money. In return they were meant to do a bit of work for you. This did not always happen.

One summer while Keith was still with us, but after he had moved out of our house, we had an American girl called Diane Leeming staying with us on this youth exchange scheme. A shire horseshoeing competition was about to take place at the Vaux Brewery and there was a spare place. Diane said she would like to have a go as she had never made a shoe for a shire horse. You were allowed a striker (an assistant to hammer the shoe into shape on the anvil) and my son Neal agreed to do that. He finished up almost making the shoe for her. I think the judge must have felt sorry for her as he awarded her fifth place.

Diane Leeming with her shire horseshoe

Diane and Neal at the anvil

Diane receiving her certificate

The day after the show at the Vaux Brewery we had four hunters booked in at the forge for 2pm. Diane disappeared the moment they arrived. My wife went to look for her and found she had gone to bed. We told her this was not a holiday but an educational programme. Diane then asked would it be OK if she stayed at Keith's next week so that she could study a bit of anatomy. I am not sure whether she meant horse or human anatomy. Fortunately, this was the girl's final week with us before moving on to the next host in the chain, and life went back to normal after she had gone.

Stewart Faylan the Third

Stewart from Arizona was another student on the youth exchange scheme. He had started off by working for two weeks with Ed Martin FWCF in Scotland. Ed phoned me as I was the next in the chain and asked if I could pick the lad up at the Sheffield coach park on the following Sunday lunchtime.

"Will do, Ed. How will I recognise him?"

"Do not worry – you will."

Joan and I sat in the car as the coach arrived and watched as the passengers disembarked. A tall young man emerged wearing a Stetson and carrying a suitcase and a large hat box with a spare hat in it. He wore a light blue jacket, and on the back of the jacket in big letters were the words STEWART FAYLAN THE THIRD.

Stewart was a very polite young man, but he did not say much and didn't take his hat off even at the dining table. I think he must have slept in it. I offered to cut a hole in the bedhead for his hat to fit in, but he appeared to lack any sense of humour and didn't respond. During his stay he became very homesick. He was not interested in the horse side of the business, just the blacksmithing part. After two weeks I took him to Stoneleigh to spend further fortnight with the next farrier in the chain. The American farriery team happened to be at Stoneleigh for an international farriery competition. That seemed to lift the lad's spirits a bit, but it did not last and he returned home before his time was up.

Andrew Frudd

Our next full-time apprentice was a young lad from Sheffield. He came to see me with his father and uncle one night to enquire if there were any chance of a job. All three of these people were a bit on the small side. In fact, all three sat on a two-seater settee with the lad in the middle. I remarked to Joan that there was more fat on a cold chip than there was on this lad, but I felt he could make a good craftsman.

Andrew stayed with us in the house and proved me right. He had a great sense of humour and soon became the life and soul of the workforce. Joan and I set no hard and fast rules for the lads, only that they must behave themselves in the town. One night Andrew came back from town with a pocketful of money. "How about that, boss?"

"Where have you got that from?"

"I dropped the jackpot on the fruit machine in the Cannon pub."

I said "But Andrew, you are not old enough to go in a pub."

"I only have a soft drink, boss, and the landlord says that is OK."

Andrew wins his first shoeing competition at the Vaux Brewery

Andrew at the anvil

Andrew on his 18th birthday. Neal got him a strippergram whilst we were at dinner at the Hunloke Arms

About a week later the same thing happened again, and we heard the same tale.

"Either you are very lucky, Andrew, or there is something else going on."

"No there isn't, boss. All I do is to put a 50p piece in my mouth and wet it and when I put it in the slot I give it a spin. It slides through the interior gates and comes back out, but as it passes through it gives you five credits. So, I have been playing all night with the same 50 pence.

I said, "If you get caught, you will get sent to hell."

"No, it's all right, boss. It's like when my mum plays on the Space Invaders at her club in Stocksbridge, she brings the igniter from her cooker. She just touches it on the console and it gives her five credits each time."

This does prove that masters can sometimes learn from their apprentices. In all fairness, this lad worked really hard to make his test pieces for entry to college. However, whilst he was at Hereford he got involved with some older boys who used to do a bit of drinking, and of course there were girls involved. One night they had a bet on who could get a girl into their room first. Andrew was not first or last to try, but before anything happened the landlady came home just in time to send the girls packing.

Now, we did not hear about this until it was time for Andrew to go to college for his second block-release period. About a week before he was due to go, he still had not received an accommodation address. I phoned the college to enquire why. The accommodation officer Mrs. Assweld told me she had been unable to find anyone willing to take Andrew because of the previous incident. That was the first I had heard about a previous incident. She explained in detail. I gave my word it would never happen again and that I would get Andrew to write a letter of apology to the landlady.

I made sure he wrote that letter, and off to college he went with it. He had written it himself and it did a lot of good, because for some years afterwards the accommodation officer used to quote from it in the talk she delivered to every fresh intake of apprentices. I happened to meet Mrs. Assweld some weeks later when I visited the college in my capacity as a senior examiner for the WCF diploma. She thanked me very much for the way I handled the matter with the boy and said she wished there were more masters like me.

As Andrew became better at shoemaking, Neal asked him if he wanted to go to some local and county shows. Andrew said that would be great. Neal used to take another mate along too, and Joan and I would sponsor the lads by paying their entry fees. Most of the time our two worked together quite effectively. I would strike for Neal or fire for Andrew and together they had a lot of success.

Not a day passed by without Andrew telling jokes and doing impressions of the customers. His best one was of Ted Parker in Ripley, who had to use a specially adapted car and would lean out of the car window saying, "Give us a light, Doug." My three-year-old granddaughter kept a toy Noddy car in our yard at the time, and Andrew would climb in this toy car then lean out croaking, "Give us a light, Doug." Everyone would fall about laughing.

One day we had an appointment in the village of Youlgreave. We found we were going to have to see to the horse in a gateway between two sets of roadworks, where the gas board and the electricity board had each got the road up. Andrew said he would go and get the horse and proceeded to do a cartwheel over the wall into its field. Halfway over he saw there was a drop on the other side of about 15 feet. The look on his face was priceless. The gas and electric workmen all stood up and listened for the crash. A few moments later Andrew popped up further down the field grinning all over his face and shouting, "I am OK, boss!"

Steven Bradshaw

Whilst Andrew was with us, we were asked if we could find a place for a boy from Lincolnshire by the name of Steven Bradshaw. He was a friend of a friend of mine called Bert Flatters and had been going to Bert's forge at the weekends. The metalwork he brought to show me was of a very high standard, so I decided to give him a chance and offer him a trial period. We were soon to find out that he loved the forge work but would not do any homework or anatomy studies. His parents were very nice, but Steven could twist them around his little finger. One day when they came to see him, he sent them back home to fetch his motor bike.

Steven fancied a girl he saw at a stable yard in Bakewell and thought he might go and chat her up one night after work. He found out that the girl worked in a pub in Bakewell and decided to ask if she would go out with him. We urged him not to go as it was a terrible winter night, with icy roads and falling snow. We even told him there was a ghost on Beeley Moor by the name of Basil of Beeley. Undeterred, he refused to listen and off he went.

Steven Bradshaw and Andrew Frudd at dinner on Sunday night

Steven Bradshaw with Andrew Frudd tied up at the junction of Thanet Street after misbehaving

He was back fairly soon, covered in snow and with his gloves frozen solid to the handlebars of his motor bike. He looked like a walking snowman.

"You haven't been gone long. Did you see the girl?"

"Yes."

"Was it worth the trip, then?"

"No." She had told him to piss off and not bother her.

Steven had a bad habit of staring at people. One night he and Andrew went to a disco at a pub called the Three Fishers on the A61 at Stretton. They spotted two girls standing alone. Fixing his gaze on the girls, Steven muttered to Andrew, "We're in there with them two, mate." What they did not know was that the girls' boyfriends were waiting for them outside. They both got beaten up and tossed over the wall at the back of the pub. Back home they told us they were not going to that pub again as the music was rubbish. They did not need to explain further. We could see by their faces what had happened.

One day Steven was acting stupid, larking about and setting Andrew off, and it was getting tiresome. Neal and I first of all tied his feet together and hung him upside down from the beams in the roof. This did not work, so we took him and Andrew across the road from the forge at the T junction and tied them to the halt sign whilst we had dinner. Two policemen drove past and grinned.

Steven Bradshaw was given every chance to do the required homework but did not bother. So, I decided to terminate the trial period and off he went.

Gordon Howett

There were always boys looking for apprenticeships in farriery. Our next lad, Gordon Howett, came from Biggleswade. We took on Gordon as a full-time apprentice following a trial period. He lived in the house with us and Andrew. They each bought a car and after a succession of crashes they seemed to settle down. Gordon was very stiff in his wrists, and when I was teaching him the art of nailing the shoes on he used to bend so many that I began to think he had bought some shares in the nail company. One day I counted over 50 bent horseshoe nails.

As I said before, we used to work in the Sheffield area on Sundays. Gordon met a girl he liked at one of the yards and asked her out on a date. He told us she was a bit older than he was and had just broken up with a college boy, who had left her in debt. She made Gordon an offer: if he could help her with the bills, she in return would teach him all about sex. You can guess his answer. Straight after work each day he would zoom off to Sheffield, picking up more than one speeding fine on the way.

As for shoeing horses, Gordon was a quiet lad who got on with the job and did as he was told. He went to a few shows with Neal and Andrew but did not have quite the same spark. He was placed in several competitions but never won first prize.

One of these events was the annual shire horse shoeing competition at the Vaux Brewery in Sunderland. The show was held in the brewery yard. The fires were all coal hearths with a hand fan on the back. (That's the reason the lads in the photograph below are looking a little black.) In the brewery

Gordon Howett

yard was a small public house. This was open all day to supply the competitors and their guests with free beer, and the presentation took place there at the end of the show. Everyone had a good time at the Vaux Brewery show, and I must say I never saw anyone the worse for wear.

Gordon passed his diploma exam with a B grade. Just before he took it, we found a second-hand forge for him. It was going cheap at a yard in Matlock, and his dad came up to collect it. So, Gordon left our company to start up on his own back home. His girlfriend went with him and we never heard any more from him.

Three sooty lads – Neal, Andrew and Gordon

Big Dave from Canada

David Compton was a Canadian mounted policeman who wished to change his career. He said he had done a short course in horseshoeing at one of the many schools in America that offer such courses. Having completed this course, his plan was to come over here and start a business in Northumberland, where he had relatives. But he had failed his English language assessment, a test that all persons wanting to enter the farriery profession have to pass. The registrar of the FRC (Farriery Registration Council) asked me if I would take him on for six months to improve his practical skills in clenching up, nailing on and finishing the job off, in fact in my view all aspects of the job.

Dave was a big man, over 6 feet 6 inches tall, so we called him Big Dave. He had a new set of tools and he would sit down and polish them after every time he used them. I think that someone had been telling lies about this man having a background in the Mounties, as he was very green around horses and at times had a very intimidating manner. I offered him board and lodging with Joan and myself, as his wife had not yet come over to this country and he had not sorted out any accommodation.

Our first call on Monday mornings was regularly at Jenny Fisher's riding school at Alton from 9am until 12 noon. This particular Monday was Dave's first day with us and I wanted to assess for myself what he could do. First up was a little pony about 12.2 hh. I told Dave to make a start while I went to the van to fetch some shoes for it. Next, I heard a crash, and whipped round to see the pony scrambling up from the

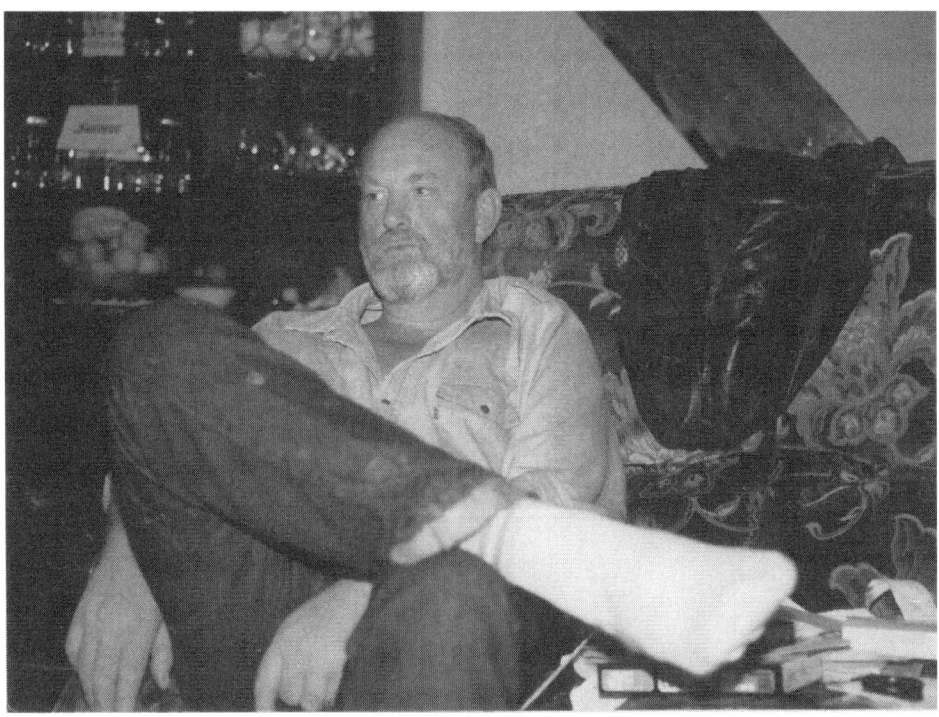

Big Dave

ground. As Big Dave had approached to pick up the pony's foot, it had jumped so he just threw it on its back. The owner saw it happen and shouted, "Never bring that man to my yard again!" The pony never forgot the experience and was always nervous about being shod after that.

I was convinced that Dave had not had much to do with horses, so I restricted him to clenching-up duties for the rest of the week. The following week, one of our calls was at Jane Smallwood's yard, just up the road from our forge. It was a dream of a place to work, with a large loosebox used only for clipping and shoeing at the end of a stable block. That day we had two of Jane's dressage horses to shoe. I let Dave start on one while I stood at his side to watch. All was well until it came to the nailing on. The horse suddenly jumped up in the air. Dave called, "Doug! There's blood here."

"Shit – come out the way and fetch me the peroxide from the van." I started to take off the shoe. The horse must have been in a lot of pain as every nail had entered the sensitive structures. As I was wiping the hoof Dave arrived and I told him to put a bit of peroxide on one spot. By now he was panicking and he poured it all over my hands.

I said, "Just go and sit in the van whilst I attend to the horse."

When it was done, I went over to the van. I took one look at him and he must have known what I was about to say. He said, "Take me home and I will leave."

Dave never did go any further in the farriery profession. As I said, someone had told some lies about his past experience. I was told he went to work in a furniture factory in the north of England. It shows that the English system of approved professional farriery training is the best.

7

FELLOW OF THE WORSHIPFUL COMPANY OF FARRIERS

Grant spurs me on

I mentioned earlier that Grant Moon encouraged me to aim higher in professional qualifications. Grant was using my forge to practise for his AWCF examination and one day he suggested, "Doug, why not do your fellowship exam at the same time, so then we can practise together." He knew it had been some years since I took my associateship exam (known at the time as the AFCL – Associateship of the Farriers' Company of London) and since then I hadn't really pushed myself to go any further. Until he suggested it, I had not in fact given the fellowship examination much thought. Practising at home with Grant did seem a good idea – and also the best offer I was likely to get as there was no one else in the Chesterfield area who could help me train for the exam. The nearest person holding the FWCF qualification was Graham Sutton at a village near Ashbourne. He was willing to help, but it would have been too far to go after work. So, I stopped at home with Grant, and I can tell you we put in a lot of extra hours each night to make all the different types of shoes named on the syllabus. For the fellowship exam you also had to write a thesis of 2,000 words or more relating to farriery, and submit six copies to the Worshipful Company of Farriers six weeks before the examination.

One advantage I had was my keen interest in photography (an interest that has stayed with me now that everything is digital). At branch meetings of the NAFBAE at the pub in Ripley, I had often noticed how, whenever anyone said they were doing a special type of work on a horse, someone else always said they had done one the same way. But no one ever had any photographic evidence to prove or disprove whether they had done it successfully. So, I had decided to buy a camera and use it to document some of my farriery cases. Besides, you could claim tax relief on the cost because it was work related. To improve my skills, I attended evening classes in photography with my wife at our local adult education centre. Our tutor was a police forensic branch photographer, a very interesting man and a good friend. I carried my camera everywhere, including in the van, and built up an extensive collection of slides on the work of the farrier and all the different types of remedial shoes used in the cases that came our way. Some of our treatments had been successful and some not. The camera proved to be a good investment, as I have had photographs published on several occasions and have been paid for their use.

Grant and I practising tooling and fullering each night after dinner

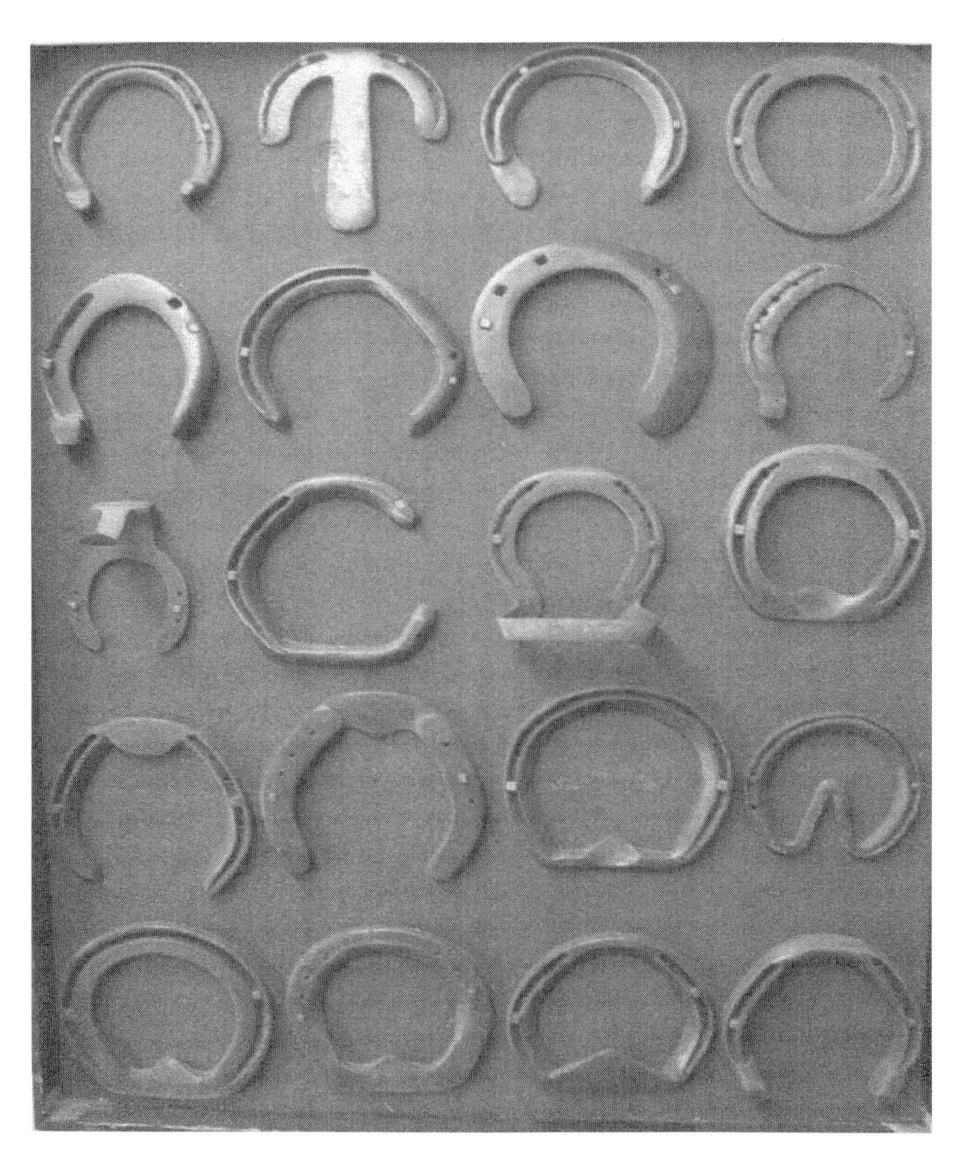

Display board:
This is the board of handmade horseshoes made by me and submitted to the examination team as a part of my fellowship exam in 1983.
No 1 Caulk and wedge, No 2 Anchor shoe, No 3 Set heel, No 4 Egg bar,
No 5, Caulk and feather, No 6 Speedy cut, No7 Side bone, No 8 Cross fire,
No 9 Extended toe, No 10 G shoe, No 11 Pattern bar shoe, No 12 Rocker bar,
No 13/14 Tooled full set for toe-horn tumour, No 15 Tooled full bar shoe, No 16 Heart bar,
No 17 Full bar shoe, No 18 Plain stamped deep-seated shoe,
No 19 Tooled full fracture shoe, No 20 Tooled full spavin/curb shoe

I then planned how to write my thesis. I decided it would be a dissertation entitled 'A description of some actual cases requiring special consideration' by D. Bradbury AFCL and that it would contain the following four case studies along with a full set of 35mm slides on each case:

1. A study on a horse with a horn tumour (keratoma).
2. A study on contracted tendons, congenital and acquired (as we termed the condition in those days). It is now referred to as ballerina syndrome.
3. Ruptured or lacerated tendons.
4. Fractures of the third phalanx (pedal bone).

Case study 1: Keratoma (horn tumour)

Keratomas are horn tumours which develop on the inner surface of the horn wall. Tumours are not common nowadays, but when they do appear the seat of the tumour is at the toe area. It is believed to be a result of a chronic inflammation of the sensitive wall, with a separation between the sensitive and horny lamina of the hoof. The pus is retained, causing partial degeneration of the sensitive lamina, which in turn causes separation of the horny and sensitive lamina. When the pus escapes, either through a passage caused by the pressure or through an artificial opening, an empty space is left which allows hard horn to form on the free margins of the sensitive lamina, thereby causing a keratoma to develop. The tumour gradually occupies the formerly empty space. The size may vary from about half an inch in diameter up to one-and-a-half

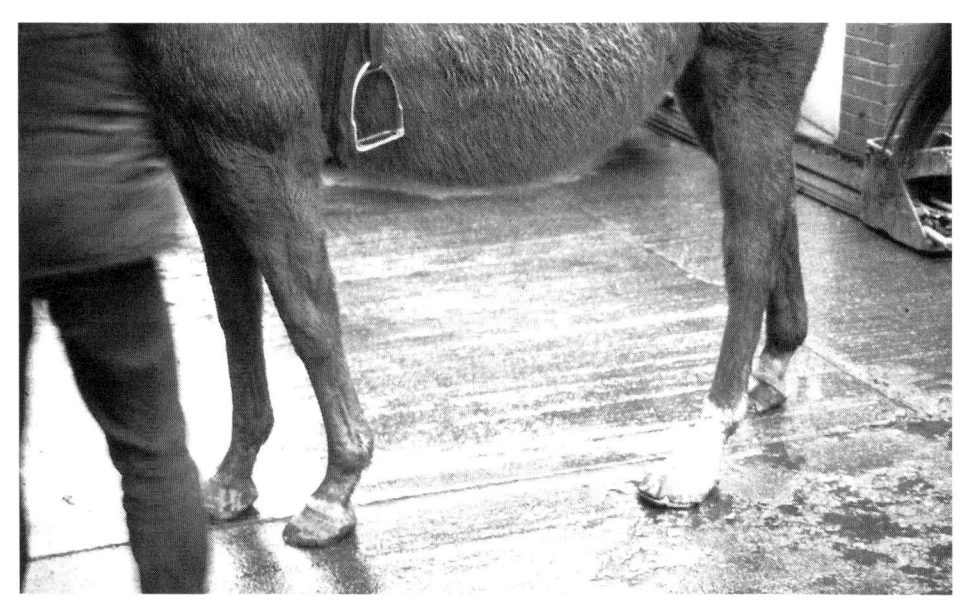

The horn tumour was found in the near hind of this 16.2hh chestnut gelding aged 11 years

The horse is standing back on his heels and growing a lot of hoof

inches. This in turn causes pressure on the anterior surface of the third phalanx. A tumour is first detected at the bearing surface, usually at the toe area, where it appears as a hard mass of horn between the sole and the wall of the hoof and in turn deflects the white line inwards. This can be seen in the photograph on the previous page. It is composed of hard grey glistening horn, waxy looking and mushroom in shape. The new growth occasionally undergoes degeneration, producing a depression of varying depth, with dark-colour walls from which a greyish-black pus is sometimes discharged.

Symptoms

Lameness gradually develops, with the horse or pony standing back on its heels. When lameness is present there is an increase in warmth and pulsation of the digital artery, and sometimes it may be mistaken for an attack of laminitis.

Causes

Chronic inflammation of the sensitive wall may be caused by:
1. Bruising
2. Pricks from shoeing
3. Corns or treads
4. Pressure from an extended toe-piece shoe
5. One of the main causes years ago was when farriers used to hammer the large clips on a shire horse's shoes back to the angle of the hoof, on some occasions using a 2lb hammer.

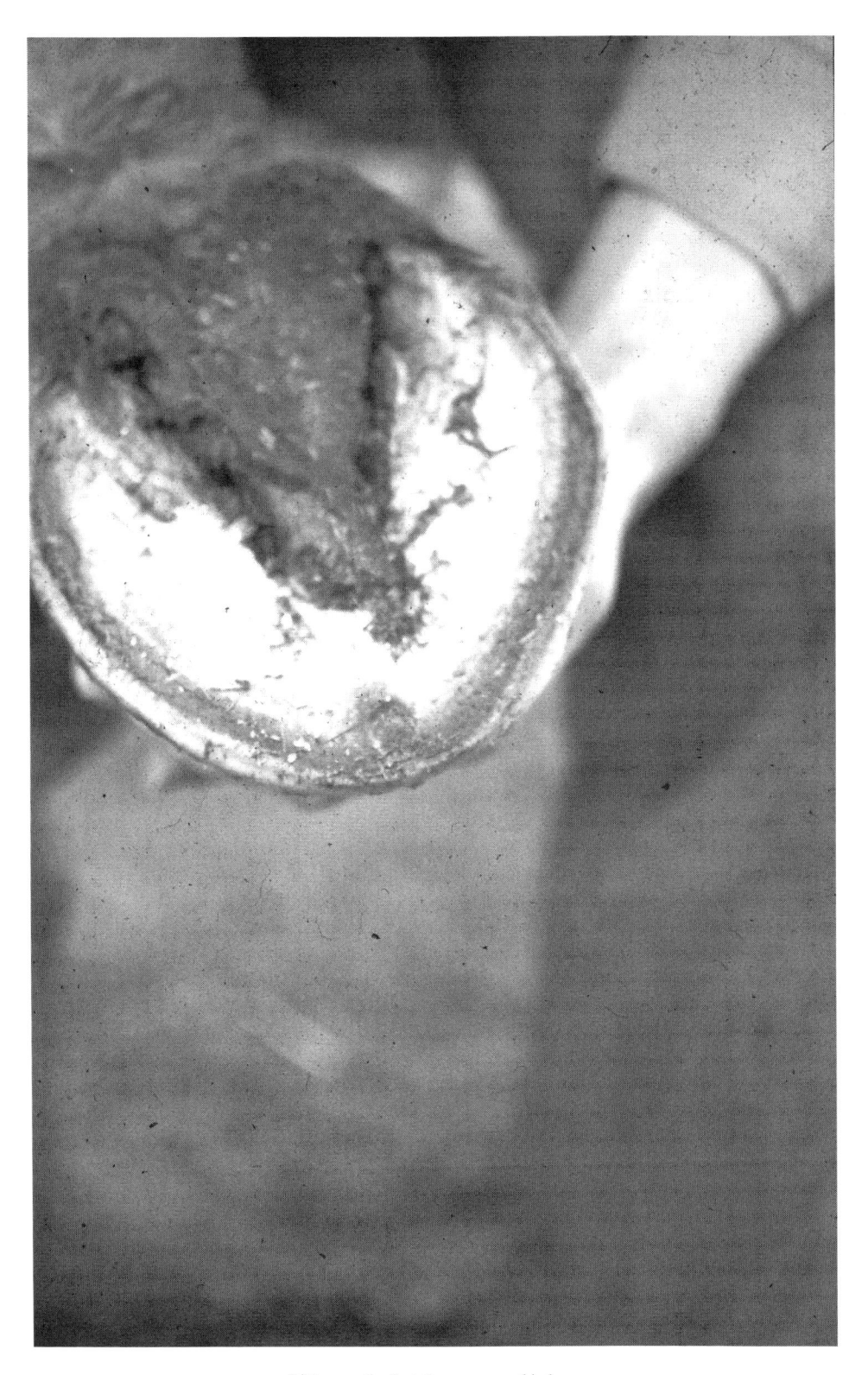

This was the first time we saw this horse

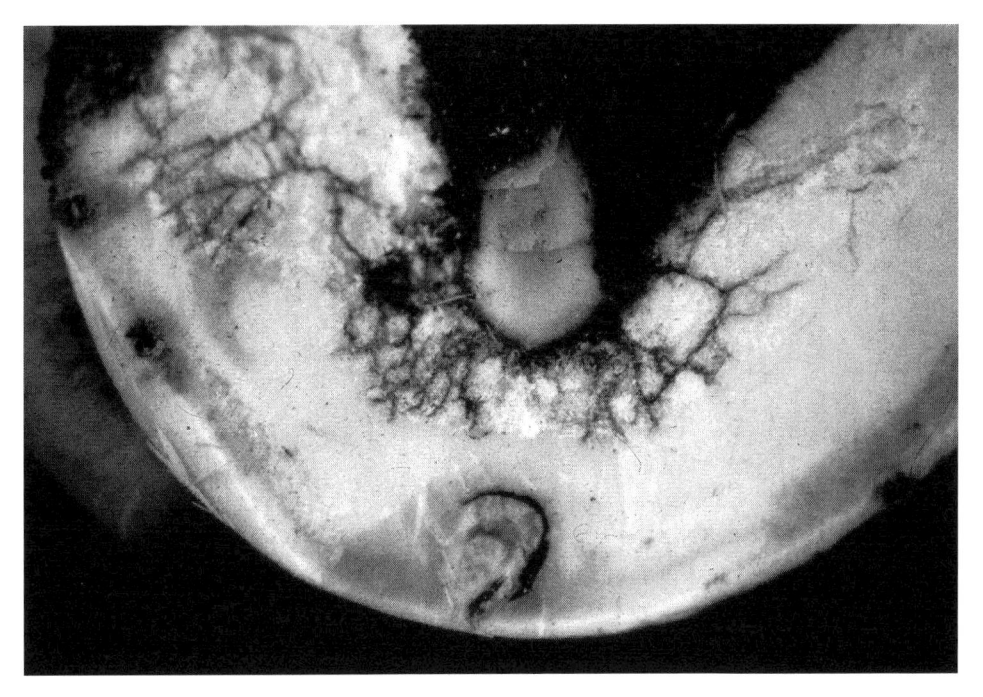

The tumour leaking greyish or black pus

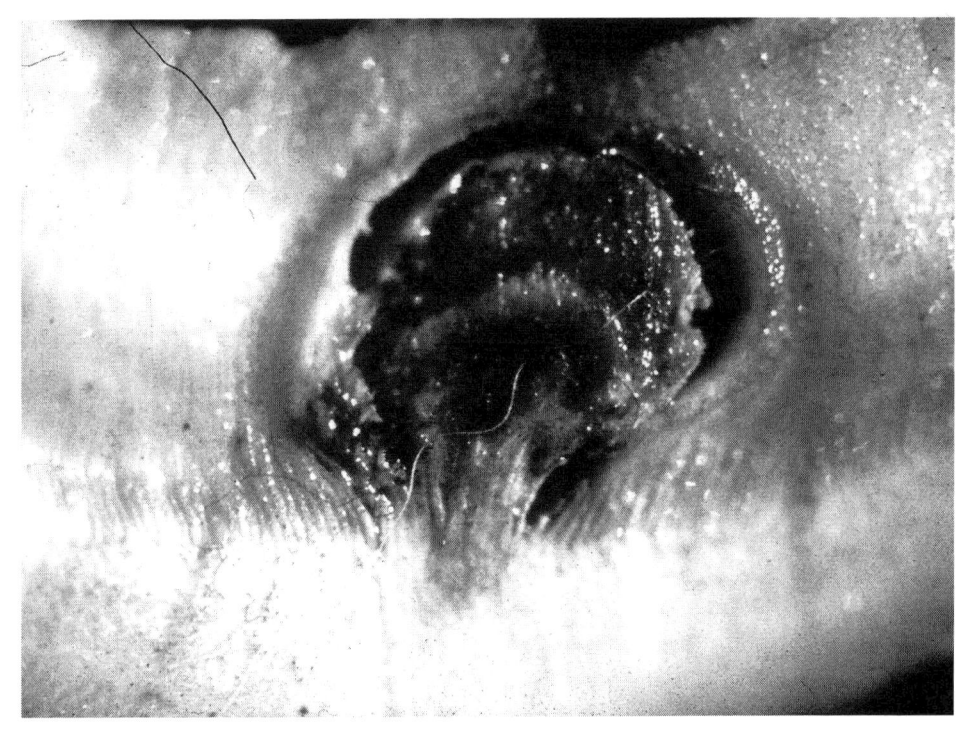

A close-up of the horn tumour, which is composed of hard, glistening, waxy-looking horn.

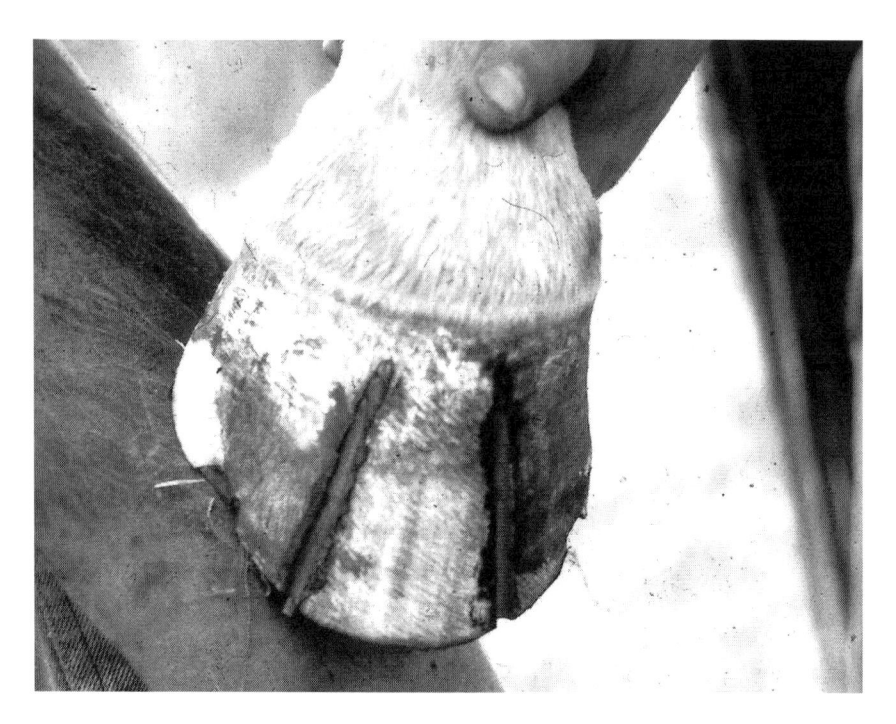

The hoof after grooving to weaken the wall

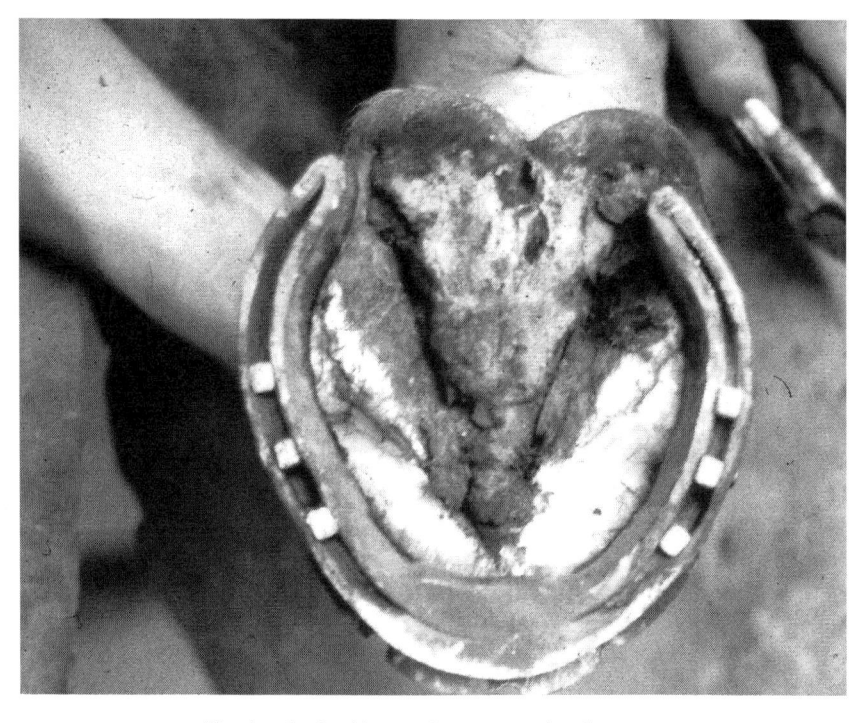

The shoe fitted, with a set-down toe covering the tumour

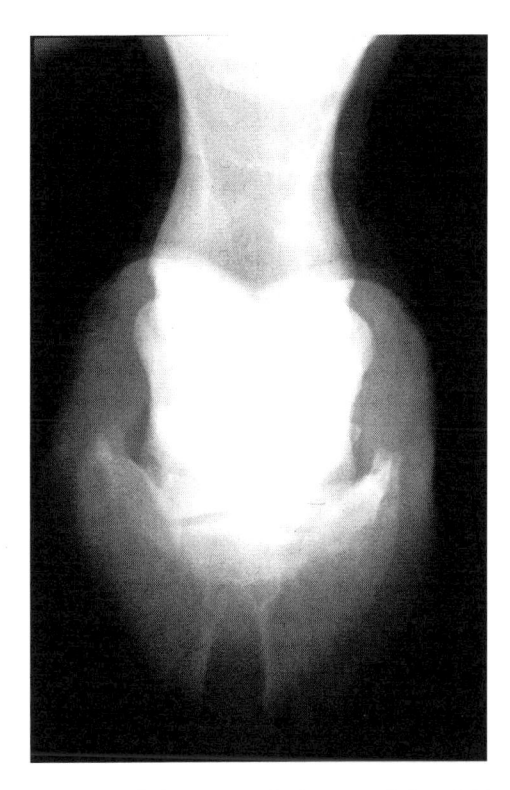

X-ray showing the horn tumour in the centre of the pedal bone

The grooved hoof and the tools I used: the T iron to burn in the grooves, and the grooving knives

Treatment

It is important to try and relieve the pressure from the immediate area of the tumour with a shoe designed to alleviate it. These photographs from 1978 are of the first case that I came across. The horse was a 16.2hh chestnut gelding, 11 years old, not in the best of condition, and the property of Mr. T. Smith of Sutton Springwood. When I first saw this horse I was not sure exactly what the problem might be. So I spoke to a couple of vets and did some research, and found that it might be a horn tumour. The symptoms shown in the books were just as I have described (a long toe, and standing back on the heels).

After giving the hooves a good trim, I sought advice from the vet, as this was something I had not dealt with before. The vet suggested that I cut two or three vertical grooves in the hoof but should start with one horizontal one first to relieve any pressure. This should weaken the outer wall, ease the pressure on the third phalanx and in turn relieve the lameness. The grooves would also facilitate the removal of that section of hoof should it be necessary at a later date. When I made the shoe for this horse, I set it down in the toe area and spread the metal to cover the area around the tumour and protect it from any foreign bodies that might enter at that location. The clips were quarter clips set well back, with no nails near the toe area.

I advised the owner to have the horse inspected at short regular intervals. This advice was ignored, as I was not called back to see the horse for a further ten weeks, and the amount of hoof growth in that time was astonishing. Unfortunately, the horse had reverted to the stance it had adopted when I first visited it. You can only do your best, so I gave it another good trim and then re-grooved the hoof to make it more comfortable. The tool I used to put in the grooves was one I designed myself: a four-inch nail welded onto a piece of flat iron, which could be placed in the forge. The grooves could be burnt into the hoof in parallel lines, then finished off with the Hauptner grooving knife. This made the hoof more presentable.

After several visits this horse was going a lot better, but from time to time it would secrete a black pus. This subsided after a time, but I noticed a change to the anterior surface of the hoof wall. It seemed to me the outer wall was so weak that the pressure had been reversed from the pedal bone to the outer surface of the hoof and had created a bulge. The horse was doing so well by then that the vet decided not to remove that section of hoof but to carry on with the shoeing at four-week intervals. Within six months the owner had sold the horse and I never saw it again.

One good thing did come from that job: I had a great collection of 35mm slides and kept them in the hope that one day they would form part of my thesis. I have had requests for copies of the close-up of the horn tumour from as far away as Australia, as these tumours are so rare and not many people have seen such good clear photographs of them as those I took.

Case study 2: Contracted tendons (deformities of the flexor tendons) or ballerina syndrome as it is now referred to

From the outset it should be said that little is known or has been written about this condition. Contracted tendons fall into two main categories:
1. Acquired – this type usually happens in foals from about 4 months up to 20 months of age.
2. Congenital – which happens at birth.

Acquired contracted tendons can occur at any time of year and are most common in yearlings or rapidly growing foals. One or both feet may be affected. All breeds of horses and ponies and also donkeys appear to be susceptible to this condition. The first signs that will be evident are the pasterns becoming rather upright and the fetlock points becoming straight; also the coronary band may become warm and puffy and the wall of the foot may flake away at the toe. Some separation of the wall from the sole may be evident at the white line. The syndrome progresses rapidly and will cause the animal to stand on its toes with its heels raised from the ground. There is only wear on the toe area and the heels grow long, so that as the toe wears the hoof becomes boxy or club footed. The animal stands with its forelegs out in front and well apart, a stance referred to as the A frame, which becomes more extreme as the condition progresses. If effective treatment is not started early and the condition is allowed to progress, the hoof will pass the point of

This foal had this problem on the near fore

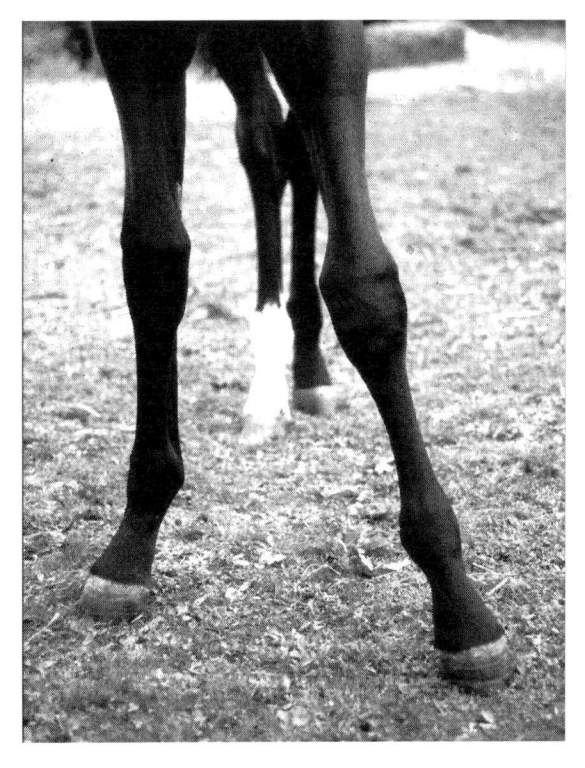

Typical stance referred to as the A frame

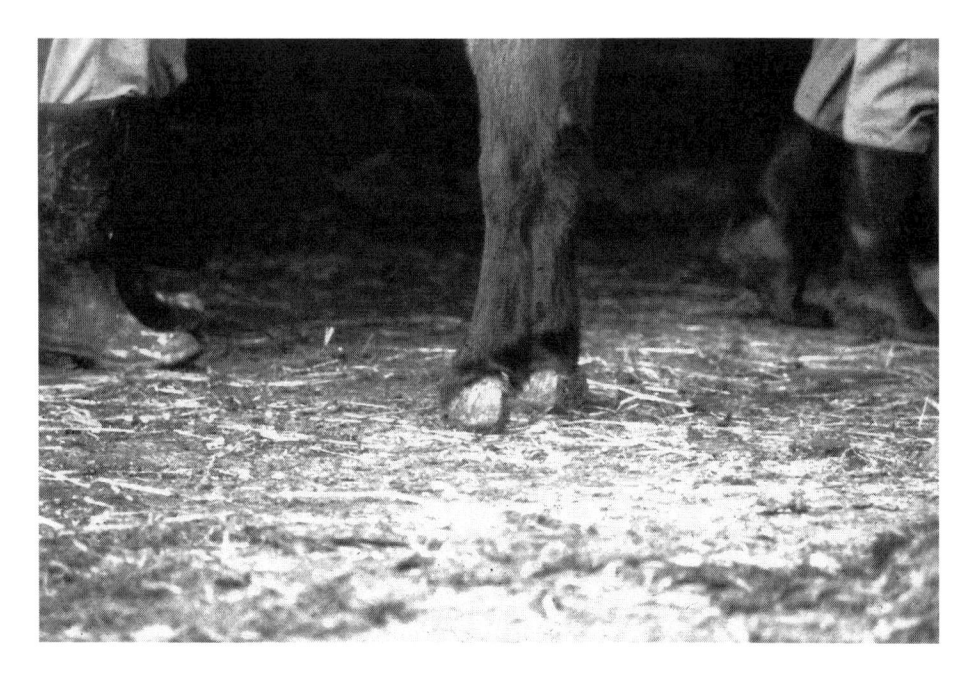

Foal before tendon operation

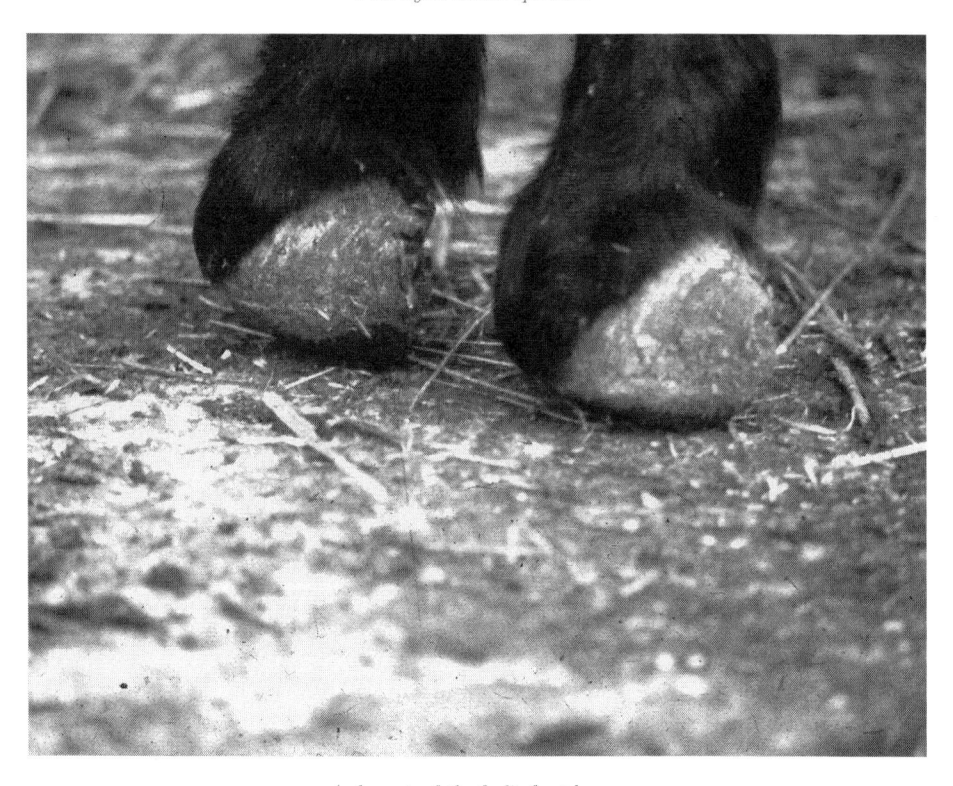

A close-up of the foal's front hooves

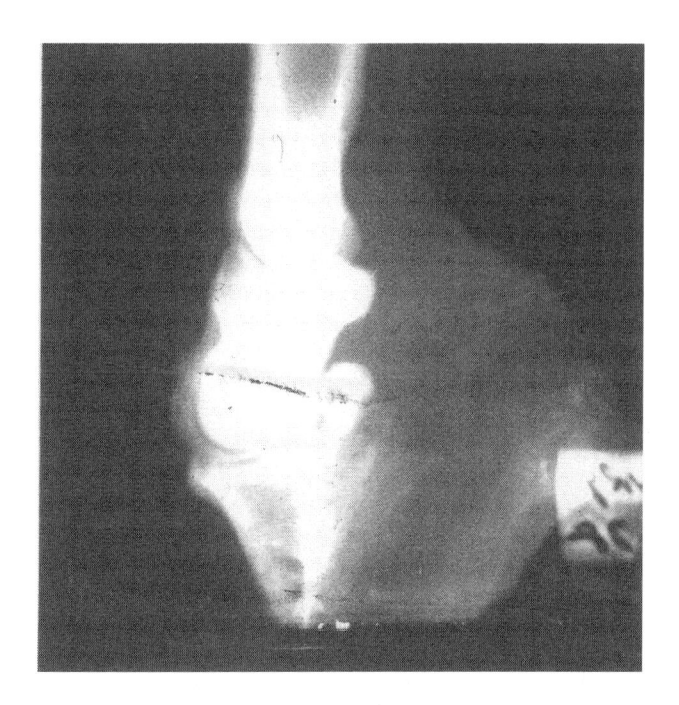

The x-ray of the foal's front hoof

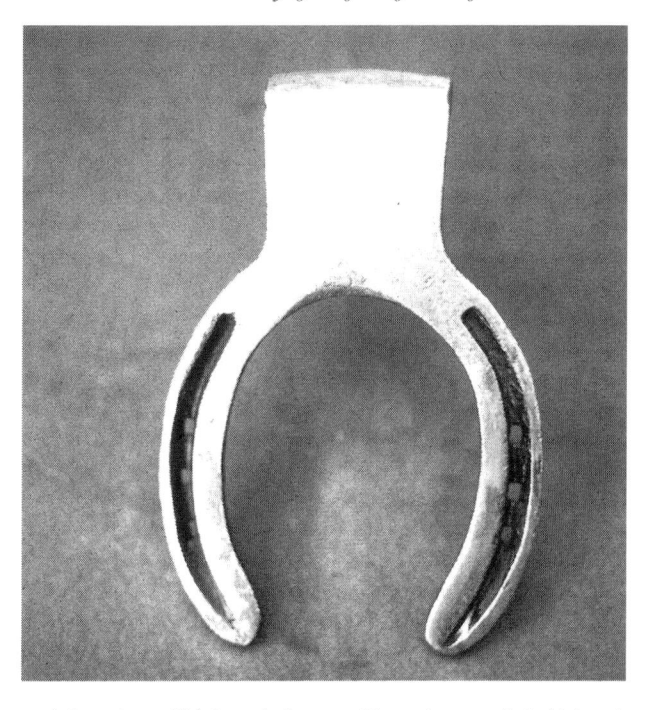

An extended toe shoe, which is made from an old rasp because of the high carbon content and will stand refitting

Anvil with rasp and shoes

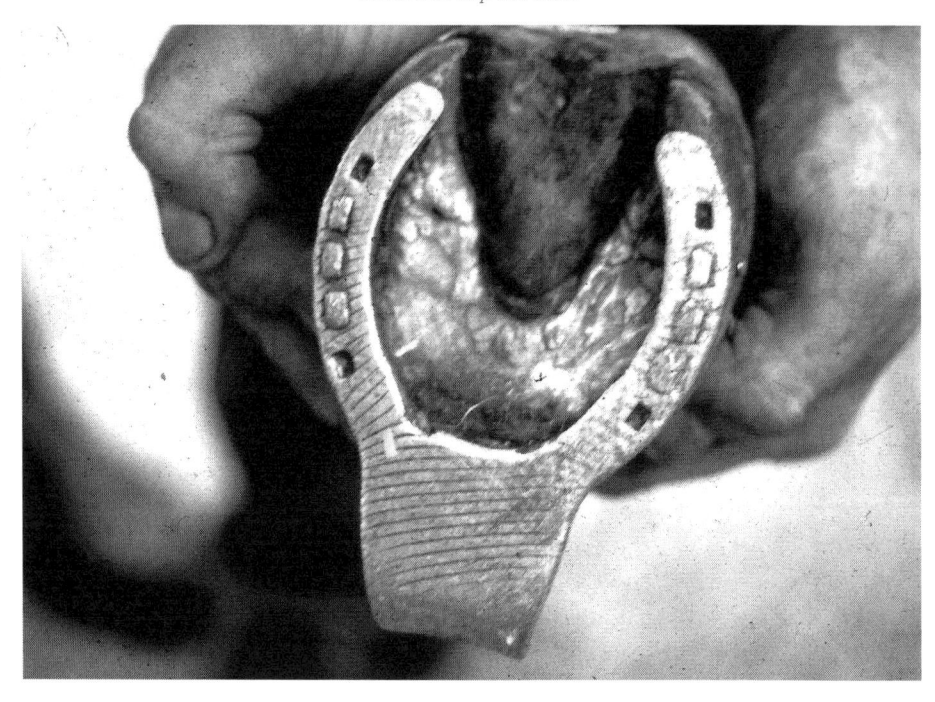

A shoe made from an old hoof rasp, left on for three weeks and showing wear from heel to toe

A new shoe made from an old foot rasp

no return and the horse will start to walk on the front of the wall rather than the sole. The prognosis is not good. Only one foot is affected on the foal pictured above, but in some foals both forefeet can be affected.

The very first case I saw was in 1977 at the yard of one of my clients at Tibshelf, who had some show ponies. She asked me to look at a foal she had bred. This foal had been on deep litter for some considerable time, most probably since it was born. I think this was the first time the owner had seen its feet and she could not understand why they looked like they did. I advised her to call in the veterinary surgeon straight away. The vet was a young man and he had not seen anything like it before, so he phoned Colonel John Hickman MR.CVS at the veterinary college for advice. The advice he got was to cut both the deep flexor and the superficial tendons and see what happened. The vet did just that and the result was nothing at all. The two hooves stayed where they were pre-operation.

Both front hooves were past the point of no return and the hind heels were becoming deformed too. The vet re-stitched the leg, brought the foal round from the anaesthetic and said that he would be back in two days' time to check if there had been any movement in the limb.

As you can see there was no improvement, so the vet decided to put the foal to sleep. I had taken photographs of this case and asked if I might have one of the legs so that I could get it x-rayed.

Over the years I have had to deal with about ten cases of contracted tendons. Only the first animal I saw with the condition – the foal just described – was put down, as both feet were past the point of no return.

The term 'contracted tendon' covers a number of related conditions, therefore the sequence is not always exactly as described. In some cases, the fetlock will knuckle forward with the hoof position remaining normal. In others the hoof and third phalanx will rotate with the fetlock remaining normal. However, in a large proportion of cases both fetlock and hoof are affected. In these cases there is an excessive pull on one or both flexor tendons, and possibly also the suspensory ligament. (The suspensory ligament is an elastic ligament giving support to the fetlock joint.)

The reason for this excessive pull is disputed. To this day no one seems to know the true cause of this problem in foals. The common theory ascribes it to a contraction or shortening of the tendon. This may occur in the suspensory ligament, and there are many theoretical reasons why it might occur. A second theory is that in rapidly growing foals the bones grow disproportionally faster and longer than the tendons.

However, a number of people find this explanation untenable. A third possibility is that there is excessive tension on the tendons from their muscle. This may be due to some problem with the muscle itself.

Dr. Van Hoosen writes in 1977 that his observations strongly indicate the cause is not a tendon inflammation, but primarily a muscle inflammation caused by an infection, a nutritional imbalance or an allergy (e.g. to oats). The remedy is to use an injectable vitamin E and selenium supplement, plus antibiotics and a prescribed diet, with corrective shoeing applied as early as possible. Extended-toe or swan-necked shoes can be used to support the hoof or pastern. One other important point is that the foal should be weaned off the mother and kept in a crew yard or some other similar place with a hard surface to get maximum leverage on the shoe. On a soft surface the toe extension would not work to its full potential.

(Some time after I worked on these cases, I think in the 1990s, the first glue-on shoes came on the market. These were the Dallmer hoof protection cuffs, and fitting them was a damn sight easier and less risky than nailing.)

Case study 3: Ruptured or lacerated tendons and the use of a swan-neck shoe

Occasionally horses and ponies meet with accidents in which both deep and superficial flexor digital tendons and even the suspensory ligaments may be severed. This can happen in both front and hind limbs and anywhere from the carpus to the fetlock or the tarsus to the fetlock.

Causes

Lacerated tendons may be caused by numerous types of accidents. Examples include over-reaching and thus cutting the tendon of the foreleg; kicks from other horses; and backing into sharp objects such as wire. If the flexor tendons are cut above the middle of the metatarsus or the metacarpus, the inferior check ligament may also become severed. When only the superficial flexor tendon is cut, the fetlock joint will drop but will not touch the ground. If the superficial and the deep flexors are cut, the fetlock joint will Dr.op to the ground and the toe will point into the air. When the suspensory ligament is also cut, the fetlock will rest on the ground. If the wound is below the distal end of the first phalanx, only the deep flexor can be involved.

The swan-neck shoe

I have had several occasions to use this type of shoe. The first time I used it was at the request of a veterinary surgeon in 1978. One of my clients needed a new horse for her riding school and bought a 15hh light bay. On arriving back home late at night she put it in a field next to but separate from

A swan-neck shoe

the rest of the school horses so it could get used to them. The following morning she found the new horse with a very deep cut midway down the hind metatarsus. The toe of the hoof was slightly raised and there was blood everywhere. The vet was called immediately, a young man by the name of Ian Taylor MR.CVS. He placed a large piece of wood under the heel of the hoof and taped it to the hoof. He then did a lot of work on the wound, stitching the tendons back. He told the owner to phone her farrier and ask him to come and take a look and then fit a swan-neck shoe for her in a week to ten days' time.

I had never made a shoe like this before and I read up on it before going to fit it. Hickman's Farriery was my main source of guidance. There is one very important factor that the books do not tell you: the shoe must be fullered to enable you to withdraw all the nails individually and so remove the shoe with ease. I duly made the shoe and went along to fit it. Everything went well. The only problem was to estimate the size of the hoof, as the foot and leg were heavily bandaged. As the horse had to rest its weight on the other leg, it would not have been wise to try and lift that one to take measurements. Length was not a problem, as in this case you shoe to the leg and not to the foot. Although I say this myself, I didn't make a bad guess. I had estimated the height at the back of the hoof at five inches, plus the pad, and that was bang on. One thing I got wrong was the angle up the back of the hoof to the fetlock. This I did not find out until the day I took the shoe off for the first time, and found a small pressure sore at the bulb of the heel. I dressed this with wound powder for a few days and all was well.

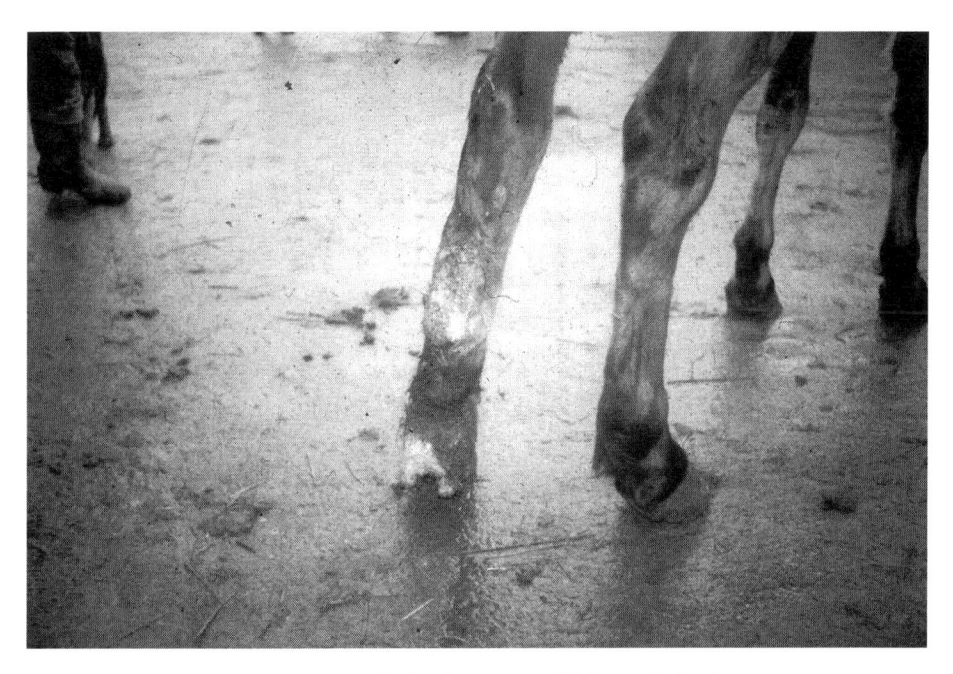

About a week after the vet operated it became infected

The leg with the shoe removed

A small pressure sore caused by the shoe

When this shoe was first fitted, the vet advised the owner to bed the horse on sawdust as straw could have built up around the shoe and caused a problem. The horse quickly adapted to the shoe and began to move around quite freely. However, about a week after the operation the wound became infected. The leg swelled to almost twice its normal size and really looked very bad; in fact, everyone who saw it said "Why you don't put the horse down, as it must be in a lot of pain?"

The vet was not too concerned at this point and said that the infection was working in the horse's favour by pressing everything together. He wanted to wait a bit longer so as to give the horse a chance. After a time, the infection subsided and the animal was able to walk out in the yard. Then after about 12 weeks we noticed a small gap appearing between the pad on the shoe and the tendon when the horse moved. It would stand for a while and then Dr.op back onto the pad.

Over the following weeks the leg got stronger and the gap got bigger. At 18 weeks we decided to take the shoe off, trim the hoof and refit the shoe for a few weeks more. That is when I saw the small pressure sore on the bulb of the heel, caused by pressure from the upright of the shoe, but this soon healed. So, to recap, this shoe had been on for 18 weeks before we decided to refit it and see just how strong the leg was. At this point we were all very pleasantly surprised at the progress the animal had made. At 20 weeks the owner decided to try putting someone on its back and walking it around the yard. Lots of young girls queued up for this job. It went well and the horse was put into light work to prepare it for the job it was bought for.

One girl at the riding school fell in love with the horse and named it Red. After a few months of working with Red, she came over to me when I was on one of my weekly visits and said "Mr. Bradbury, would you believe me if I told you that Red and I are going over the jumps in the outdoor school?"

I said, "Really? If that is so, put on your clean jodhpurs on Sunday morning and I will bring my camera and take some pictures of you and Red in action."

You can see from the photos that Red could jump, but it took a few attempts before he consented to do so. The rider was really embarrassed as he would do everything she wanted other than go over the jump. When he finally did, he jumped well clear. The girl knew I might want to use my photos in giving talks and slideshows to pony clubs, and said "Please do not show me on Red when he was refusing, will you?"

I said that actually I would, because it showed the pressure on those back legs when he came to a stop. She was quite happy at that explanation. You may think that farriery is a dirty smelly back-aching job, but there's a lot of job satisfaction when you see the joy on a youngster's face at getting a result like this, and that makes you realise what an important the job the farrier does.

First attempt

followed by a second attempt

and a third

then finally room to spare

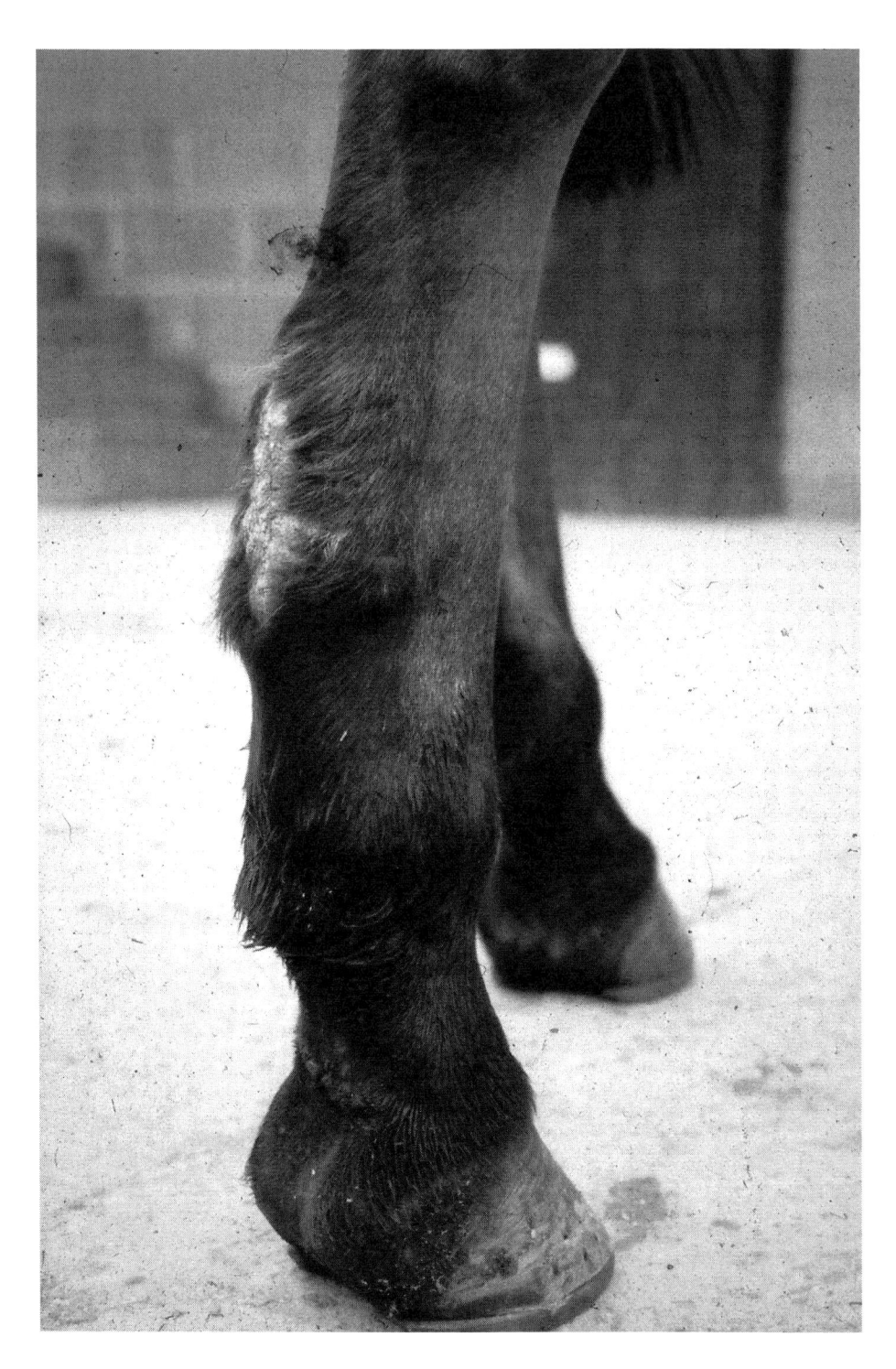

Red's leg one year after his accident

A very happy young girl

The following case was not part of my thesis, but I am including it as a point of interest.

The last swan-neck shoe I made was in 1999 for a seven-year-old Irish draught mare that had never been shod. She was kept at a riding school that was quite near Sheffield but not in my usual area. The owner told me that the horse had been trapped in a five-barred metal gate and had cut the tendons in her hind leg. She was 16.2hh and had never been shod as she had misbehaved so badly in the past when the owner's usual farrier tried to shoe her that he had refused to try again and had left her unshod. The owner told me it was her vet who had advised her to phone me, as he remembered having worked with me many years ago when he was in practice with Bill Bacon MR.CVS in Alfreton. He had said, "If anyone can help you, it is Doug Bradbury. Tell him your vet is Ian Taylor and I am sure he will come out to see you."

The last time I fitted one of these shoes for this vet had been 20 years earlier, and that was on the horse called Red that you have just read about. I told this lady I would pop over to Killamarsh that afternoon and have a look. It was again difficult to take any measurements as the horse was heavily bandaged and not sedated. So, I made a guess and chose for the base a factory-made shoe 6½" across and 7" long. I made the rest of it in sections in the shape of a chair, with the back support held in place by two wing nuts so the vet could remove it when he returned the following week to change the dressings. Mr. Taylor came to sedate the horse while I fitted the shoe. I did ask the owner to invite her usual farrier to come and watch what I was doing as it might be of use to him in the future, but he never came. I returned to this horse some six weeks later and did a refit. Progress was good, though the animal still needed to be sedated for the work to be done safely. Three months later the mare was ready for another shoe. She continued to progress well and was able to walk normally in this shoe. After that I said there was no need for me to come any more as the owner's regular farrier would be able to manage the work now. I did not hear any more about this horse from the owner but I have since seen it out on a ride with a child on its back. The mare seemed to be walking reasonably well, though I thought the leg did not seem to flex as easily as it should.

The inside of this horse's leg

Outside of the same leg

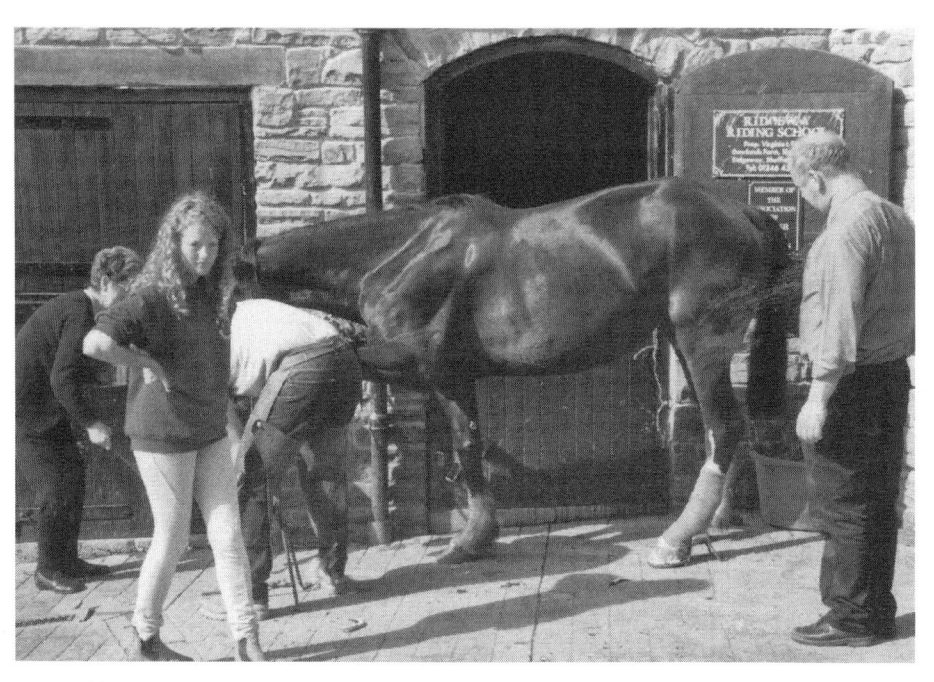

The shoe is on but not finished off at this point so a trim all round before the horse wakes up

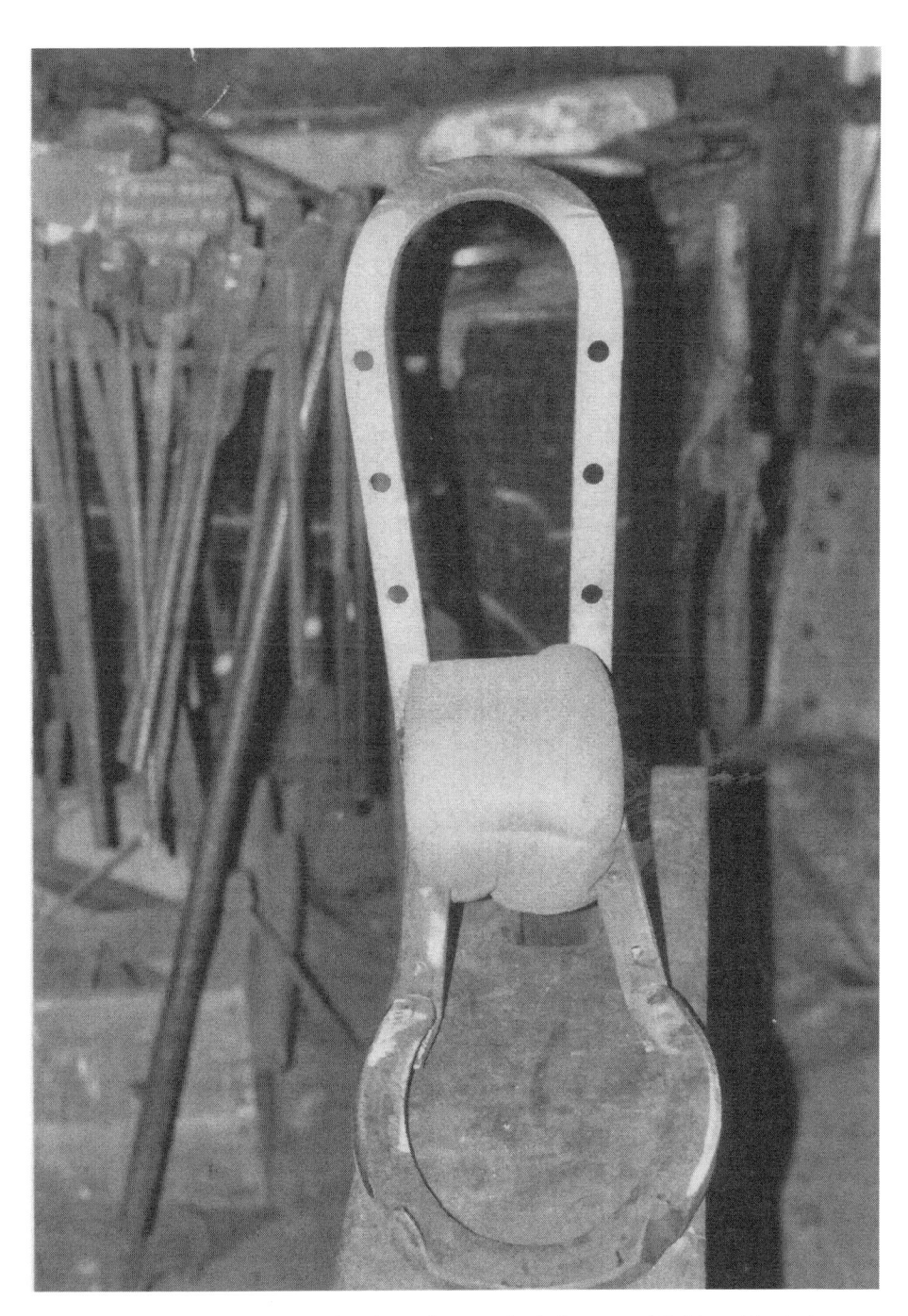

This is the same type of shoe as I used on the previous case for the horse named Red but with a back support held by two wing nuts so the vet could remove it to redress the leg each week

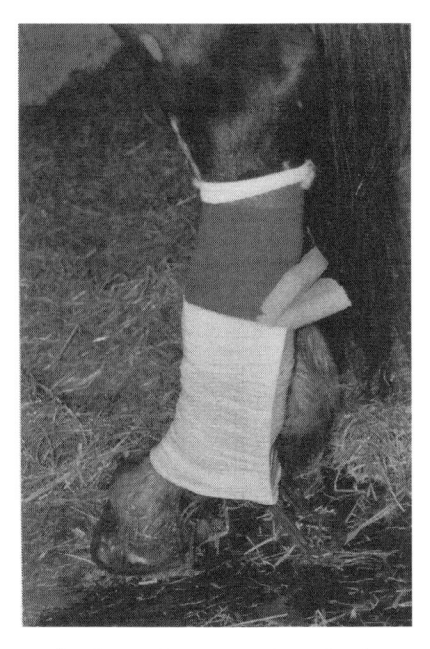

The shoe in place supported by a bandage

Case study 4:
Fracture of the third phalanx

In 1979 I was visiting one of my clients in the village of Crich to do some routine trims. There was a very attractive palomino mare by the name of Cameo in the next stable. I said to my customer, "Have you bought a new horse?"

She replied "No, it belongs to a friend of mine. It's 15.2hh and only seven years old but it's going to have to be put to sleep as it has been diagnosed with a fracture through the lateral wing of the pedal bone. The vet doesn't think anything can be done to save it."

At the time I happened to be reading a book by an American vet called O.R. Adams, describing how he dealt with fractures. I thought that if the owner would agree, I would like to have a go at curing the horse by fitting a special bar shoe as recommended by Dr. Adams. My customer offered to contact the horse's owner and tell her what I had suggested. That night the owner phoned me and said, "Please would you have a go at trying to save my horse?" She promised to get me the x-rays from the vets. She explained that she had been out riding on Cameo and on their return turned her out in the field. Being in peak condition and feeling full of herself, the mare reared and bucked, and in doing so she crashed her hoof onto a large rock.

Before starting any work, I consulted the Oakham Veterinary Hospital and they thought it was well worth a try with this special type of bar shoe. They suggested the mare could be put in foal whilst she was resting afterwards.

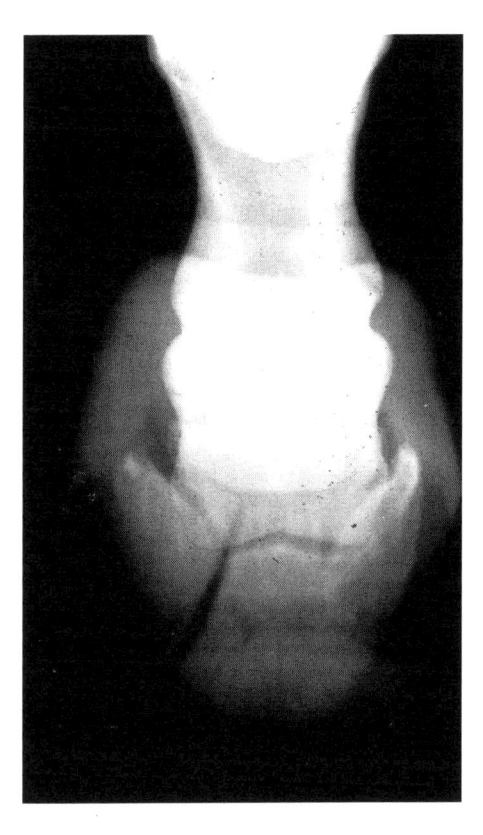

X-ray of Cameo's hind hoof

The owner and Cameo, 1979

Causes of fractures

Fractures are commonly caused by some form of force or violence.
1. A fracture may result from direct force, for example when a severe blow breaks the bone at the point where the force is applied.
2. A fracture may result by indirect force, in which case a bone breaks at some distance from the point where the force is applied. In such cases the force is transmitted along the intervening bones, which may escape injury.
3. Occasionally, the third phalanx (also known as the pedal bone, coffin bone or P3) may be fractured as a result of penetration by a foreign body through the sole.
4. The third phalanx may also become fractured as the result of trauma to a large sidebone, in which case the P3 may break through one of the lateral wings.

Symptoms

If the third phalanx is fractured through the centre of the bone and the fracture involves the articular surface, the lameness is acute and the horse will refuse to put the hoof to the ground. There will be increased pulsation and heat in the affected hoof. If the fracture has been present for some time, signs of lameness will not be evident and x-rays will be necessary to diagnose the problems, as these are sometimes mistaken for nail pricks and nail binds.

Treatment

When treating this type of fracture, the third phalanx should be immobilised as effectively as possible by using a fullered bar shoe with quarter clips as well as clips on either side of the fracture. The bar should be recessed so there is no pressure on the frog or surrounding area. Clips can be welded to the outside of the branches of the shoe near the heel quarters to stop the heels from expanding. This type of shoe should be reset every four to six weeks for a period of nine months.

After Cameo was shod in this way she walked out sound and continued to do so all the time she was carrying her foal. In fact she had twins, but sadly one of the twins only lived a few hours before it died. The other filly grew up to be an eventer just like her mum. I re-set Cameo's bar shoe every six weeks for about 18 months. A final x-ray of the fracture in her hoof was taken on 25th March 1981 and showed the bone was clinically healed. This horse went on to compete as an eventer for many years after this setback.

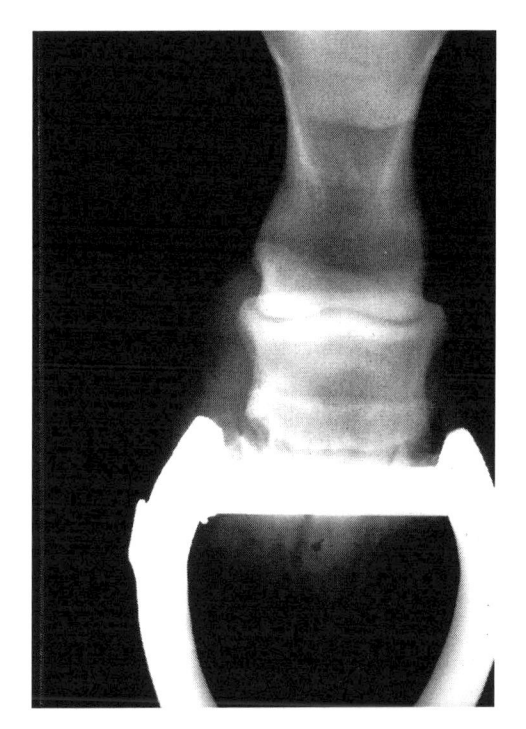

X-ray showing bar shoe and support clips

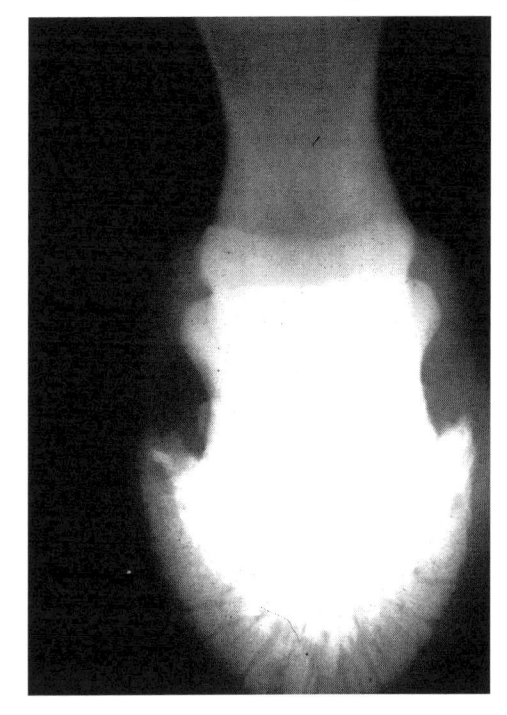

Final x-ray shows fracture clinically healed, 1981

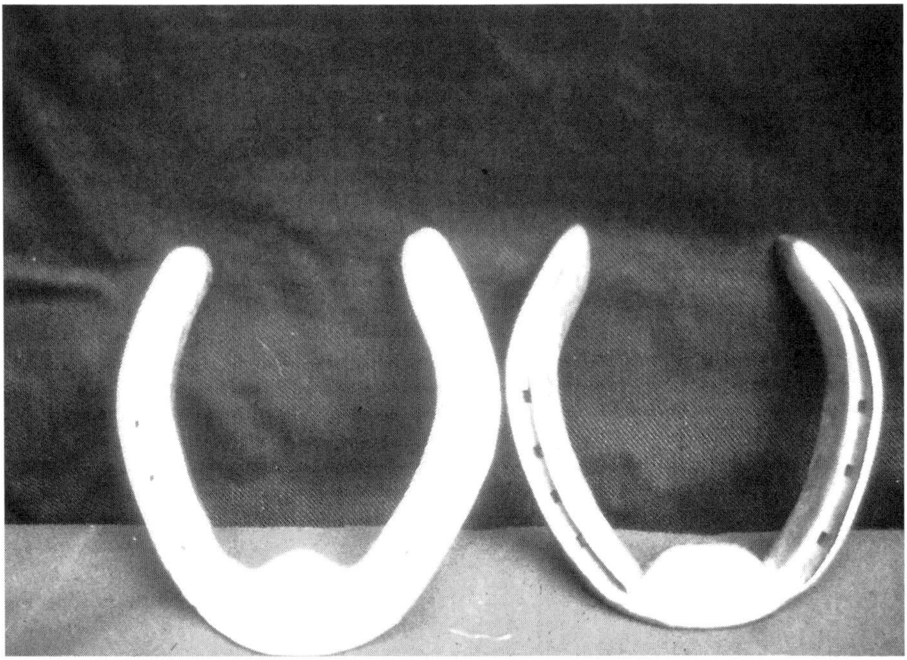

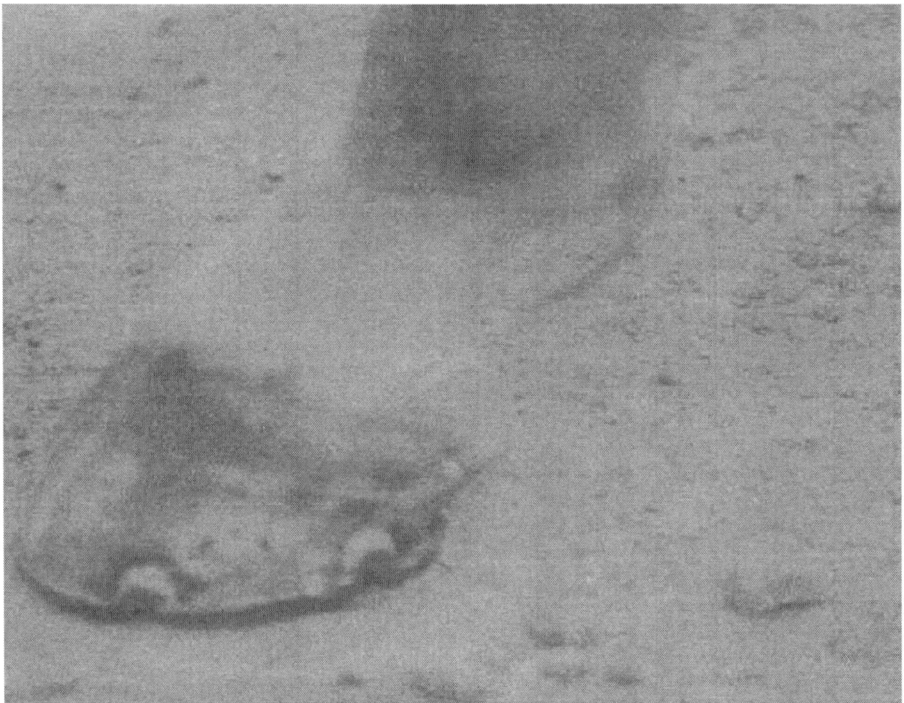

Fracture of the pedal bone
second example

In September 1981 we were asked to look at a 16.2hh grey gelding that had fallen whilst doing a cross-country event. There was a large swelling around the hock, so the vet was concerned about damage to that area. The swelling did not go down until several weeks later. At this point the leg looked good but the horse was still lame, so the vet decided to do an x-ray of the lower leg and hoof. That is when the fracture of the pedal bone was discovered.

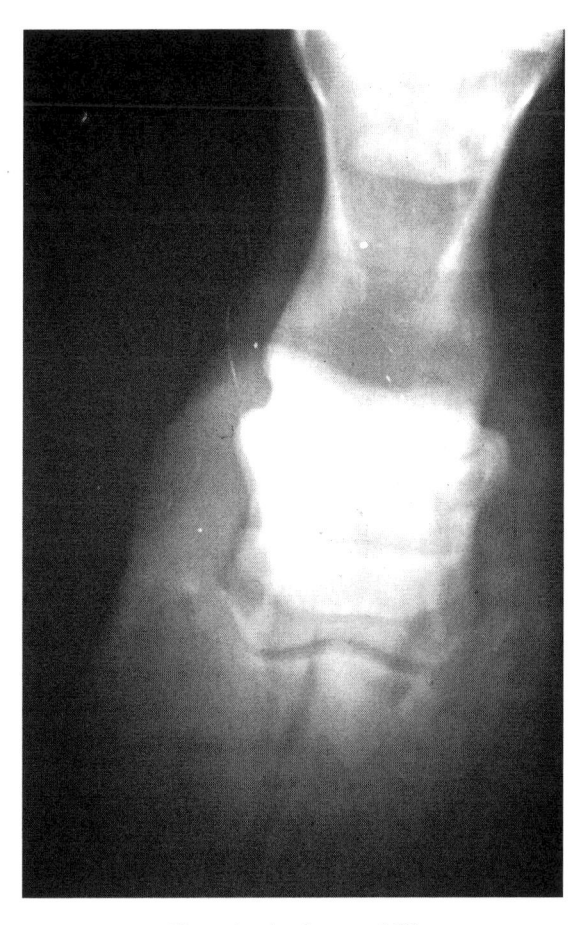

X-ray showing fracture of P3

On the day of the x-ray by our local vet Mr. Chris Charlesworth MR.CVS

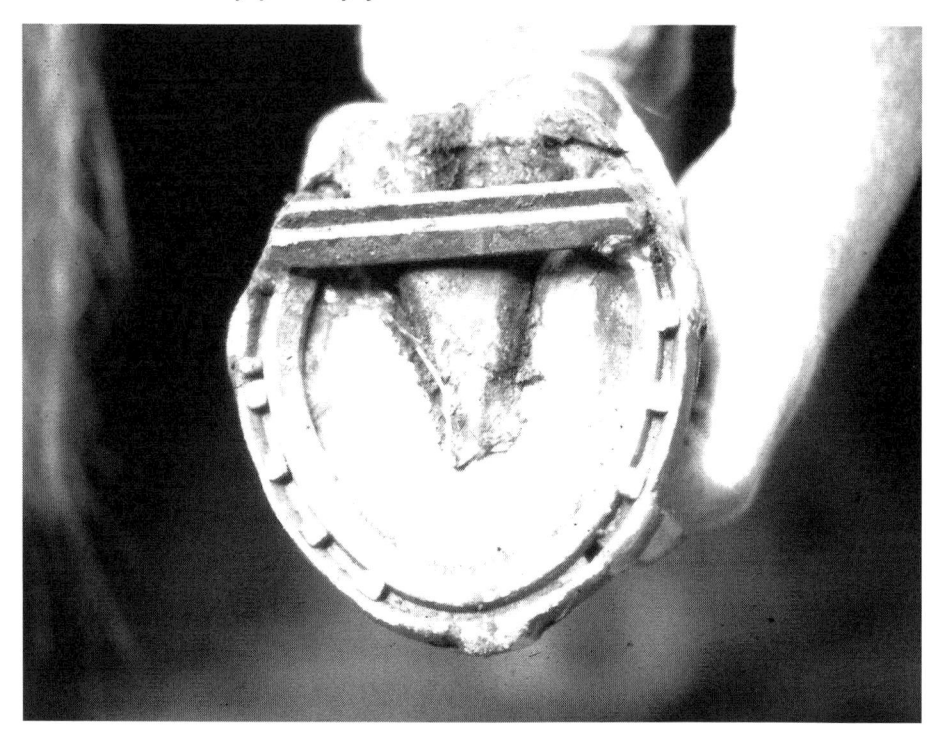

The bar shoe fitted

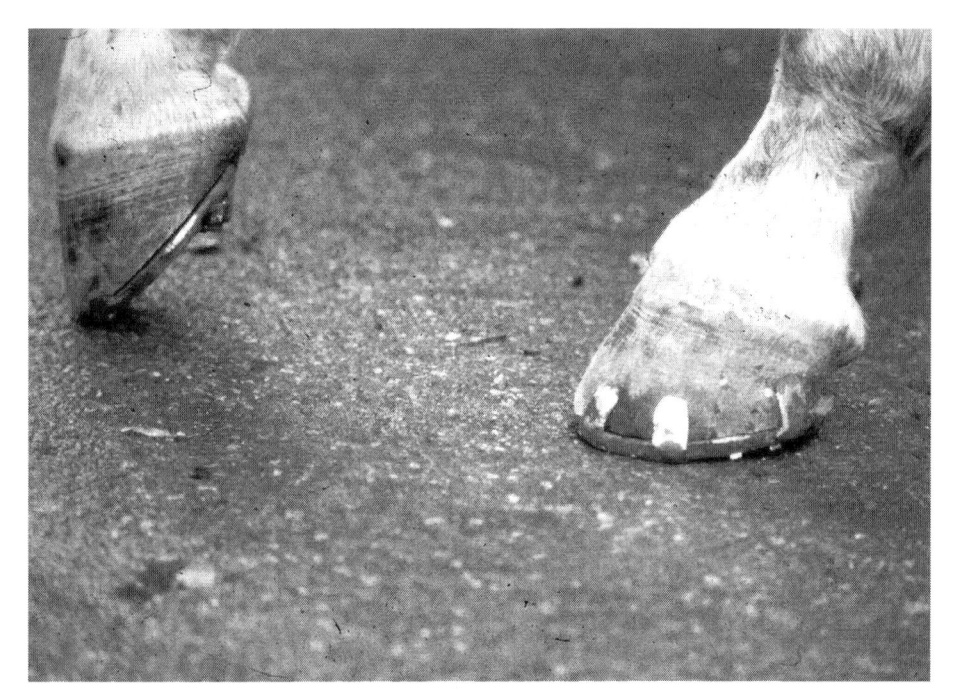

Newly shod hooves

The horse competing again in the job he loved

The owner of this horse was a dear friend of mine but his son was a very hard forceful rider and wanted to work the horse almost straight away after we had shod it. Our advice was to take it slowly and give it a chance to recover, but we doubted he would adhere to our advice. We shod this horse in a heavier section of concave iron than we would normally use and placed a bar of the same iron across the back of the shoes. I say "shoes" because we shod both feet the same to keep the animal level and avoid putting any more strain on the previously injured hock. The vet marked the hoof just where the fracture was and we put welded clips on the shoe to support that area. The bar across the back of the shoe was to prevent any pressure on the frog and avoid forcing the bulbs of the heel to expand and contract, which would in turn have moved the fractured pedal bone. With that bar and the extra clips on the shoe, we successfully prevented any movement in this area. When the job was completed, the horse walked sound and the lad rode it back home. It remained sound and within eight months was competing in cross-country events again.

The FWCF examination

Completing all six copies of the dissertation was a mammoth task. I hand-printed all the photographs in my dark room on Ciba chrome paper from the 35mm slides in my possession. My wife and daughter typed it all up for me. I was now ready to attempt my FWCF examination at the School of Farriery in Hereford. Grant was to take his AWCF in the same week.

At my first attempt I passed with my thesis and lecture but failed on the practical test. I was told to re-take the practical part in six months' time. The reason I failed was that my deep-seated bar shoe was not dressed to the angle of the heels of the foot.

My second attempt was a bit of a farce. Edgar Stern FWCF was the senior examiner with Roger Clark FWCF as second in charge, and a vet called Denis Oliver. Three of us were taking the exam: Ron Wear, Colin White and myself. The examiners came into the forge bringing a dead leg for each candidate. We were allowed one minute to look at the foot and do the measurements, then the leg was taken away and we were not allowed to see it again until we had made the shoe and taken it to the classroom to try it on the hoof. I finished my shoe in plenty of time but when I was given the leg to fit the shoe I could see immediately that the shoe was too big. I knew at once I had failed again. But this was the first time they had ever done it that way – removing the shoe and leg from the forge – and it has never been done since. I was very disappointed and went home saying the Worshipful Company could get stuffed as it seemed that to satisfy their demands your face must fit.

Only thanks to my wife, who pushed me on to take the examination for a third time, plus some bloody-minded persistence on my part, did I eventually pass. This time the test was a 3/4 fullered egg bar shoe. The leg was left in the forge, the job was completed in about 25 minutes and yes, the shoe did fit. The veterinary examiner Denis Oliver came over and congratulated me, and the two WCF examiners did the same. My son acted as my striker as he was at the college on his diploma course at the time of the exams. As you could only have an apprentice to be your striker, I was lucky Neal was there and available to do this job. We had been practising at home together for the shows he was to enter as well as my forthcoming examination, and he was of great help.

Now I was a Fellow of the Worshipful Company of Farriers of London and my name was entered as such on the register. I was the only person in Derbyshire able to call myself Citizen and Farrier of London. It took a few weeks to come back down to earth.

A sequel to my case studies, involving a flight with a veteran fighter pilot

Before I came properly down to earth, however, I was treated to a day of excitement that included a horse with a cartilage injury and an aerial view of my forge. The horse would have made an interesting study alongside the records of similar cases I had collected over the years. How I came across it, and with whom, makes a story in itself.

One of our clients was a young lady from Bamford called Nicky. Her father Roger had been a Second World War fighter pilot and was now in his 80s. Nicky told me her dad had his own aircraft and went flying in it most weeks. She promised she would ask him to take me for a flight, but no more was said at the time. One day in 1989, I had just finished shoeing Nicky's horse when she asked if I would go with her dad to look at a horse in Market Harborough. It was one his granddaughter had been riding whilst she was at college down there. Granddad Roger had offered to buy it for her on condition that a vet and a farrier both checked it over to their satisfaction. The seller wanted around £4,000 for the animal. Roger came to see me himself about going to inspect the horse one day the following week. Preferably on the Wednesday, he said, as he was having a new car delivered on the Tuesday, a Volvo sports model, and the run to Market Harborough would be a good opportunity to put it through its paces.

Roger had been involved in a car accident a couple of years earlier, when his Range Rover was turned on its side and he lost his right arm. He was in St James's Hospital (Jimmy's) in Leeds at the time the television people were filming there. The series featured various doctors, nurses and patients, and Roger with his major operation and subsequent progress was one of the stars. He was a big tall man, somewhat similar in build to me, and he had a prosthetic arm but rarely wore it.

Roger turned up at my front door as arranged for our trip to Market Harborough. I did not know until we set off that he would not be using his prosthesis to drive but relying on just his left arm. The steering wheel had a knob on it so Roger could control it with his left hand. But through the corner of my eye I could see that every time he needed to turn the wheel the stump of his right arm would move in his shirt sleeve as though his right hand were also on the wheel. My immediate thought was, *Bloody hell, shall I be all right?* Leaving my home, we headed south on the M1 and at 70+mph it was quite a ride.

On arrival, it did not take long to judge that the horse would not serve Roger's granddaughter well. It had suffered an accident a couple of years ago on a hind hoof, a deep wire cut which had left an ugly scar through the hoof and fetlock. The owner said the horse had been going lame intermittently but was now recovered. Feeling around the hoof, I could tell that the cartilages of the distal phalanx had started to ossify and would therefore result in more permanent lameness in future. The granddaughter wanted the horse for three-day-eventing and I said straight out that in my opinion the horse would not be suitable for this purpose.

Roger said, "OK Doug, that's that. Let's go and have some lunch." We pulled up at a pub, and after a couple of pints it did not seem to matter anymore that Roger had a disability. We came back up the A1 instead of the motorway because he wanted to buy a new trailer for his farm at a place he had seen advertised in a magazine. He parked in the yard, went to the office and said, "I want a trailer. Where are they?"

The man in the office said their salesman was not in.

Roger reared up at the man. "Do you sell trailers or not?" he demanded. "I have come to buy a trailer so get off your arse if you want to sell me one." He spotted the one he wanted and said "OK, you can deliver it tomorrow to my address. I will pay you now if you can do that. If not, good day to you."

By now the man was falling over Roger to please him, and promised he would have the trailer as he had said.

We set off again for home. As we were nearing Retford, Roger said "Doug, do you fancy a flight in my plane?"

I thought, *What the hell?* After two pints and watching him do business, who was I to say no to this man?

Roger got his phone out whilst driving, wedged it between his shoulder and his ear, and called the airfield. "Hello, Roger here. Can you have my plane ready in 30 minutes?" I just sat there with my mouth open.

We pulled into a small private airfield at Gamston. Some

kids were playing with their remote-controlled cars on the runway. We went into a small room and Roger said, "Excuse me a moment whilst I put on my flying suit." That was when he put on his prosthesis, a length of 3/8" round metal with a hook at one end and a cup fitting over the stump of his right arm at the other. We strode off to the hangar where the plane was kept. My heart was beating fast.

"Right Doug, in you get. Place your feet where I tell you as she's an old bird from 1980 and the wings are made of thin wood."

With trembling voice, I said "Right, Roger," and sat down.

"Do not touch those things by your feet as they are the rudders." He reached over and fastened a large array of belts between my legs, over my shoulders and around my waist. Then he got in beside me.

I thought, Bloody hell, there's not a lot of room in here. In fact, it was such a tight squeeze that if we had flown upside down we would not have fallen out. There was no parachute, but then a parachute would not have been much use as we would not have had room to deploy it.

By this time, the kids had been moved off the runway. A voice came over the radio: "You are clear for take-off. Roger and out."

Roger said "Doug, set the altimeter."

With trembling voice: "Yes Roger. Where is it?"

"On the far right. Set it at 1,000 feet. Just turn the knob in the middle of the dial. We do not want to run into any hills, do we?"

I thought, *Shit, it's up to me now.*

By now we were moving down the runway at speed. I

opened my eyes and the first thing I saw was the piece of metal on Roger's stump hooked over the joy stick. He pulled it towards him and up we went. Our flight plan was to head over Worksop and Whitwell to Chesterfield, then Chatsworth to Ashover to Clay Cross to Hardwick Hall and follow the M1 back to base at Gamston.

My first thought was, It's bloody cold up here. We wore leather hats with radios inside so our conversation went something like this:

"OK Doug?"

"Yes Roger."

"It's lovely up here."

"Yes Roger."

"Doug, look how green it is."

"Yes Roger."

"Doug, we are heading towards Chatsworth."

"Yes, Roger and out."

This was most certainly a wonderful and exciting experience, and by then I was just beginning to appreciate it. That was until we flew over Clay Cross, when Roger put the plane on its side and said "Look Doug, there's your house just below us."

"Yes, Roger and out." I forced my eyes open and saw my blue van in the yard. As we dived down we were so close I could see the rust patch on the roof. But that was not all. I did feel a bit uncomfortable from the waist down; in fact, I think I shit myself. Then it was on to Hardwick and the M1 and the business of landing. Before we could go down, Roger had to get on the radio to the control tower to give them a bollocking and tell them to move the kids off the runway where they were playing with their remote cars again.

Finally, the plane taxied to a stop and Roger switched off the engine. "Did you enjoy the day, Doug?"

"Yes, Roger and out."

We still had to get home from the airfield. On the way back, I could not help but notice a pile of blueprints on the back seat. I said, "What are you planning now, Roger?"

"Well, Doug, they are plans for a friend of mine that has lost his legs. He wants to fly and I am designing the controls he will need."

Apparently innovative design was Roger's forte, as he had been the one who designed the adaptations to his own prosthetic arm whilst he was at the hospital in Leeds. His daughter told me in November 2010 that he was still flying to that day but not as much as he used to.

Thank you, Roger and out, Doug.

Roger's plane

Roger sent me this photograph of his latest plane. He told me the photo was taken not far from Clay Cross and you could see the M1 just by the wheels. He had had this plane from new, having collected it from the Mudry factory at Bemay in France where it was built in 1988. It was a rather famous type of aeroplane called a CAP 10 (because it was developed as number 10 in the CAP series). A two-seater, it was adopted by the French Air Force as its standard aerobatic trainer because it was powerful and well balanced. The flying controls were very responsive and suitable for training and precise aerobatics. The plane had a 180 hp Lycoming engine and was fully equipped with full blind flying instruments and airline radios, so Roger had been able to fly all over Europe by day or night. It cruised at about 130 mph and at up to 1,100 ft altitude. The range between refuelling was about 650 miles, but Roger usually tried to make each leg of his flight about 400 miles then have a stop. He had to allow for the wind if it was strongly behind him and sometimes, he could cover 200 miles in one hour, but if the wind were from the other direction then his ground speed would be much slower. Roger told me he was flying to Bordeaux in France one day above the railway lines and a TGV high-speed train overtook him. His furthest trip was to Ankara in Turkey, a journey down the Danube Valley that would take about three days to do comfortably.

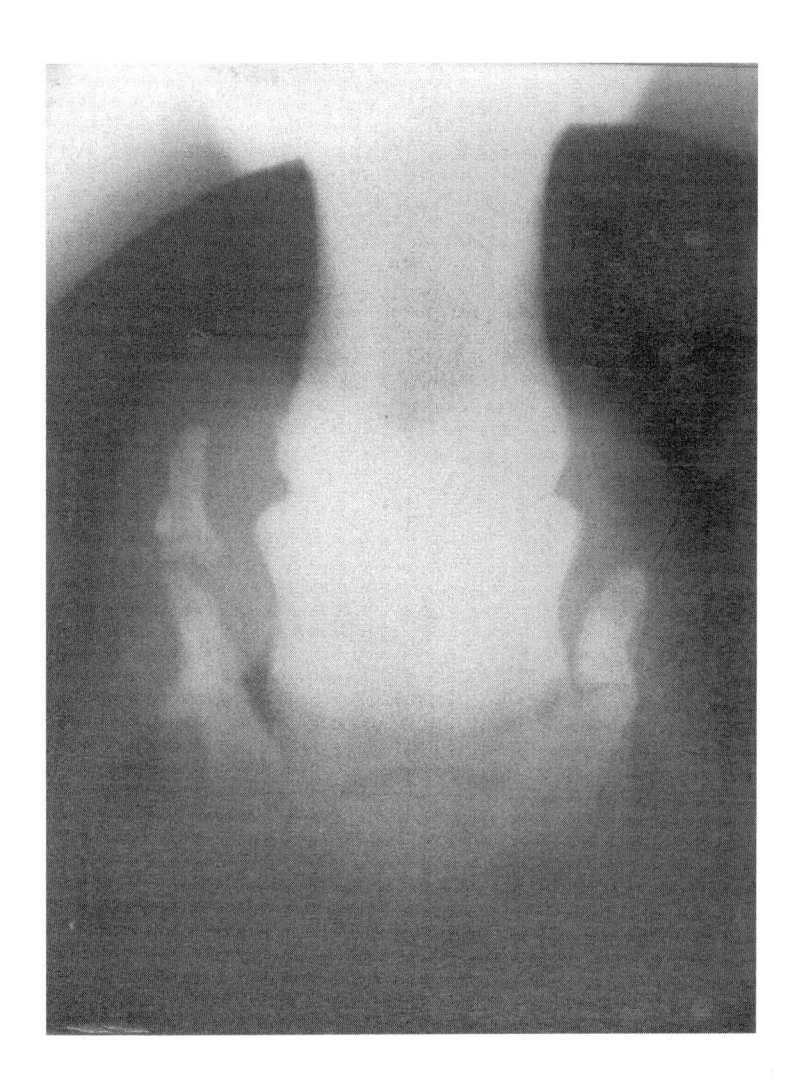

This photos are of a horse that had suffered a similar wire cut to the one I saw at Market Harborough. As you can see, the cartilages of the distal phalanx have ossified and turned into bone over a period of time (a condition called side bone), causing intermittent lameness during the period of change from cartilage to bone. I am sure this would have happened to the horse that I visited with Roger.

The photo features an x-ray showing of a horse with side bone, showing a fragment of cartilage that has broken free from the distal phalanx.

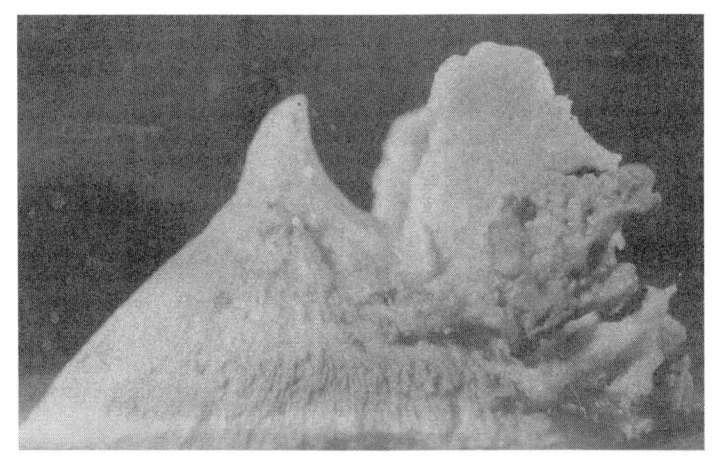

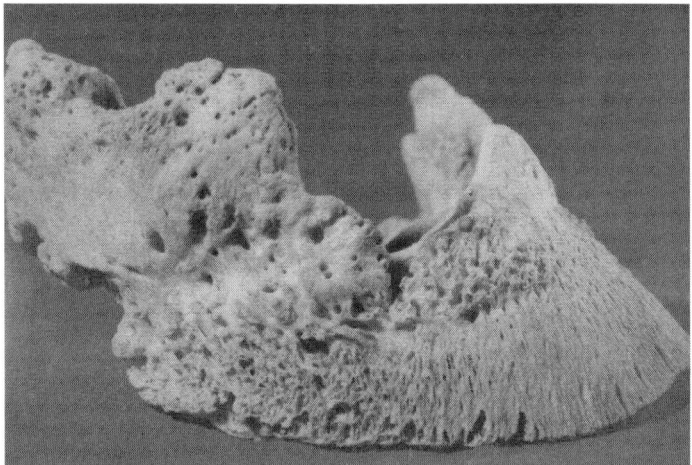

Below is a pedal bone that has been removed from a shire horse that was euthanised because of continued lameness. It shows the changes that were taking place within the hoof capsule. First you can see normal cartilage that has not yet turned to bone, then an area of cartilage that has turned to bone, and at the distal border there is cartilage and bone.

Below shows a pedal bone and a lateral cartilage that has completely ossified. This would be known as unilateral side bone.

The two cartilages of the distal phalanx form part of the posterior section of the hoof and play a big part in the expansion and contraction of the hoof. They are non-vascular and are grey and glistening, and arteries and veins pass through them. A simple test is to press your thumbs around the coronary band and they should yield to the pressure. If there is no response I would guess that there is some form of side bone. Causes include direct trauma to the area and excessive road work. The specimens in the photos are from horses that had worked in the railway yards pulling the large wagons – typical working conditions for horses in heavy industry. The area just above the coronary band would have been catching on the rail lines day after day. See the photo below showing the effect of pressure on the cartilages.

This horse had worked in the railway yards for many years before it was put to sleep. The skeleton shows unilateral side bone, also high and low ring bone.

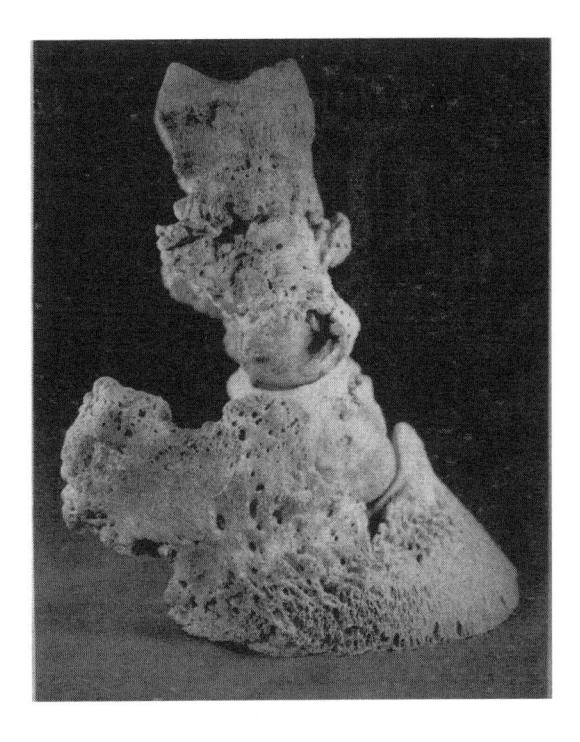

View of a carthorse leg skeleton

8

LECTURES AND LIVERY

Lecture tours for the FRC

About three months after I passed the FWCF examination, my friend Mike Cox called and asked if I could do a lecture with him in Lincolnshire. At that time, he was travelling the country on behalf of the Farriers Registration Council giving talks on the finer points of horseshoeing and also showing a film that the Worshipful Company of Farriers had produced entitled The Farriery Craft. This was all about the company and its involvement in the profession. The FRC would offer these lectures for free to pony clubs and other groups of people interested in the welfare of horses. This request from Mike was to help him out on one of those evenings.

All went well and evening lectures became a regular job for me. Mike would phone and say, "We're booked for such-and-such this week. The FRC are providing a car and you'll get £30 a trip." Although I enjoyed doing the talks, travelling around the country to deliver them sometimes became a bit of a bind.

One week, for example, we did three talks in Hampshire, Wiltshire and Surrey, so I would be getting back to my home at one or two o'Clock each morning and then having to go to work the following day.

However, some days out with Mike Cox were definitely too good to miss.

A jaunt to Ireland

One evening around 6pm, Mike phoned to ask if I fancied a trip to Ireland. The American Horseshoeing Team were to give a demonstration at the Irish National Stud School of Farriery, and Mike was to go as a representative of the FRC.

This was in 1987, and I had recently been back in hospital for a further operation to straighten my right ankle. This one I paid for, and I chose to go to the Park Hospital just outside Mansfield. The surgeon was Mr. Edwards and it was his second attempt on this joint. After a week in hospital they had let me out on crutches with a short leg plaster and told me to come back in six weeks. Meanwhile my son and the lads were running the business and I did what I could from home.

"Ireland? OK by me," I told Mike.

He replied, "Right, we leave tonight. I will pick you up at 8pm and we are due to catch the ferry at midnight from Holyhead. We will leave the car there and get a taxi to the National Stud when we arrive in Dun Laoghaire in the morning."

Mike and I shared a weird sense of humour and we spent the night at sea telling jokes and downing cups of free coffee. When we arrived in Ireland, Mike called a taxi and asked how much to the National Stud.

"£40 to you, sir."

Mike said, "No thanks, we will catch the bus."

So, we went to the bus stop, waited for the bus and found we were the only passengers on it. Well, you would have thought we were royalty, the way the driver and his conductor treated us. We sat at the front with them and they gave us a conducted tour with commentary, taking us around all sorts of places that were way off their regular route. Arriving at the stud, they dropped us at the main gate and drove off with a cheery wave.

That was when we had a shock. The drive stretched ahead of us into the distance like an empty M1. Remember, I was on crutches. Mike set off at his usual army pace leaving me hobbling behind. After some time, a car came along. The driver stopped and told me to jump in, "But what about your mate?"

I grinned, "Bugger him." The driver gave me a wink and accelerated past Mike. You should have seen the look on his face as I waved to him. When we stopped to wait a few yards further on, he rushed up to the car, full of gratitude to the driver.

We had a fantastic day and the organisers even arranged for a car to take us back to the ferry later that night. At the docks Mike said, "I will take you for a pint of Guinness. This will be the true taste of Guinness as it does not travel too well." He was right, and it didn't need to. After a couple of pints, we boarded the ferry home, arriving the following morning completely knackered. That was to be the first of many such trips with Mike.

Fancy a trip to France?

"I shall be going over on the ferry and driving the FRC car." This was another of Mike's phone messages. "If you and Joan fancy a trip to France, come to my home for 8pm tonight. Put on some strong boots or shoes and I will show you where to get some excellent night-time photography."

Mike lived at Shenton in Leicestershire. We got there for 8pm as he had said, and off we set. We were to sail from Dover early in the morning, and as we were approaching the town, he explained about the photo opportunities he had mentioned. He took us right up on the tops of the cliffs overlooking the harbour. It was all lit up, and what a brilliant sight. It was pitch dark where we were, with grass and weeds above knee high, which was why we needed the strong boots.

Carrying on down to the docks, we prepared to board the ferry for Calais. Mike said we were heading for a small town by the name of Epernay. I sat in the front and Joan was with Mike's wife Gwyneth in the back as we drove onto the car deck. By chance I put my hand down by the seat and discovered several pairs of new GE farrier tools, which Mike had omitted to disclose to the customs and would be selling through his contacts in France. We arrived about midday at Epernay, where we met Stewart Taylor and a girlfriend (not his wife) and also one of Stewart's apprentices for a drink and some lunch. Mike disclosed that he was to be one of the judges in a big horseshoeing competition, alongside his friend Edgar Stern FWCF.

Mike had arranged accommodation for us all at a grape-picker's house for £6 each per night. We all arrived at the same time: Edgar and his wife Joyce, Mike and Gwyneth, Joan and I, Stewart Taylor and his girlfriend plus the apprentice. The lady of the house came out to greet us. "Monsieur Cox, this is your room."

It was a small box room with a four-foot bed in it. Mike said, "I cannot sleep in that bed. It is too small for me and my wife."

No problem: the lady phoned a friend and they brought a metal hospital bed over.

"Monsieur Stern, that is your room." It was on the next floor at the apex of the house with a bunk bed on either side of the apex. Edgar and Joyce had to crawl in backwards. We were all laughing at them when it came to my turn. "Monsieur Bradbury, you will sleep on that mattress on the landing next to Monsieur Taylor and his wife, and the boy by your side on another mattress."

Well, the girl that was with Stewart threw a right tantrum. "I am not sleeping on a mattress on the floor! I demand a hotel!" Stewart had no choice but to take her to find one. What do you expect for £6 a night?

The shoeing competition was being sponsored by Baron de Rothschild's champagne company.

Things were proceeding nicely when who should turn up but David Gulley FWCF and his wife Judy. I was busy taking photos when I noticed David eyeing me. He said, "I need a striker for this class." The task was to make a pair of tongs and then fit a shoe to the horse provided.

I said, "I have no working clothes with me."

"Do not worry about that, boy, you will be all right."

I agreed to help David and he brought out sweatbands and other kit. The start bell went, and we were off. David kept telling me, "Do not burn it, boy, do not burn it."

After a time I got fed up listening to that, and replied "I's a working boss, I's a working boss." One of the other judges, who hadn't met me before this trip, said to Mike "Who's that Isa fellow working up there?"

"It's only Doug pratting about with Gulley," said Mike.

David was placed fourth and won 25 kilo of French horseshoe nails, which were different to the ones we used in the UK. He gave me a two-and-a-half kilo box, saying "Doug, I always pay my strikers." After that it was party time. And next morning it was time to set off back home and get some horses shod.

Mike Cox looking at David Gulley and me. Gulley kept saying "Don't burn it, boy," and I kept telling him I was a working boss.

All the farriers took part in a tug of war with this horse. They said they could pull it over, but the horse won

Joining the livery

One day in 1988 Mike Cox and I each received an important invitation. We were asked if we wished to join the livery of the Worshipful Company of Farriers. This honour is reserved for a limited number of eminent and experienced members of the WCF, who may be farriers, veterinarians or others committed to the welfare of the horse and the continuation of the farriery profession.

Joining the livery proceeds in two stages. First you become a freeman of the Worshipful Company, a title which also confers Freedom of the City of London. This status is rooted in the historical traditions of craftsmen's guilds in the city. Then, once you have your Certificate of Freedom and have taken your oath of allegiance to the Lord Mayor of London or his deputy, you are summoned to a court meeting of the Worshipful Company of Farriers to be robed in your livery gown and to swear allegiance to the Queen and to the Company.

You have to be nominated by one livery man and seconded by another, and the whole procedure takes about a year. You go to London, first for an interview at the WCF and then to the Guildhall. Here you apply for your Certificate of Freedom by redemption (paying a fee) or completion of apprenticeship. This application takes several weeks to process. In due course you are called back to London to receive a certificate endowing the Freedom of the City. In this ceremony you take your oath of allegiance to the Lord Mayor and the sheriffs of London, and then the Lord Mayor or his deputy presents you with your Certificate of Freedom. Next you take your certificate to a court meeting of the WCF. The WCF does not have its own hall, so it holds its ceremonies in one of the many old livery halls in the city. In my case it was at the Innholders Hall in Cannon Street. At the hall I was met by the beadle (a livery company official) and taken into a small room where a black-and-white cloak was placed around my shoulders. Then I was taken into the court, where I was told to kneel and read out my oath of allegiance to the Queen and also to the master and wardens of the WCF, and to swear to attend all court meetings in my livery gown when summoned to do so. This is the second of the declarations you must make before being admitted to the WCF as a liveryman of that company, the first declaration having been made at the Guildhall to the Lord Mayor of London. Following the oath, you are introduced to the other members of the court before dinner. At dinner, the master of the WCF will take wine with the new livery members.

WCF declaration by a freeman

WCF declaration by a liveryman

The Deputy Lord Mayor presenting the Freedom of the City to me

Daughter-in-law Karen, granddaughter Kirsty, my wife Joan, myself, our son Neal and my sister Annie. The two certificates in the background are those of Winston Churchill and Admiral Lord Nelson

The Deputy Lord Mayor with my wife and I, being presented with a book of life with my Freedom certificate in 1988

My first mentor had been my friend Fred Varnam, but after he died I was introduced to a gentleman by the name of Eric Guy Plant RSS AFCL FWCF (Hons), who was to be my guide in entering the livery of the WCF. Eric had gained fellowship of the Worshipful Company with honours. A giant of a man, six feet tall, 16 stones in weight and as gentle as a baby, he was willing to help anyone who was interested in the profession of farriery. He was married to Daisy, a small gentle person, and they lived at Normanton near Leeds. They had no children and were regular churchgoers.

Fred Varnam and Eric Plant having a chat

Eric's father and grandfather had come north from Shropshire to find work in the mines in the 1930s. Eric also started off in mining, and as a lad was taught his craft in the blacksmiths" shop at the pit. In those days the coal industry was facing short working weeks, and to help supplement the housekeeping Eric worked on local farms. Here he often found himself teamed up with a pair of shire horses to do the drilling or sowing. As a young lad his job at the pit included helping the two farriers and their mates to look after 460 ponies and 18 shire horses. Apart from taking shoes off, he had to help break in the new horses and ponies bought by the mine owners. He learned a lot from those colliery farriers, but it was during the evenings spent at Whitwood Mining and Technical College that his lasting interest in the finer arts of his profession began.

Eric started competing in farriery events at local shows before entering the Great Yorkshire Show in 1952 and winning his first major trophy there. He told me he could well remember humping his tools onto the train to Halifax to compete in the novice class and how proud he felt when he won. He was presented with a set of carvers and a silver medal. The same year he qualified as a registered shoeing smith (RSS), passing with honours and a distinction in anatomy. Among his later successes was the title of Yorkshire champion farrier, which he held from 1953 to 1958.

In 1968, following the gradual closure of the Altofts mine, Eric moved on to looking after shire horses for Tetley's Brewery and police horses from Leeds and Bradford, not to mention shoeing top-class three-day-eventers for royalty at the Bramham Horse Trials. He also took on a range of repair jobs – from harnesses to carts and lorries. Once his work inspired a ballet by a young choreographer, who taped the sounds going on in the forge and requested sketches of Eric's working positions. Eric and Daisy got a special invitation to see the finished result. Eric said although he did not know a lot about ballet, he could follow that one well enough. On the competition circuit, his successes continued, especially in 1976 when he won the carthorse shoemaking championship. However, he decided to stop competing the following year to concentrate on judging at shows such as the Great Yorkshire and many more, some as far away as Scotland.

Eric qualified as an Associate Farrier of the City of London and in 1978 became a Fellow of the Worshipful Company of Farriers, again with honours. He also served on the Yorkshire District Committee of the Farriers Association and was their delegate for many years at the AGMs. He was one of the founder members of the Yorkshire Farriers Education and Demonstration Association.

Eric with a Leeds police horse

Eric at work on one of Tetley's shire horses, 1960

He trained one apprentice, David Goldthorpe, who worked alongside him at Tetley's Brewery. David started his winning ways by achieving first place in the apprentice horseshoeing competition at the Great Yorkshire show, the same competition that Eric won back in 1952. The trophy he brought home had been passed from one winner to the next each year for fifty years. David went on to become Yorkshire champion and top English farrier at the Royal Show.

Eric and I became very good friends, and when I entered the WCF livery he continued to mentor me. The numbers of those invited to the court dinners were limited and the names were taken in alphabetical order, so it would be my turn at the beginning of the year and Eric's at the end of the year. Eric used to say, "Go to all the dinners and let the company see you are interested, and you will be surprised at how much good it will do you. So that we both get to as many events as possible, you take me as your guest in January and I will take you as mine at the end of the year." We managed this dining partnership for many years.

Each year all the livery companies receive an invitation to a dinner at the Lord Mayor's residence, the Mansion House in the City of London. This is one of the most prestigious events of the year, and it is quite a spectacle to see the men in their dinner jackets and the ladies in the best dresses their men can afford. The dinner is served in the Egyptian room and the orchestra is usually a military band playing through the meal. At the end of the meal the loving cup is passed around the table.

The Egyptian room at the Mansion House in London where the dinner is held

The first Mansion House dinner my wife and I attended was with Eric and Daisy. Eric issued our instructions: "We do not travel on the train in our bow ties as people will think we are bouncers. Daisy takes her dress in a bag. We go to the Great Northern Hotel next to King's Cross Station, have a pot of tea and get changed in the ladies and gents' rooms. It is much easier to get a taxi from the hotel than the station. We travel back on the last train and we will be in a bit of a rush to catch it. As there won't be many people about by then, we will not need to change out of our evening wear."

Joan and I arrived back in Chesterfield that night around 2am. After a few such late nights at successive dinners, we decided there was no need to rush around so much. We found a small hotel in Gower Street near to St Pancras Station, just somewhere to get your head down and have a good breakfast next day before travelling home mid-morning on the Saturday. If we wanted more food, we could go to Chinatown early or late for it. At a later date we found a nicer hotel, the Ibis, and now we use this hotel whenever we go to London.

Eric and Daisy with my wife Joan and I at the Mansion House, 1989

ERIC G. PLANT
R.S.S. Hons., A.F.C.L., F.W.C.F. Hons., Reg. F.
CONSULTANT FARRIER

27 High Green Road
Altofts
Normanton
West Yorkshire WF6 2LF

Telephone
Wakefield 892076

One of Eric's business cards from the 1950s

The Worshipful Company of Farriers is proud to call itself the mother company of the Princess Royal, who was its master in 1984-85. I went to several WCF meetings with Eric when Her Royal Highness attended. Eric would say, "Good morning, Annie," (I used to think, *Bloody hell, what next?*) and she would answer, "Morning, Eric, and how is Daisy?"

On 4th January 1990 Daisy suddenly passed away, leaving Eric on his own. He became a very lonely man and he looked to Joan and me for company. He used to phone me just to see what I was up to. Around that time, I was doing quite a few lectures in Yorkshire and I would ask if he wished to come. He jumped at the invitation every time, so Joan and I would pick him up and then drop him off at home afterwards.

On the first such occasion, when we stopped at Normanton to drop Eric off, he stayed sat in the car for a while and then said "Will you come in for a cup of tea?"

I was in a hurry to get home, but Joan said, "We would love to, Eric."

Some weeks later, Eric told my wife, "Thank you for coming in for tea that first night." It had been the first time that Eric had returned home at night without Daisy there to greet him. After that we got phone calls almost every week around lunchtime on the Friday: "What are you doing, Doug? Are you busy?"

Either Joan or I would say, "Why not come down for a few days?" We never had to say it twice. It would take Eric 57 minutes from his home in Leeds to our yard. He would stay three or four days and liked to travel out in the van with me and the lads. He used to sit on the tailgate of the van chatting to the customers. This happened almost every week, and my kids wrote "Eric's room" on the door of the bedroom he used.

We weren't to know that Eric was a poorly man. Some days he would say "I will stay in bed a bit if you do not mind," and we assumed he was tired or just feeling his age. Staying in bed was OK by us, and Joan would look after him while I was at work. Then, about ten months after Daisy died, Eric was visiting his brother in Blackpool when he developed a severe pain in his head and was taken to hospital gravely ill. While he was there, the Princess Royal wrote to him wishing him well. Eric died on 9th November 1990, just eleven months after his beloved wife Daisy. The funeral was a big one and the Leeds police put a guard of honour at the church door. The church was full, with lots of people standing outside.

A few weeks later, Eric's sister Rita and his brother-in-law (also called Eric) phoned to ask for my help with the farriery stuff he had left. He had donated £500 to the National Association of Farriers for the benefit of apprentices and £500 to the WCF, also for apprentices. Rita said I could have whatever else I wanted from Eric's belongings, except that the books were to go to Hereford School of Farriery. I took them along in two large boxes, along with the journeyman certificate he had been awarded on completion of his apprenticeship. I handed them over to the senior tutor Tom Williams, with Mike Roberts, Howard Cooper, David Wilson, Franklin Birch, Simon Curtis and Howard Ellis looking on. All the books had Eric's stamp on the inside, but that did not stop them from disappearing from the college library. By the time the college closed its Hereford site and transferred to a new campus at Holme Lacy, not one of those books remained. Fortunately, I was able to assure Rita that I did manage to retrieve Eric's certificate, which is now in my care and on show in my museum along with some more of this great man's work.

Ben Deable

We entered the 1990s with business continuing to build up well, and I reckoned we would have work for another pair of hands. About this time, my friend Mike Cox phoned to say he was looking to place a boy called Ben Deable, who was serving his time in London with a farrier called Mr. S. Craig but needed a change of master. Mr. Craig used to have several boys working for him at once. He would put them forward for an apprenticeship two at a time and the rest had to work on a shoe-making machine whilst they were waiting for their turn to go forward. He did provide them with sweatshirts with the firm's name on them, on the understanding that if they were lost or damaged it was their responsibility to replace them.

Accommodation is often a problem for apprentices, but Mr.

Ben Deable

Mementos from two of the happier days we had with Ben: a new rasp and a best-shod rosette

Mementos from two of the happier days we had with Ben: a new rasp and a best-shod rosette

Craig seemed to have the answer. He had some garden sheds on his land and said, according to Ben, "You lads can take it or leave it." On hearing this, we decided to give the boy a chance. The first problem was that he had no P45, in fact had never had one. My wife phoned Mr. Craig to ask about the matter and she was just given a load of blether and no help. We had to put Ben on an emergency tax code until it was sorted.

Ben was not a happy lad, and being so far from home did not help. The field officer often used to send them elsewhere in the country for the simple reason that it was not always the masters that were at fault for the breakdown in the apprenticeship. If a lad did not like the new job, he was free to leave it. Ben could not afford to go home every weekend as his parents had now moved to South Devon. After one weekend when he did go home, he spent the rest of the week telling the rest of our boys that his father had been reading the Wages Act (the replacement for the Truck Act) which spelt out exactly what masters could do and could not do about paying you. Then on a further occasion he came back asking for a transfer nearer home. He said this was on his doctor's advice as he was suffering from stress. I said, "OK, give me your doctor's phone number and I will discuss this matter with him." Just as I thought, he was bluffing and the stress evaporated.

Ben stuck out his apprenticeship and eventually managed to complete his time with me. There were good days and bad; he was very moody and the rest of the lads did not want a lot to do with him. Things improved when he found an ally in the next lad we took on, a boy very much like himself by the name of Craig D'Arcy. Towards the end of his contract with me, we found a second-hand forge for sale, which I bought for him because it was going cheap and would give him a good start when he set up his own business back home. I told him he could pay me for it when his father came to fetch him. His dad duly arrived to pick him up at the end of his apprenticeship and off they went, and we have never seen or heard from him to this day. He did meet a girl from Chesterfield who went to live with him, but the relationship did not last and she came back home after a time.

Alan Bailey, the new FRC field officer

Ben Deable was the last boy Mike Cox sent us, as he got so fed up with all the paperwork in his FRC post that he left the industry completely. He got a job as the head gardener at Woburn Abbey, something he was also very good at, and he is still there to this day.

Mike's successor as field officer was Alan Bailey AFCL, a former teacher at the School of Farriery in Hereford. Alan had had one attempt at his fellowship examination but failed and did not try again. Instead he left the college and became a field officer for the FRC. I had been one of his FWCF examiners, and he came to see me one day whilst he was travelling around the country. He told me he had expected the exam to be a rubber-stamp exercise, as someone in the company had led him to believe it would be. Alan was a brilliant teacher of anatomy and we could not fault him on that part of the exam, but we had had to fail him because his practical was not to the standard required. The specimen shoe that he had to make was a pattern bar shoe. The bar was not properly welded and he was out of time. Failure had left him very bitter and he told me he would never go for the exam again.

However, he was enjoying his new job. Besides having a moan about the FWCF exam, he had come to ask if I could I do him a favour as he had a boy that he needed to move. He must have been talking to Mike Cox on the subject of transferring apprentices. This lad Craig D'Arcy came from Blackburn in Lancashire and was currently working with an ex-army farrier who had a family problem. Also, the boy had been placed too near home and his parents kept interfering. We did have room for one more, so I agreed to look at the boy.

Craig D'Arcy

At this time, we had my son Neal, Andrew, Gordon, Ben Deable and I shoeing horses. Martin Bridge, Steven Hardaker and Martin Elliot had passed their exams and left to set up on their own. We were able to fit in Craig D'Arcy as our new apprentice. He was partway through his training and needed some sorting out.

Craig D'Arcy

The boys stayed at our place and used to pay my wife £30 pounds a week board. This included breakfast, a packed lunch every day and a cooked dinner. All their washing too, so I do not think that was a bad deal for them. On weekends when they did not go home, they would ask if I could find them some work. A veterinary surgeon had asked us to do some weekend jobs in the Sheffield area and very soon these built up to a big round on Sundays. For the lads this meant earning £25 cash and a meal at the Hunloke Arms. For their pub dinner they would get a starter, a steak and a pudding plus drinks, and thought it an excellent arrangement.

One bank holiday weekend, Craig said he would stay for Sunday dinner then go home to Blackburn as he would not be at work on the Monday. He told me his sister's horse had cast a shoe and asked if he could take one from our forge to put on the horse for her. I agreed to that. After we had eaten at the pub, it was our custom to stay around the bar for a while. There was quite a party of us, with my daughter and her husband, Neal and his wife, Joan and me and all the lads, and we'd have a few drinks and a laugh – it was a happy time for us all. But on this occasion Craig jumped up straight after dinner and said he was off. I cannot explain it, but I had a feeling from the way he was in such a hurry that something was not right. I said to my wife, "Drink up. We are going to follow Craig's car at a distance." He headed not for the M1 to go home, but back to my forge. I parked up the road and walked to the yard. Craig was just coming out, and lo and behold he was carrying two handfuls of horseshoes.

I said, "Hello, Craig, and how many feet has your sister's horse got?"

He had been caught red handed. I told him to return the shoes and that would be the end of the matter.

Things returned to normal after that incident. Craig made friends with Ben Deable, which helped them both settle down. One day Craig told the lads he knew where there was a big flat for rent in the town. He said he and Ben were going to move into it and the others could join them if they liked as it would be cheaper than living with us. They asked my wife if she would mind. Joan said certainly they could leave; she was delighted for them and she would be better off without all the extra work.

Then Craig wanted to know if we would still be taking them out for a meal on Sunday nights even though they would no longer be working on Sundays.

I said, "Not bloody likely!"

Nor had they realised that they would have to pay council tax, do their own washing, pay for a TV licence and electricity and cook their own meals. Andrew soon left the flat, went home and travelled each day to work. Ben got in trouble with his council tax and could not pay. So, Joan and I paid it and then stopped the equivalent amount per week from his wages.

At Penistone Show: Craig winning second prize in the apprentice class, Neal first in the masters, Andrew first in the apprentice class

Craig was not a happy lad, but he did his work and took note of what he was taught. One thing, though – he did not show feelings for the horses. This became evident while we doing a local call for a lady that had just moved up this way from Hereford with two horses. It was the first call of the day, and I was working on one horse while Craig was shoeing the other one. That night the owner phoned me to say the horse Craig had shod was lame on the hind hoof and "I want you to come out now and see to it." It was 9pm and I told her I would be there first thing in the morning.

She said, "Very well, but do not bring the lad that did it onto my yard again."

I removed the shoe and told the woman to consult her vet and keep us informed on the horse's progress.

We put the shoe back on a few days later at the request of the vet, but the whole case became a nightmare. That weekend my wife and I were due to go off on holiday to Australia, leaving

Neal in charge. The lady demanded that Neal should go to her yard every day for ten days. When I got back, she called me on the Sunday night to say her horse was still lame. She wanted me, and not my son or any other lad, to see to it there and then. I told her I would be there in the morning. Apparently, she had taken the horse to a show and there had been a mishap in the horsebox on the way. The horse had somehow pulled off the shoe and broken its hoof so badly there was nothing to nail the shoe to.

I had the horse's leg up and was inspecting the damaged hoof while the woman stalked up and down. Finally, she stopped stalking and started shouting. "Your work is atrocious. I am not made of money and I am sick of this." Now, Neal and I between us had been out to her yard a dozen times and never yet charged her for any work or visits. The lady went on ranting until in the end I walked out on her. I told her to stick her horses up her ass and went off to my next call. I was told later that she had caused the injury to the lame horse herself because of the way she had driven the lorry: you could hear the horses falling about inside it. Also, the same horse had a previous injury to the stifle joint.

The point I was making earlier about Craig in relation to this client was that he never asked and did not care about the horse he had lamed. This indicated to me the lack of a professional manner. However, he carried on towards his diploma. In the exam he was just below the pass mark with 59% (the pass was 60%). The chief examiner Edgar Stern asked the senior tutor who Craig's master was. When he heard it was me, he said, "By the end of the lad's time with Doug Bradbury he should be OK, so we will lift him the points to pass him."

Craig finished his apprenticeship with us and left. We did not hear from him for a long time, but he must have done well enough for himself as he became a member of the National Association and served as its president from 2009 to 2011.

National stable management conference at Stoneleigh

In 1996, I was asked to do a talk and slideshow at Stoneleigh, the home of the Royal Show in Warwickshire. The talk was part of a national stable management conference for horse care advisers. It was sponsored by Robinsons Healthcare, who were represented by Clive Wetherall, their business manager for animal healthcare. This two-day event was attended by over 50 delegates and followed a syllabus based on the British Riding Club's phase 1 and 2 examinations. The two days combined talks with practical exercises conducted by qualified master judges, who would assess the candidates' potential as horse care advisers. In exceptional circumstances the judges might recommend candidates for further training based on part 2 of the syllabus.

I was one of a long list of speakers. Mike Wells of Warwick College spoke on soil tests, acreage, fertilising and growth promotion. Stuart Hastie MR.CVS, an extremely experienced equine veterinary surgeon, talked about ailments and stress-related injuries. Mr. R. Thursby-Pelham MR.CVS presented a paper covering the care and handling of brood mares, foals and youngstock, including the currently topical subject of equine viral arteritis, an infectious disease that can cause abortions. It was my turn straight after lunch. I quote from the Horse and

Rider magazine: "Mr. Doug Bradbury is guaranteed to wake any delegate up after lunch. He is a working master farrier, a Fellow of the Worshipful Company of Farriers and a livery man to that company of London. His encyclopaedic knowledge of farriery and corrective horseshoeing kept delegates riveted to their seats, and his sense of humour and amusing anecdotes always make him a firm favourite with knowledge-hungry members."

By then I was well accustomed to waking up audiences. I used to give talks on, 'The Life and Times of a Farrier' to riding clubs, Women's Institutes, U3A, Probus clubs and the like. Joan would accompany me and often our daughter Gale would do the driving, so between them they made sure I kept the talk reasonably decorous. I would show my pictures and get the audience laughing, and saw it as a way to educate people about farriery and its importance in the horse world. It was also a way to raise funds for charity – I generally donated any fees from the talk to the Air Ambulance service, Cancer Research or the Friends of Clay Cross Hospital. Donations raised from my museum of horseshoeing went the same way.

Doug lecturing at Stoneleigh in 1996

Craig D'Arcy, who was president of the British Farriers and Blacksmiths Association in 1996

Mark Thomas Jones

We had had mixed feelings about Ben and Craig, our last two apprentices. A lot of the happiness had gone from our company and we needed to change that as soon as possible. Once the Stoneleigh conference was over and Joan and I had taken our holiday to Australia, I got back down to work at the forge. I reckoned we had room for another lad, as long as we found one that was keen and promising. At this point we started getting calls from a boy in Wales called Mark Thomas Jones.

Mark Thomas Jones

Mark was from Merthyr Tydfil and he said he had got my phone number from Hereford School of Farriery. When he first called me, it was in fact just before my wife and I were going on holiday, so I told him to phone again on my return. Neal said that he called every day I was away, asking if Mr. Bradbury had returned yet. He was so persistent that we asked him to come for an interview.

Mark's father brought him up to Clay Cross. The family seemed to be what we call wheeler dealers, maybe from a gypsy background. We had the feeling that, in every deal they did, they would always ask for cash back as luck money and always try to pull one across you. Mark had been trying to work for himself with computers but now seemed very keen to be a farrier, so I told his father to leave him with us for a week and we would have a look at him. He asked if he could stay over the forge where the previous lads had stayed, as he had never been away from home before.

During the first week Mark cried almost every night because he was homesick. His father told him he had to stick it out after going to so much trouble to get the job. This seemed to work, and thereafter he stuck so close to me that people said, "If you ever drop dead, Mark will go over the top of you." He was not the brightest of lads but very keen to learn. He had a slight nervous tic that tended to make him suddenly jerk his head. Of course, the lads made fun of this, but he put up with the teasing.

Before apprentices could be accepted on the farriery course at college, they had to make several shoes as test pieces from a pattern book they were given. After a trial period at their master farrier's forge, they would be invited to an interview at college and would take their test pieces with them. Whilst they were there, they would watch a demonstration on one of the pieces from the list and then they had two hours in the college forge to reproduce the same or as near to it as they could. Next, they would go in front of a selection panel made up of two farriers and a vet. I was a member of the panel on some occasions, but not the one Mark was due to attend. Nevertheless, I was able to give him some tips on the questions he would be asked, so over dinner every night I would make him go through a mock interview with me.

The time came for Mark's college interview. On the panel were Edgar Stern FWCF, David Wilson FWCF and a vet. The candidates had to take the piece they had made into the room with them and place it alongside the one that had been made in the demo. When I asked Mark how he had gone on, he said, "I think I might have done well enough to pass, and my head did not shake once." He certainly did pass, and about a week later, I saw Edgar Stern at an examination board meeting. He said "Hello, Doug. We had a lad in front of us last week and he gave us the answers before we gave him the questions. And to top it off he walked out with his test piece and the demo one as well." He added with a chuckle, "Someone had most certainly been getting the lad ready for the big day."

Mark could drive so he went home at the weekends, as he and his father had some trotting horses they liked to race on Saturdays. I told him that he must give up harness racing if he wished to be my apprentice, as the sport was too dangerous, and he needed to devote his time to the job in hand. He was not too good at anatomy or at writing things down, but was to become a very good worker and was eager to learn. He would ask to come with us when Joan and I went out doing lectures to pony clubs or the like.

Mark continued to do well for the next three-and-a-half years. At shows around the country he was so successful that he was selected for the Welsh apprentices' team. When he learned that his team was to compete in Scotland at the international championships, he spent weeks beforehand on a high with excitement. The week before the show, I was at a livery dinner in London and told a few friends about Mark, and within a few minutes they had offered to sponsor him to the sum of £80. Besides that, David Gulley said he was taking a minibus up to Scotland with the English team and would have room for Mark so he would pick him up at junction 29 on the M1.

Before long it was time to get ready for Mark's final examination at college. We had a horse booked to come into the forge on the Sunday morning before his test, so I ran a mock diploma exam.

Mark doing his mock exam on a local horse

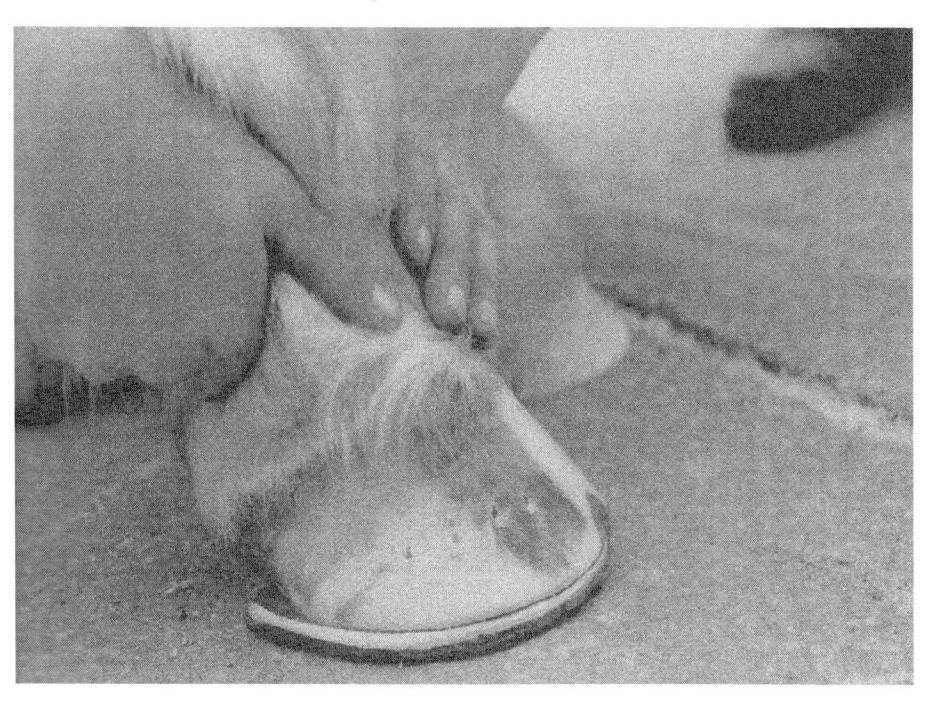

The finished front hoof

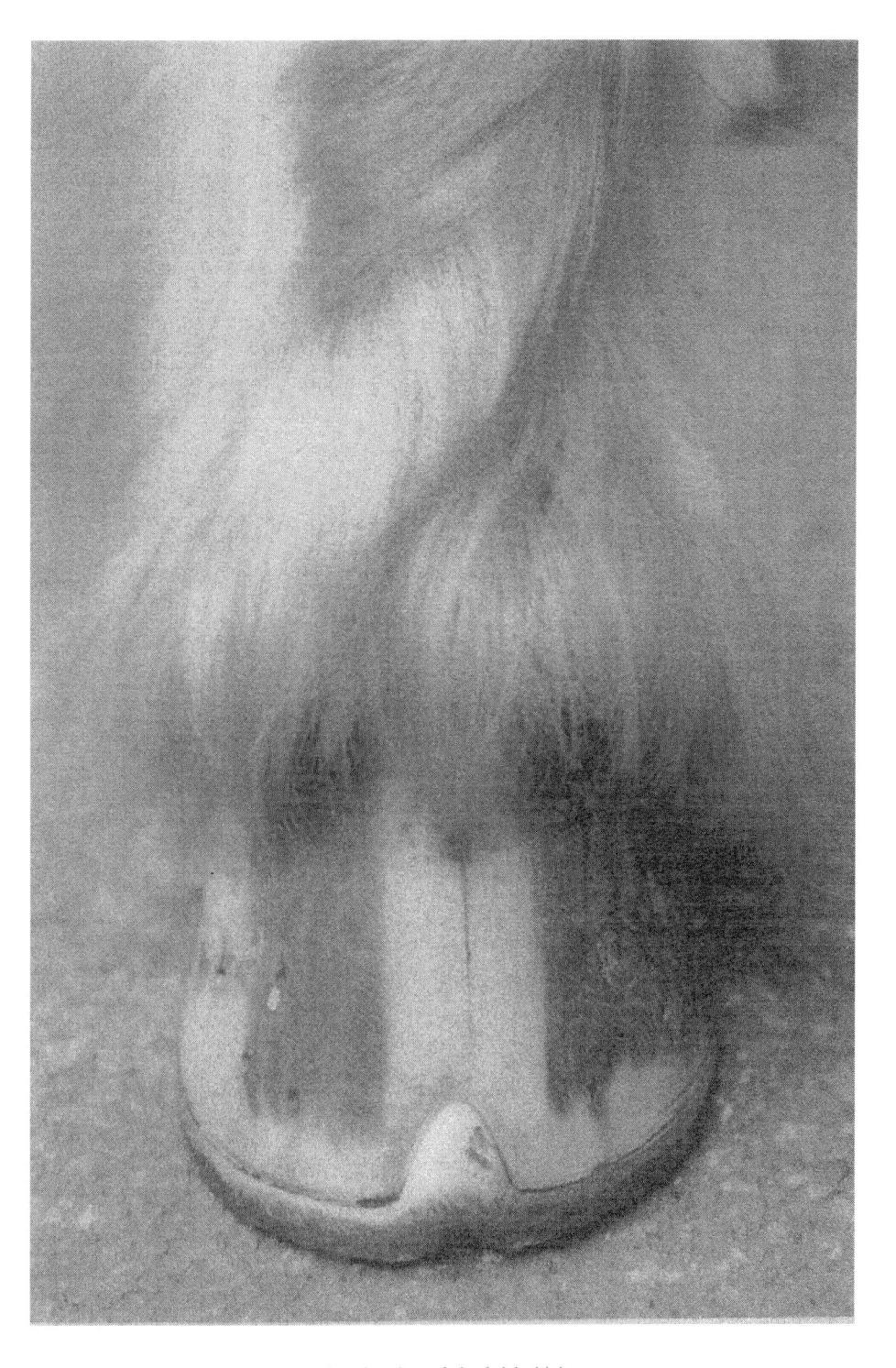

Anterior view of the finished job

Mark's job on the foot for his mock exam

I told him there was to be no overtime and no rough cutting. He had two hours to make and fit two shoes, starting at 10am and finishing at 12 noon. He had to make a 3/4 fullered front shoe and a concave hind shoe. He finished with some time to spare and as you can see, he did a very good job. We hoped he would be able to repeat it next day at college.

Mark made the test-piece shoes needed for the exam and took them to show the examination team on the day. Before the exam, the college tutors always went through all the shoes the candidates intended to put forward. I would tell my boys, "Put in something different that you can talk about, as well as the set test pieces, so as to impress the examiners and show them just what you are capable of doing. Examiners get bored with looking at the same type of shoes 20 or 30 times over." With this in mind, I had taught Mark how to tool and fuller concave shoes from 5/8 square metal. This is not a requirement for the diploma, but it keeps the skill alive. The tutors at college would not have allowed Mark to submit the tooled and fullered shoes for the exam itself as they would have said it was unfair to the boys less able to do this work. I told him not to be put off by such restrictions, as it was his job to show the examiners exactly what he was capable of producing and also to show that he was a true craftsman. So, Mark kept the shoes he had made in his pocket and did not show them to the college staff.

The day arrived; Mark did his practical test and it went well. Now it was time to answer the theory questions and to show the shoes he had made during his time with his master. On the panel on this occasion was James Ferry FWCF, a very keen competition farrier from Scotland. The first thing Mark did was produce from his pocket a tooled and fullered hind preventer shoe (used to correct brushing, when the horse's hind foot interferes with the opposite foreleg). There was a silence. Then Mr. Ferry said, "Are you trying to impress me?"

Mark said, "Yes, sir. I have another one here." He produced a tooled and fullered speedy cutting shoe for a front foot.

Mr. Ferry said, "I am impressed."

The following morning Brian Kavanagh, the Registrar of the FRC, phoned me. (I was a member of the Farriers Registration Council at the time.) "Hi Doug, just to tell you that your boy has passed his diploma with honours. Congratulations, but do not tell him yet. He will get a letter in day or two." Honours! You could have knocked me down with a feather. I could not believe this boy could have pulled it off. Well done, Mark.

Mark posing

"*Mark – you are supposed to hit the nail*"

Successful apprentices were invited to London to receive their diplomas at the Guildhall in the City. Mark was allowed to take his parents and grandparents as well as his girlfriend. None of them had ever been to London before, so this was to be a special trip for them all. I put on a serious face and told Mark that he would have to make a speech in front of the Lord Mayor. I had him rehearsing every night after dinner. Well, I tell you, he was shitting himself over it.

Not until we were at the Guildhall did I tell Mark he did not have to give a speech after all. He just laughed and said, "You rotten sod, I was crapping myself." After the ceremony we all went for a Dr.ink and dinner, and had such a good time that his family missed the last train back home and had to find a hotel for the night.

Mark stayed on working for us for a short time, but he had a girl back in Wales and it was not long before he was on his way back home to marry her and start up on his own. One day he phoned to ask if Joan and I would go down to Wales to do a lecture at a pony club in Merthyr Tydfil and spend the weekend with him and his wife. He said, "I will show you around Wales."

Mark was a great lad, but he did get a bit mixed up at times. On the first night we were driving back from dinner when Mark pointed down the valley to some caves and said "You see those caves down there? They have got satellites in them."

Mark's wife said, "Mark, you mean they have got stalactites and stalagmites, not satellites."

The following day he took us to see the widow of the late Eddie Thomas, world champion boxer. Mark had bought his cottage from Eddie, who had been the mayor of Merthyr for a short time and with his brothers had owned several drift coal mines in the valley. Mrs. Thomas was a very interesting lady and showed us photos of her husband with Jack Solomons, Randolph Turpin and many other famous people in boxing. My lecture went well and it was a very good turnout; in fact it filled the village hall with people standing around the sides. We did not charge any fee, and the pony club presented us with a small clock set into a statue of a miner made from Welsh coal. We had a great weekend and set off back on the Monday morning. Mark still keeps in touch by phone and he comes up to see us all from time to time.

Mark receives his diploma from the master, Dr. John Garnham

Past master Denis Oliver MR.CVS HonFWCF gives Mark his silver medal for passing with honours

Joan, Mark and Doug. It was a great day for this lad and one he will always remember

Steven Arnold

Our next lad Steven Arnold, or Arnie as he was to be known, came from Stoke-on-Trent. He too had trained at the School of Farriery at Hereford, where he had just finished a blacksmithing course (as it was called back then). With lucky timing, he phoned to enquire about vacancies just when we had decided to look for another apprentice. Also, by luck, Steven was at college with a young man from Annesley in Nottinghamshire, who knew where we lived and offered Steven a lift to Clay Cross for a trial. The trial went well so we took him on as our new apprentice. The photograph shows Mark Jones making him welcome. The two lads got on very well together. I think this was partly because Mark could now move another step up the ladder and leave the shit jobs to Steven.

This lad was quite bright and always attentive, and we never had any problems with him. He managed the big hunt horses well even though he was a bit on the small side and not especially strong. I don't think all was well at home, as his parents had separated and he had a new stepfather, but that was none of my business.

Steven was about halfway through his apprenticeship when he came to me very upset. He had received a letter from the Farriers Registration Council stating that he had been reported for shoeing horses in the Scarborough area after his working hours. This was obviously a load of nonsense – for one thing, Scarborough was over 70 miles away – but what a nasty letter to send a young lad. I told him not to worry and to leave it to me to sort out. I got on the phone to the FRC straight away to demand a written apology for Steven. I told them, "When my lads finish work each day they have no energy for anything else, let alone travel over 70 miles to shoe more horses. I can clearly state that this young man is not at fault. May I suggest that you check your information more thoroughly before writing to anyone else in future." About a week later, Steven received a letter apologising for the mistake. They said there was another boy with the same name in the Scarborough area and they were very sorry for the upset they caused.

Mark has a new roommate and friend

Steven learns to fit his first shoe

Steven worked steadily towards his diploma exam and passed it with no trouble. The presentations were held in London, and all lads and masters plus their parents were expected to attend. Steven said he had a small problem: he did not own a suit so would we mind if he did not go? My son Neal said immediately, "Problem solved. I will loan you one of mine. You will go to the presentation and we will all go to support you." And all was well. When Steven's time was up he expressed a wish to leave my employment and have a go on his own. This is what most apprentices want, so we all wished him well and off he went, making room for another boy hoping to become a farrier.

Brendon Hogan

Just before Steven left us, we heard about two boys at Hereford School of Farriery who had not yet secured an apprenticeship. They were Brendon Hogan from Scotland and Austin Leahy from Ireland. As we were fortunate in always having lots of work on, I asked them both up to my forge for a few weeks. My son was now an approved training farrier (ATF) and if these lads were any good he would be able to supervise one while I took the other. Both boys stayed in the flat above the forge and had their meals with us in the house.

No photo of Hogan – he was not with us long enough.

That first weekend, Brendon's father came to see him on the Sunday morning around 10am. He had booked bed and breakfast just up the road from the forge. The first thing he said to me was, "Where is the nearest pub?" I told him but said it would not be open until midday. Father and son disappeared but I do not know where they went. The same thing happened the following week. On that Sunday evening, my wife made a roast beef dinner for the boy. As Joan and I would be going out, I called him down to eat around 6pm. Getting no answer, I went up to the flat over the forge. And there he was, flat across the bed, drunk as a lord and unable to stand up. I gave him a piece of my mind and put his dinner on the table by the bed. My wife and I went out, and when we returned, I went to see the lad. He was fast asleep, with the dinner partly eaten and the sink full of vomit.

Brendon came down to breakfast the next day as though nothing had happened. I told him he was no longer welcome at our address and would not be joining this company. He must pack his belongings, phone for his father to collect him, and leave that morning. When Mr. Hogan arrived, he apologised for the state he had left his son in but asked whether I would reconsider if he paid me to keep the boy on to complete his apprenticeship. I told him he had not got enough money to make me reconsider and that was the end of the matter.

I had not been present each time Brendon travelled out to clients' yards with the team, but the other lads told me he had used bad language in front of the customers. Some of our customers had complained to Neal and insisted he must not bring the young man on their yards again, so it was a good thing that we terminated his trial with us.

Austin Leahy

Austin was just the opposite. He was very shy and did not speak much at all. When he did, it was hard to make out what he was saying in his strong Irish accent. He was not the sharpest knife in the drawer, but he did as he was told and we offered him a job.

Austin would spend hours on his own in the flat. One morning he came down for breakfast wearing a child's cap on his head with small flowers on it. I told him to remove his cap whilst he was at the table. When he did so, we all stopped eating and stared. He had shaved his head. And he had done it with some Lister horse clippers that I kept in my small museum in a room next to the one he slept in. I said, "What the bloody hell have you done?" Austin never answered. Well, I could not take him out to the customers looking like that, so I left him in the forge making shoes for about three weeks until there was some growth on his head.

Over the next year all went reasonably well. Austin did his work and he joined a local boxing club just down the road from us. One day he asked me to take a look at his hand as it was swollen. I could not see the reason for the swelling and there were no points of entry from nails. My advice was to go and see the doctor. The GP thought there must be an infection and gave him some antibiotics. These had no effect. After a week, his whole arm was swollen so we took him to the hospital. They admitted him with a thrombosis. He told them it could be from a prick from a horse's nail, but they said it was more probably caused by a direct blow from boxing and advised him to give it up.

Austin holding the pony's leg too high

My wife went to see him at visiting times. She said he would just sit there and not speak. In fact, on one occasion he got a phone call from Ireland and just left Joan sitting on her own for almost an hour. He had no one else to visit him as all his folks were back in Ireland. He can't have been all that thick as he tried to blame his job for his problem and made an attempt to get compensation from me (no chance).

In due course Austin recovered and returned to work, and one day he and I went to a call in Cutthorpe near Chesterfield. It was at a large house with a swimming pool in the garden. The pool was covered over with a green plastic sheet as it was only April. The lady said, "Good morning to you both. I will go and get the horse." She returned and tied the horse to the place where we were to shoe it, and we started work. At that point, her other horse decided it wanted to be with its friend. It jumped the gate and trotted up the garden toward the yard.

But it stepped on the green sheet that was covering the pool. In went the horse at the deep end with a great splash. The animal was floundering in the water with the sheet around its legs. The next thing I saw was Austin pulling off his shirt and jumping in to save the horse. But Austin could not bloody swim. So now we had him and the horse thrashing about in the deep end of the pool. I shouted to the lady to phone the fire service but to save the horse first as it was the horse we'd be getting paid for.

Later that summer, Joan and I went out to dinner one Sunday night and returned to find all the alarms going off. My neighbour was waiting for me. He told me he had seen someone go in the yard and offered to come with me to investigate. I found nobody in the house or forge, so I turned the alarm off. I noticed Austin had a light on in the flat so I went up to see him and found his brother Dennis there with him. Dennis was a jump jockey who rode for Jenny Pitman. He apologised for setting off the alarm. He had come looking for Austin and opened the wrong door. But, he said, it was really important he saw his brother as soon as possible. He had to tell him some bad news: his sister had drowned in a river accident. They had gone for a walk by the river on a sweltering day and had been paddling in the water to cool off when the current swept her away. Dennis had come to take his brother home for a time.

Austin had two weeks off. Afterwards he returned to work and carried on training for his diploma exam, which he passed. He left our company and did some locum work for different farriers. Later we were told he went to America, and that was the last we heard of him.

Billy Bartlett

Billy was a local boy from the village of South Normanton. He was a very pleasant lad with a good sense of humour. He worked well and was very attentive to all he was told. This lad was indentured to my son Neal, with me assisting when needed. He lived so near to us that he could travel from his home every day. He mixed in well with the rest of the lads and we became one big happy family again.

Billy liked a drink and a fag. None of the lads ever smoked or drank at work, and Billy understood the rules but realised he could make up for it after work. The way Joan and I saw it, they were grown lads and what they did after work was their own business. Within reason. I found out that Billy used to call at a pub in the next village after work each night because they opened at 6pm. Some nights he would still be there at 8pm without having been home for dinner. He was addicted to the fruit machines and he never had any money. He would very often ask for a sub until Friday when he received his wages. He always paid it back, but he told his mum and dad he had to work late every night. So his mum and dad thought I was a rotten boss to work for.

Billy did well at work, but his private life was something else. He had a string of girlfriends and eventually moved in with one young lady who was separated from her husband and had some children. She was a pretty girl and he was well pleased. He used to tell us that she was a fantastic masseuse and would give him one most nights. This lasted a few months, and then he went back home for a short time. Next,

Billy Bartlett

he moved in with a girl from Grassmoor, and then found out one of his previous girlfriends was pregnant with his child. You can guess how mixed up this lad was. His mum ran a dance school and his dad worked long hours at the pit. His brother was a schoolteacher and a musician and had his own small band, which was doing very well. Sometimes Billy would play the drums in the band.

Then a blow fell on the family. Billy's brother committed suicide at a hotel in London. By now Billy had finished his apprenticeship and set up as a farrier in his own right, and was living with his previous girlfriend and their child. We realised the loss of his brother hit him hard, but he was getting a bad name in the horse world for letting customers down and not keeping his appointments. This was bad news for us as he worked in the same area as we did, and people would say,

Andrew, Ben, Billy, Gordon and Mark (kneeling). The framed certificates are of some of our previous lads who have passed their diploma and moved on

"That lad you trained" etc. At one time Billy phoned my son and asked if he and his girl could come to see him. Neal said "Yes, of course." He asked if Neal could find him some work two or three days a week as he had few clients of his own, did not like working alone all day and missed the companionship he had enjoyed with us. Neal said he could start next Monday and booked in some extra work for him to do.

On the Monday, Billy did not show up for work until 9.45am and said he would have to finish at 2.30pm. The following day he did not show up at all and left Neal to cope with the extra work on his own. After that Neal said he was not going to try to help him anymore. Billy still works in the same area, but we never see him – we only get his dissatisfied customers complaining he does not care about their horses. Of all the lads we have trained, it is so sad to see one let himself down like that, and to have it happen in the area where we work is both difficult and soul-destroying for us.

Billy and Mark and the horse's owner Lenny Harvey on a practice test before Billy's exam the following week. The photos that follow are of that day

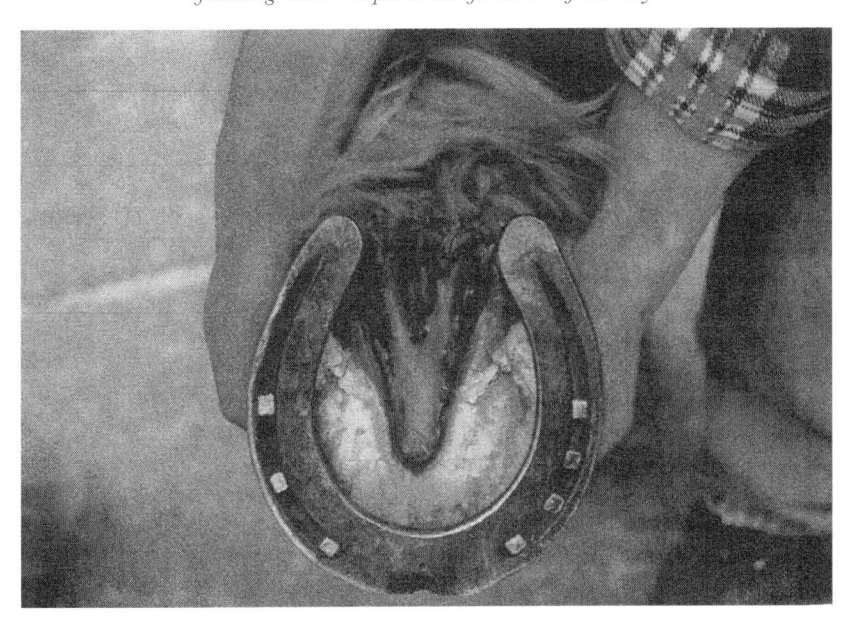

The test I set was a ¾ fullered front shoe for a riding horse and a concave hind shoe with a toe clip. The time allowed was two hours with no rough cutting and no overtime, starting at 10 am and finishing at 12 noon

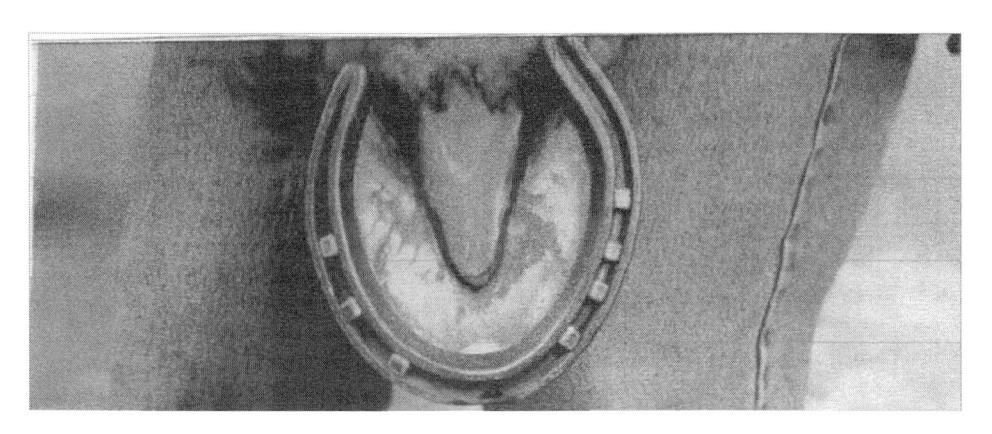

The concave hind was finished on time and overall the job was worth a possible B pass

Billy, Mark and AnDr.ew Frudd in the Queens Pub at Mark's leaving party, where a good night was had by all

Billy receives his diploma from the master of the WCF, Roger Johnson MR.CVS

Steven Arnold and Billy with the farriers' float on London Wall 1995

The farriers float on Gresham Street at the start of the Lord Mayor's Parade 1995

Bill Poor on the youth exchange scheme

This time it was the turn of a young man from Texas by the name of Bill Poor, the son of Jim Poor who, you may remember, visited us when Grant Moon came over with the American Farriers Team to compete at the international team event at Stoneleigh, Warwickshire in 1989.

This young man Bill Poor was obsessed with the tales of our folk hero Robin Hood. He had seen the film on the television back home. He wanted to see Nottingham Castle and if possible Sherwood Forest. My wife took him to Nottingham on the train and showed him the castle, and they joined the tour through the tunnels and then had a drink in England's oldest pub, The Trip to Jerusalem. The following day I took him to the grave of Little John in the village of Hathersage. We also took him to see the Major Oak at Edwinstowe. He was overcome with gratitude because we took the time to help him fulfil his wishes. For our part, we reckoned it was good for us to have these young people to stay as we could all learn from one another. This lad Bill was to become a world champion at the Calgary Stampede in Canada some years later. Steven Arnold, when he finished his time with us, went over to America and stayed with the Poor family for a time.

Doug, Neal, young Bill Poor, Steven Arnold, Mark Jones, Billy Bartlett

Bill joins us on the rounds

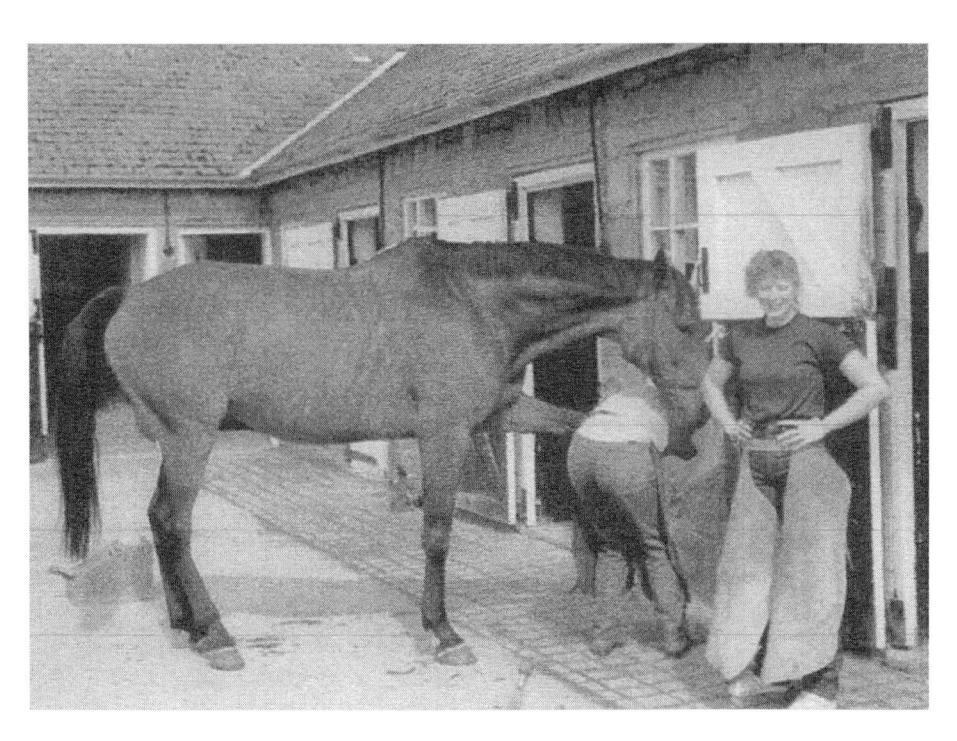

Bill's stepmother Kelly out at work with us at the High Peak Hunt stables in Bakewell. Kelly was a farrier too and came over with her husband to stay with us when they were in the American farriery team with Grant Moon. She told me the reason for the tight-necked shirt was that back home the male grooms were always trying to look down her jumper

9

SILVER SHOES AND RACEHORSES

The silver shoes

At a livery dinner in London during the early 1980s, a lady approached me for advice on an old WCF tradition. This lady was Winnie Seymour, the daughter of Harry Matthews, who had died several years earlier. For some time before his death he was not able to drive, and Winnie used to drive him to all his duties in London. Harry Matthews was a liveryman in the Worshipful Company of Blacksmiths as well as the WCF, so it made sense that his daughter should join the same liveries. She continued to support both companies after her father passed on, and used to attend every event they held. Now she asked if I would help her to restart an old WCF tradition her late father used to uphold. It was to make a small silver horseshoe for the new master each year.

The silver shoe must not be cast but had to be forged in a blacksmith's shop on the anvil. Winnie had asked Howard Cooper FWCF if he knew anyone that could help, and he said, "Try liveryman Doug Bradbury. Doug likes fiddling." She said that if I were interested, she would show me a shoe her dad had made so I could copy it. The one she produced was a plain piece of silver in the shape of a horseshoe, with two caulks and nail holes part stamped. She told me her father used to get the silver from a company of jewellers and silversmiths in Birmingham: F. Marson & Son of 90 Spencer Street. He would buy it in lengths about two feet long and one-quarter inch square. "Tell Mr. Marson what it is for and you will have no trouble, as he knew my father well," she assured me. Little did I know then just what was involved and just what I had let myself in for.

Eric Plant FWCF listened in on all this and said he would give me a hand to make the shoes. Over the next few weeks, I purchased the silver and set about the task. Having never handled silver before and being unused to working in such small dimensions, I had to make the tools first. I decided to make the shoe in the shape of a hind roadster, so I needed a fuller, a nail stamp and all the polishing tools.

At the next company dinner, Winnie made a beeline for me. "Have you made the silver shoe, Doug? Let me see it." Off she went with the sample. A short time later she returned and said "It is very nice. Thank you for making it. Now I will tell you what you do with the shoe. Each year when the new master is sworn in, the beadle will present you to him. When you shake hands you press the shoe into the palm of his hand and wish him well. That's all, and then you move on."

The first one I presented was to Arnold Scott, who became master in 1984. Winnie asked how it went. I said it was OK, no problems. She then said that as it was several years since her father had died, no shoes had been made for some time. Would I consider making all the back number of shoes for the past masters? I thought, Bloody hell, what am I doing? but agreed to make them. So, at the next several court dinners she would come over to me and say "Have you had time to do any spare shoes? If so, come on and I will introduce you to the past masters that have not had a silver shoe. When you shake hands, place one in his palm. He will know just what it is. Look around at any court dinner and you will see the past masters sitting there polishing their silver shoes in their table napkins."

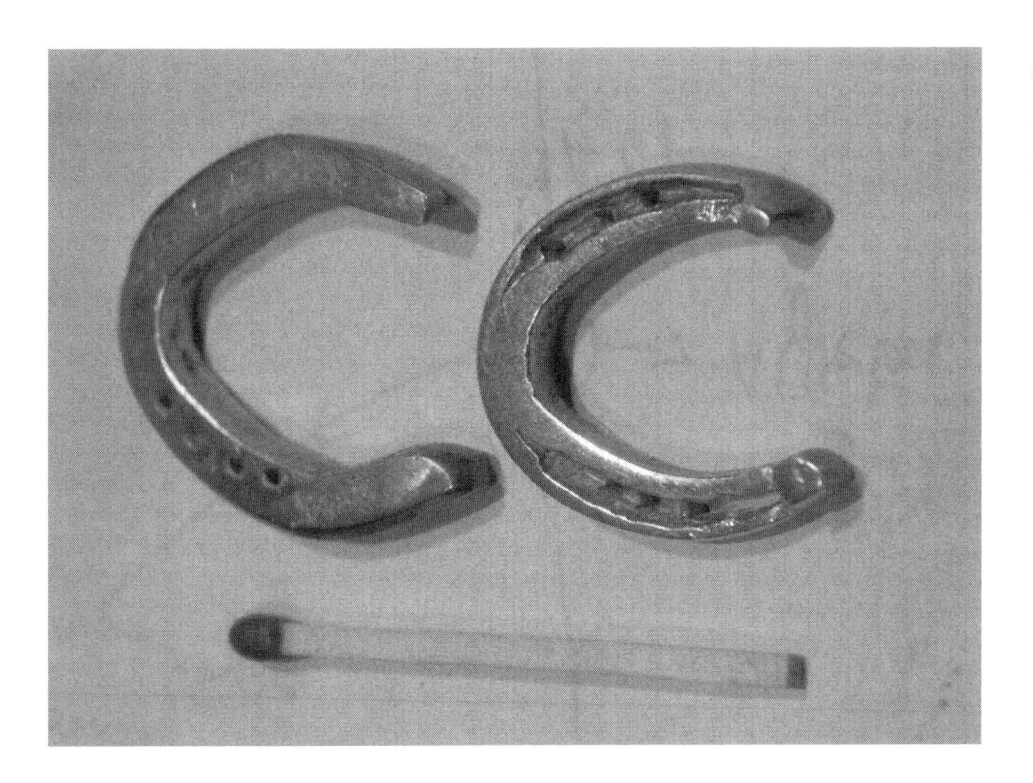

The first two silver shoes I made

Over the years I made well over 20 small silver horseshoes for the masters of the WCF and the Lord Mayors of the City of London. Also, my wife, daughter and daughter-in-law, plus a few close friends, each have one. Some of the masters concerned were A. Scott, D. Tavernor, T. Neligan, Lady Graham and John Alsford. In 1988 Roy Thompson, who was master that year, asked me if I would make one for the Lord Mayor. Then there were M. Jepson, T. (Mack) Head, Mrs. P. Halliday, J. G. Barsham, R. F. Johnson MR.CVS, Dr. J. C. Garnham KLJ MB BS MR.CS LRCP FFPM, R. F. Wallis FCA, Mrs. D. Pagan BA ACA, Howard Ellis and Sir Gordon Shattock (whose first wife was killed in the Brighton bomb attack). Ron Cocker was the last master I made a shoe for. He was not popular with many members of the company. When I presented the shoe at his installation, he just looked at it, said "What's this?" and put it in his pocket. It was the recognised custom to write to the person who had made the shoe and thank them, but not this man; he was the only one not to do so. After that I never made any more, and to my knowledge no one else has carried on this tradition.

Left to right: Roy Thompson and his wife, Sir Gordon Shattock and his wife, Dr. Garnham and his wife, Roger Johnson MR.CVS and his wife

THE WORSHIPFUL COMPANY OF FARRIERS

MASTER 1987/88
A. G. W. SCOTT, FCA
TEL: 01-693 4128

5, BREAKSPEARE,
COLLEGE ROAD,
DULWICH,
LONDON SE21 7NB

15th. Dec. 1990.

Dear Mr. Bradbury,

I would like to thank you very much indeed for making and giving to me the silver horseshoe, which you handed to me at the Court Dinner on Thursday.

My wife and sons (one of whom is a member of the Company) were also highly delighted to see it, and I think it will now become a family heirloom.

I shall prize it very highly and I am very grateful, both for the kind gift and as an example of very fine workmanship.

I wish you and yours the compliments of the season and a Happy New Year.

Yours sincerely,

Arnold Scott

Douglas Bradbury Esq FWCF.

One of the many letters from the masters thanking me for their silver shoe, followed by a letter from Winnie Seymour

Elvaston Castle 1988

Elvaston Castle in Derbyshire was the seat of the Earl of Harrington until 1939. This gothic-style castle was designed for the third earl in the early 19th century by James Wyatt, although Wyatt himself did not live to see the designs carried out. The earl wanted new gardens to go with his castle and offered the commission to the famous landscape gardener Lancelot Capability Brown. However, Brown turned down the invitation because the area was too flat. It was left to Charles Stanhope, the fourth Earl of Harrington, to finish the work, and he invited William Barron and a team of 90 gardeners to landscape the park.

Derbyshire County Council acquired Elvaston Castle and its surrounding parkland in 1969 and opened it to the public on Good Friday 1970. Before this could happen, however, the grounds required a lot of work to make up for over 25 years of neglect. Many of the trees were pruned and restored and shrubs were cleared to allow light and air to the other specimens. Unfortunately, the Bower Garden was beyond restoration.

Following the opening of the park, the lower stable yard was restored and became the home of the working farm museum, which opened to the public in 1980. The staff wore period dress to show visitors something of the lives of those who worked on the estate in the early 19th century. The top stable yard provided facilities for visitors, including a shop and information centre and a field study centre for schools.

Derbyshire County Council asked me if I would do some demonstrations for them at the castle, as part of the themed series of events being arranged for local schools. The first event was to be called 'Grandfather's harvest'. The second was 'Sheep to shawl' and the third was 'A Victorian Christmas on the farm'.

The lower stable yard housed a large number of buildings, including two blacksmithing shops with forges operated by large bellows. There was one anvil, a water bosh, a leg vice and several pairs of tongs and anvil blocks. These had been donated by people in the surrounding areas but had evidently been positioned in the smithy by people who did not understand what they were for, and the bellows needed some repairs. The yard also contained a saddler's shop, a joiner's shop, a large sawmill, an engineering shop, old tractors and many other types of farm machinery. Not to speak of the gypsy caravans donated by a Mr. Hunt.

The yard foreman met us when we arrived, showed us where the forge was and was left us to it. I made sure we were early so that we could get the forge going before the kids arrived at about 9.15am. It was lucky I did so, as the bellows were not blowing as they should and it was only thanks to a cocoa tin and some plumber's tape that we got them going well enough to make the fire. We did have our gas fire with us just in case, but it was not needed. The plan was to split the children into groups of twenty and give each group about fifteen minutes in each workshop in turn. The riding school adjacent to the yard supplied a small pony for me to shoe. The girl groom said she would bring me another pony when we had finished. I said, "Not at this price you won't. This one will last all day, thank you." I should explain that the council were paying me only £30 a day, and there was no way £30

The smithy at Elvaston Castle

Some of the children arriving

covered my costs. I was treating it as a public relations exercise for the farriery profession, as so little was taught in schools or anywhere else about our work. Indeed, I had been giving talks and demonstrations for this purpose to schools and community groups for many years – but you can see why I wasn't keen to shoe more than one pony for the price.

However, whilst I was at the castle, the rest of our staff were busy servicing our regular customers' horses as usual. This format worked well and many schools supported the council's venture. Each group of children had a teacher with them, and of all the groups that passed through the forge there was only one set that misbehaved. To restore order, I struck the anvil with the hand hammer, which made it ring like a bell, and roared "All of you, shut up and listen. I have given up a day's work for you lot. If you cannot behave, get out of the forge." That did the trick. They all stood to attention, including the teacher, and after that we had no more noise from them.

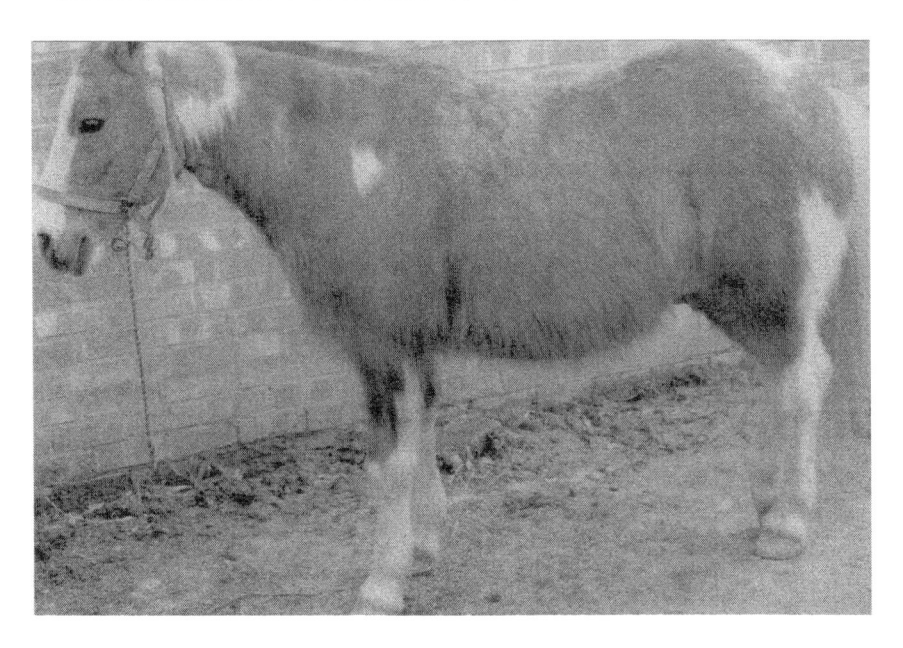

This was the first pony the girl groom brought me, saying she would get another one when I had finished

The second event followed the same pattern, with the added attraction of a man shearing the sheep, a lady spinning the wool and an exhibition of all types of knitted garments. Equally successful was the Victorian farm at Christmas. At the end of each event, all the children would line up and climb into a large farm cart, twenty at a time. Major, the shire horse that lived on the farm, would then take them around the estate.

Unfortunately, the Elvaston working farm museum closed due to lack of support. Derbyshire County Council put it up for a 150-year lease. A private company was interested in making it into a hotel and golf course complex but met a lot of opposition from a group called Friends of Elvaston Castle and the situation stuck at stalemate for a long time.

Doug goes into films

Film crews were often milling about at Elvaston. Once I was asked to take part in a scene for a TV programme, a new soap called The Bretts. I had to be seen working on the anvil in the stable yard just as two actors were walking past. My job was to be making a horseshoe at exactly the moment they went by. It took twelve takes to get it right. As the actors passed the forge, one of them was meant to say goodbye, climb into a vintage Rolls Royce on a stand, put the car in forward gear and move off in it about three feet. Instead he put it into reverse and shot off the set backwards with a loud bang. The producer went ape shit and danced up and down on his hat.

The pay was £50 a day plus lunch. Meals were served in a double decker bus fully kitted out for the job, and the food was excellent. The Bretts was shown on ITV but was pulled after only a few weeks as it wasn't getting enough viewers.

On another occasion, I was working at the castle when a man came to see me from the BBC. He said he was from the outside broadcast unit and they were planning to make a short film for schools. The company making the film was Landmark and it would be entitled *A Day in the Life of a Country Child*. They had chosen a boy to play the part of the country child, a young lad from Matlock by the name of James Twyford, and asked if I would take the part of the blacksmith/farrier. I would have to join Equity, the trade union for actors, as I had a speaking part. I said "OK, I'll give it a go" and the BBC man said he would be in touch.

Some weeks later, I received a call asking me to go to the castle for a costume fitting. They said it wouldn't take long, so Joan came along too to see what it was all about. The costume lady said, "You won't need to look much different from how you are now. Just leave off shaving for a week and all you will need is a granddad shirt – one without a collar. We just need to put on a bit more dirt." My wife said, "If you needed a dirty shirt, you should have given me a phone call."

The day of the filming was a big one. *The Day in the Life* story started at 5am on a cold wintry morning with James being called from his bed to go and feed the pigs and chickens and then fetch the water for the house, all before breakfast. When that was done it was time for a mug of tea and a bit of bacon on bread, then out to fetch the farm horse (who was Major, the castle's resident shire). James was shown learning to plough with the horse. After that he did some muck spreading, first shovelling it off the yard and then spreading it on the fields. Sometimes, he said, he was allowed to ride on the muck cart. Then he was shown picking stones off the field, at the same time telling the viewers that stones were a farmer's worst enemy and must be cleared from the land. Next, he fed the sheep using the turnip slicer.

James then had to take Major for some new shoes. He explained how the best place in winter was in the forge. "This is where we find Doug the smith. I keep asking Doug to take me on, but he keeps refusing me. He says my parents could not afford to indenture me and that I would do better in the army." With that, he brought Major into the forge and my role began. The first problem we encountered was that James was not strong enough to use the sledgehammer. The camera crew solved it by shooting the scene with my son's hands on the hammer shaft, so it was Neal not James doing the striking. Heating the forge to make the shoes took a long time because the bellows in the top stable yard had a lot of holes in them. When it came to the part where we plunged the shoe in water to cool it off and the steam rose with a great hiss, the producer shouted "Stop! Can we have that again? The smoke effect was good."

My thoughts were, *Bloody hell, it took ages to get to that heat on this forge.* But we did it.

The shoeing scene was finished off and the film moved on to the yard. Here the threshing machine was in full operation while a crowd of local people in costume stood around watching it. Eventually we stopped for lunch, but that meant off to the local pub – not a bit like the banquet set out on the ITV bus. With filming now finished, I was paid £50 for the day and thought that was the end of it.

Then one day my granddaughter, who had just turned

three years old, ran to her mum crying "Grandad is on the telly!" She was right: the film was on the schools programme and was repeated again in the afternoon. After a short time, I received a cheque from the BBC for £12, and the same thereafter every time it was on TV. I even got paid for repeats. This went on for several years and the price kept on rising. My film career was very short, but I enjoyed it.

Douglas in the forge at Elvaston

Pay chit from the BBC

This is Major, a 16-year-old shire horse, outside the forge in 1988

Major was a gentle giant with no vices whatsoever. Besides starring in the BBC film, he was used for lots of jobs around the estate. I made a lot of visits to Elvaston and this was one of the last photos I took of Major. Sadly in 1995 he suffered an attack of laminitis. For a time, he seemed to be responding to treatment but I think in the end the pain was so bad that his heart just gave up and he passed away.

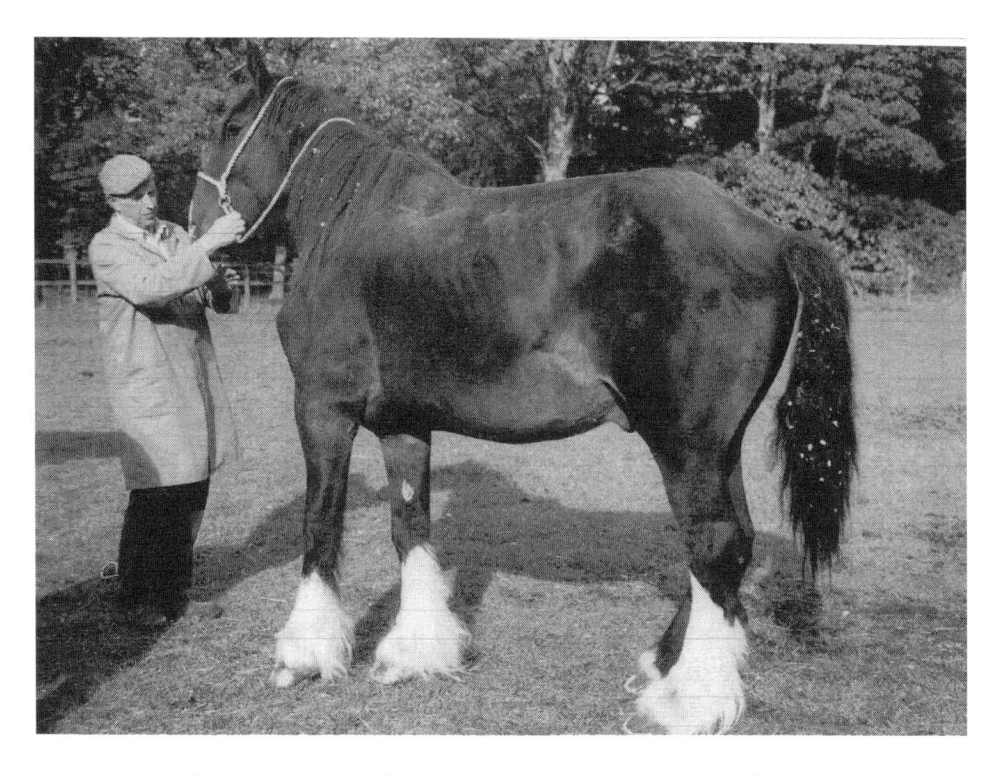

One of the last photos of Major, taken at the onset of laminitis in 1995

MAP C

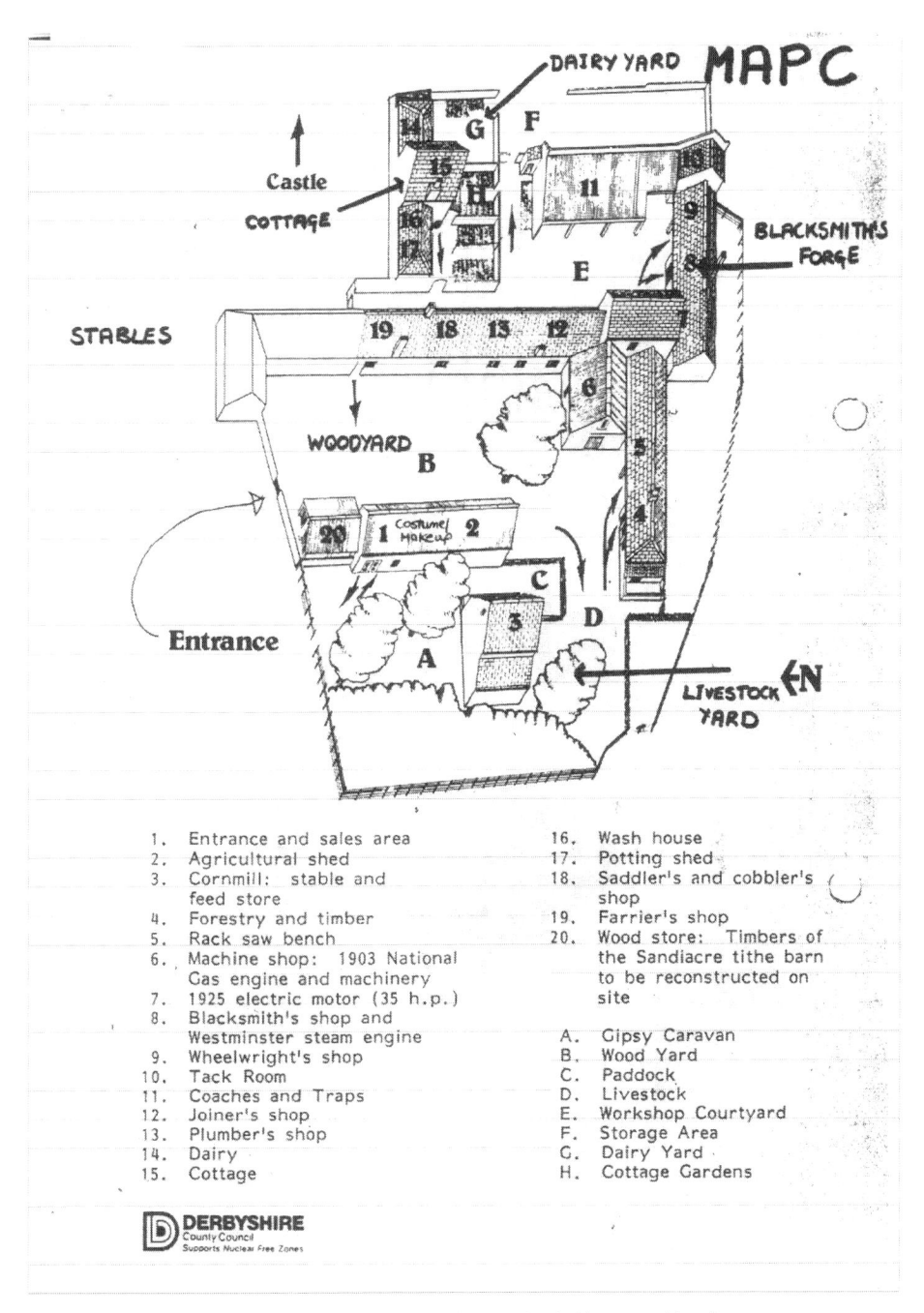

DAIRY YARD

Castle COTTAGE

BLACKSMITHS FORGE

STABLES

WOODYARD

Entrance

LIVESTOCK YARD

N

1. Entrance and sales area
2. Agricultural shed
3. Cornmill: stable and feed store
4. Forestry and timber
5. Rack saw bench
6. Machine shop: 1903 National Gas engine and machinery
7. 1925 electric motor (35 h.p.)
8. Blacksmith's shop and Westminster steam engine
9. Wheelwright's shop
10. Tack Room
11. Coaches and Traps
12. Joiner's shop
13. Plumber's shop
14. Dairy
15. Cottage
16. Wash house
17. Potting shed
18. Saddler's and cobbler's shop
19. Farrier's shop
20. Wood store: Timbers of the Sandiacre tithe barn to be reconstructed on site

A. Gipsy Caravan
B. Wood Yard
C. Paddock
D. Livestock
E. Workshop Courtyard
F. Storage Area
G. Dairy Yard
H. Cottage Gardens

DERBYSHIRE County Council Supports Nuclear Free Zones

Most of the filming took place within the bounds of this map, with a few scenes at Shipley Park Farm

The Desert Orchid Farriers Appeal 1991

By an Act of Parliament of 1975, the Worshipful Company of Farriers was charged with responsibility for securing adequate standards of competence and conduct among persons engaged in the shoeing of horses. Concerns at standards of farriery have surfaced periodically over the last century. Although there has been some improvement since 1975, the Company has recognised for some time that there is scope for further development. One project that aimed to boost the status and standards of the profession was the Desert Orchid Farriers Appeal of 1991-95.

Desert Orchid in action

The Desert Orchid Farriers Appeal Fund was registered as a charity on 17 December 1990 and lasted until August 1995. Named after the legendary racehorse, it was an enormous undertaking. The key objective was to provide better trained and equipped farriers to improve standards both in Britain and throughout the world. The immediate priority was to arrest the declining numbers of farriers by establishing an apprentice training fund, where a capital sum of £2 million would help offset the recent withDr.awal of government funding. Other goals included the establishment of an international institute of farriery, better postgraduate training facilities, and the creation of a charitable trust to relieve hardship, sickness and suffering amongst farriers and their dependents.

A committee was initially formed as follows:

The Duke of Beaufort (Vice President)	W. J. Alsford (Appeal Chairman)
The Duke of Devonshire (Vice President)	R. Moon (Appeal Director)
Earl of Westmorland (Vice President)	T. Bradshaw (PR Director)
Lord Oaksay	
Dr. P. J. Gazder	
G. Bearman	

They were later joined, on the farriery and veterinary side, by Eric Plant, Roger Johnson and his wife, Edgar Stern and myself.

How did I get involved? It came about because the appeal chairman John Alsford was the master of the WCF at the time. John was a timber merchant who had made millions from the import and export of timber. He took a year out from his company to devote to the farriers of this country. The financial cost to himself must have been astronomical; I do know it also cost him his job as chairman of his companys' board of directors. He travelled the country speaking to farriers to try and explain the problems we were facing as a profession due to the withdrawal of government funding for apprentices. He would visit any group of farriers in any part of the UK, arrange a buffet and drinks for everyone attending, and pay for the lot. John invited me onto the appeal committee he had formed, who met in his flat in the Barbican in London city centre.

Winnie Seymour, Neal and Joan at the Hampton Court dinner hosted by HRH the Princess Royal

A night to remember – dinner at Hampton Court Palace

Kate Doogan, her mum, Kate"'s partner, Gale and Paul, Karen and Neal, Winnie, Joan

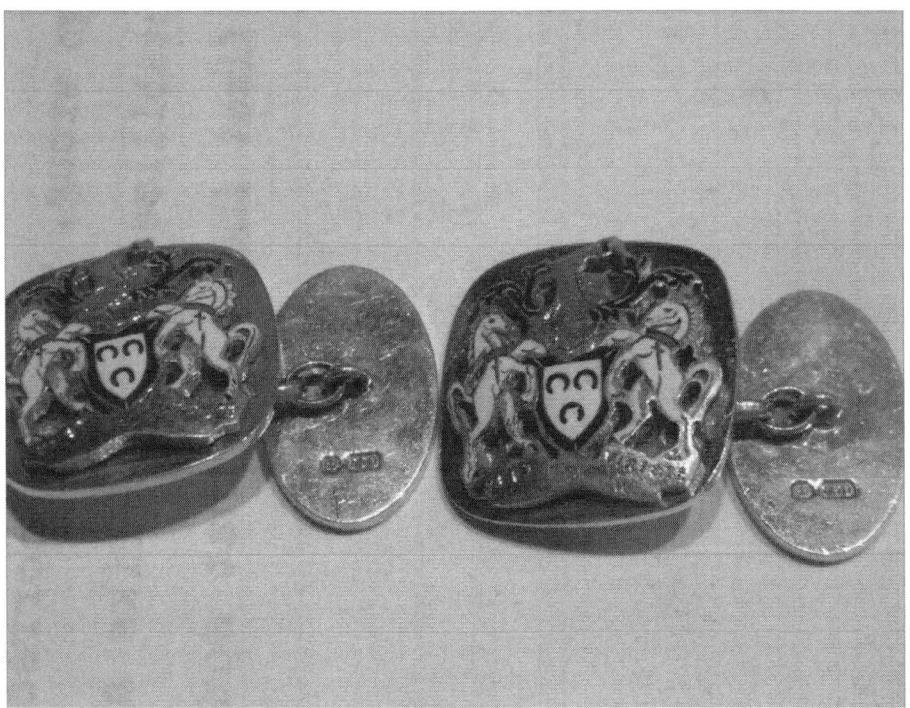

Some photos of the merchandise that was on sale for the WCF: 18-carat gold cufflinks, pill or stud boxes, and a small carriage clock

The Desert Orchid Farriers Appeal

in conjunction with

The Worshipful Company of Farriers

present a

ROYAL GALA BANQUET

in the presence of

Her Royal Highness, The Princess Royal

HAMPTON COURT
Monday, June 10, 1991

Menu and wine list

Menu

*

Potato Nest of Quails Eggs

*

Champagne Sorbet

*

Welsh Fillet of Lamb
served with a selection of vegetables

*

Trio of Puddings

*

Coffee and Chocolates

Menu and wine list

Wines

∗

Bodenham Reichensteiner 1989

∗

Chateau La Bonnelle 1985

Grand Cru St Emilion

∗

Maison Christophe

Menu and wine list

The campaign began in earnest with the official launch on 10th September 1991. It took the form of a gala banquet in the presence of Her Royal Highness the Princess Royal in the Great Hall of Hampton Court Palace.

John Alsford called to let me know he had arranged this launch event at Hampton Court for 10th September, and mentioned he had put me down for a table of ten. I said thank you and how much would that cost me? £2,000 for the table! Bloody hell, I thought. As I had my son and his wife and my daughter and her husband as my guests as well as Joan and myself – in other words, Dad will pay – that left only four tickets to sell for my table. However, we managed, and it was in aid of a good cause – all funds raised from the gala evening were to go towards furthering the craft of farriery and so promoting the health and welfare of the horse.

It was certainly a splendid night. There were 200 guests, and the banquet was preceded by a military display from the Mounted Farriers of the Household Cavalry Regiment, the dismounted Band of the Life Guards and the trumpeters of HM Life Guards in state dress. Afterwards we watched a firework display and a march past by the Grenadier Guards in the palace grounds. Helping to stage the event were the Duke of Devonshire, the Earl of Westmorland, Dr. Gazder and Brian Masterson. There were harpists, flautists and a string quartet to lend atmosphere, and a 12-piece orchestra to serenade us throughout the meal.

The Princess Royal acknowledged in her address that times were hard. "This may not be the best moment in time to start an appeal," she said. "But it is essential, and we must get on with it. This particular appeal is necessary to all horse owners and users. It does not matter whether you are interested in racing at the highest level or simply enjoy the sight of horses grazing in your field. One of the things you cannot avoid is the care of the horse's feet." Her Royal Highness concluded her 12-minute speech by highlighting the withdrawal of government funding for apprentice training. "Because of this, the importance of this appeal is very, very much more immediate," she said. "We must make it successful, not only for the owners but the horses themselves. It is important that we maintain a genuinely high basic standard of farriery in this country to save horses from suffering. If you don't have horses with feet that are comfortable and are working for them, there is not much point in having them at all."

And John Alsford as master of the WCF summed up: "Farriery is a craft which is part of our heritage and is in danger unless we grasp the anvil, plan its future, and prepare properly for generations to come."

"It was a spectacular function, and seemingly well received by all", said the event organiser Leonora Moon. The appeal was expected to host a number of other fundraising gala events over the coming two years. Despite all this, the results fell short of what we had hoped for. Of course, there were the non-believers from the start, who had no intention of helping it succeed, however much hospitality John Alsford put on for them. The only disappointment at the gala banquet itself was the fact that the majority of those who attended were already behind the appeal. There were not many new faces. Undoubtedly the current economic recession was biting hard, and many people who were approached simply could not afford to attend.

As the Princess Royal said, it was not an ideal time to start an appeal. Even the name of the country's favourite racehorse Desert Orchid could not work its magic. The project got underway at the same time as the Gulf War, and soon the Desert Storm operation was dominating the news. Lots of pledges were made but never kept. Some of the big racehorse owners who were expected to back the appeal failed to come forward. It was hoped to raise in the region of £7 million over the years but the fund fell well short of that target and closed in 1995. However, I can honestly say that I did my bit and more.

Master of the WCF John Alsford and I became very good friends and found we both shared the same birthday on 1st July. No one will know the true cost to this man of the years he put into the Desert Orchid appeal. But he phoned me a few years later to wish me many happy returns from Australia and told me that he was now able to make out a cheque again, the first for several years. So, you can read into that just what I am saying about what the campaign cost him.

My time on the Farriers Registration Council

In the early 1990s I was elected onto the Farriers Registration Council for a term of three years. It involved attending meetings at the Royal Veterinary College in London. I could only afford the time to go to meetings thanks to my son and our apprentices running our business whilst I was away.

I was also very interested in photography, and it was whilst I was at Stoneleigh taking some photos at the International

Farriers Competition in 1994 that I first met a farrier called Geoff Morris. He came up to ask about the photos I was taking, and we got talking about the National Association of Farriers and the Desert Orchid Appeal. I told him what I knew and he said he would think about joining the National Association and do something for the appeal as well. Several months later Mr. Morris phoned to ask if I would do a lecture for him in Bromyard near Hereford, where he lived. If I could do this for him, he would make it a party at the same time. He expected to raise lots of sponsors and he would share the proceeds between the Desert Orchid Appeal and the National Association of Farriers.

Geoff Morris raised over £500 from this event. Cecil Swann was president that year, and received the cheque from Geoff at a splendid NAFBAE ceremony.

Geoff and his wife have just presented Cecil Swann, president of the NAFBAE, with £500.

Just one of the raffle prizes donated at the presentation ceremony. The president of NAFBAE is holding a cake that was made by one of Geoff''s customers for the occasion. The cake is in the shape of a horseshoe and bears the NAFBAE badge

"Bradbury, am I in trouble?"

About six months after that I got a phone call from Geoff Morris asking if he could speak to me in confidence as he understood I was on the FRC. "OK," I said, cautiously.

Geoff lowered his voice. "Mr. Bradbury, can you tell me if I am in trouble or not?"

"First tell me what you have done."

"Well, I went to shoe this horse. It was a bastard, and whilst I was bent over doing its front feet it bit me quite badly. I stood up quickly and threw a punch at the horse, but the horse saw it coming and moved his head. So, I missed and hit the lady owner on the chin, spot on, and she fell to the floor spark out. Her husband was close by and he said, "That has shut her up, hasn't it?" Do you think I am in trouble?"

When I stopped laughing, I could only suggest that he leave the country. Luckily for him the lady did not report it to the FRC and nothing else was heard of the matter.

The firing of the anvil for Tom Barker, master of the WCF 1996/97

Behind the gates in the city walls of London EC1 sits Armoury House, the headquarters of the Honourable Artillery Company (HAC). This is the oldest regiment in the British Army, dating form 1537 when it was first incorporated by charter under King Henry VIII. In 1996 the solicitor Tom Barker was installed as master of the Worshipful Company of Farriers, and he chose to hold the customary reception at Armoury House because he

This is the HAC building on City Road, London. On the right is the main entrance

This is the HAC building on City Road, London. On the right is the main entrance

had served in the HAC in his younger days.

To commemorate his year in office, Tom Barker also decided to present a poleaxe to the regiment. This was a specially made, chromium-plated tool of a type that regimental farriers had carried over the centuries wherever horses were used in battle. It was the farrier's duty to go around the battlefield afterwards and dispatch any horse that was badly injured. He would end its suffering by driving the point of the axe into the animal's skull, resulting in instant death. With the blade of the axe he would remove the hoof capsule as it would have a number branded on it. He would present this to the officer in charge to register the animal's death. The tradition of hoof branding goes back to the 18th century, when it was seen as a way to prevent the theft of military horses. Troopers would say their horses had been killed when in fact they had sold them. Military horses are still branded to this day.

Master Tom Barker making his presentation to the commanding officer, who in turn presents it to the regiment

The poleaxe ready for the presentation

Luncheon followed the presentation, but that was not the end of the day. One of our liverymen was a farrier by the name of Frank Dean FWCF, who had his forge in the village of Rodmell near Lewes in Sussex. Before Tom Barker became master, Frank had told him of a very old tradition in Sussex. This was the firing of the anvil at a wedding or other special event.

Frank Dean FWCF with one of the anvils at the HAC

Frank Drills the small hole in the bung, with Roy Thompson and T. (Mac) Head looking on. You can see the wooden bung in place and the small hole made in it

Tom had listened with interest. Now he asked Frank if he would fire the anvil at the master's reception if he could get permission from the police. The police must have taken a lot of persuading, as there was a lot of trouble from the IRA at that time, with continual bomb attacks in the UK and Ireland. However, Tom managed to get the go-ahead.

Blowing things up was no obstacle for Frank as he was well acquainted with explosives, having been a member of Winston Churchill's secret army, the Auxiliary Units, during the Second World War. (The Auxiliary Units were a force of 3,500 civilian volunteers recruited in coastal counties in 1940 in case of invasion. Sworn to absolute secrecy, they were trained to hide underground and emerge at night in order to destroy German ammunition or fuel dumps and to assassinate Nazi officers and British collaborators.)

Now, the grounds of Armoury House are normally admired as a peaceful oasis of green within the city. They include a full-size cricket pitch and outdoor ménage, parade grounds and beautiful gardens, complementing the gracious dining chambers and historical exhibition halls indoors. As the guests gathered on the lawns, Frank and his son Roger began to unload the two anvils that he was to fire. In each anvil was a square hole about two inches deep. Frank filled each hole with black powder and drove a wooden bung into it with a sledgehammer. Next, he drilled a small hole through the bung and ran a trail of the black powder from the hole along the base of the anvil. In the blue van close by was Frank's gas forge with a length of metal getting hot.

Both anvils were now in place and everybody was told to stand back a few steps. No one thought to warn the people playing cricket in the grounds who, oblivious to the plot, carried on with their game. Roger placed the red-hot metal on the base of the anvil to ignite the powder. Seconds later there was one almighty bang. The cricketers hit the deck. Some of the bowlers got red scorch marks on their trousers; the non-bowlers got brown stains.

I do not think I should print what they said when they came over to ask what the bloody hell was going on.

Anvils all set and ready to fire

Frank making a big bang in the city of London

Frank and his son Roger

Frank and I were good friends and in the year 2000 his daughter brought him to see me and look round the museum I have above my forge. Frank had previously sent me some ox shoes, made to a local Sussex pattern and typical of those used across the South Downs in earlier years. Oxen and cows are still shod in Europe to this day, as I have seen for myself in France and Spain. You can get factory-made shoes for cattle in various patterns, from traditional nailed-on types to modern stick-on ones. They even make boots in rubber that completely encapsulate the cow's hoof. On the next page are photos of what I am talking about.

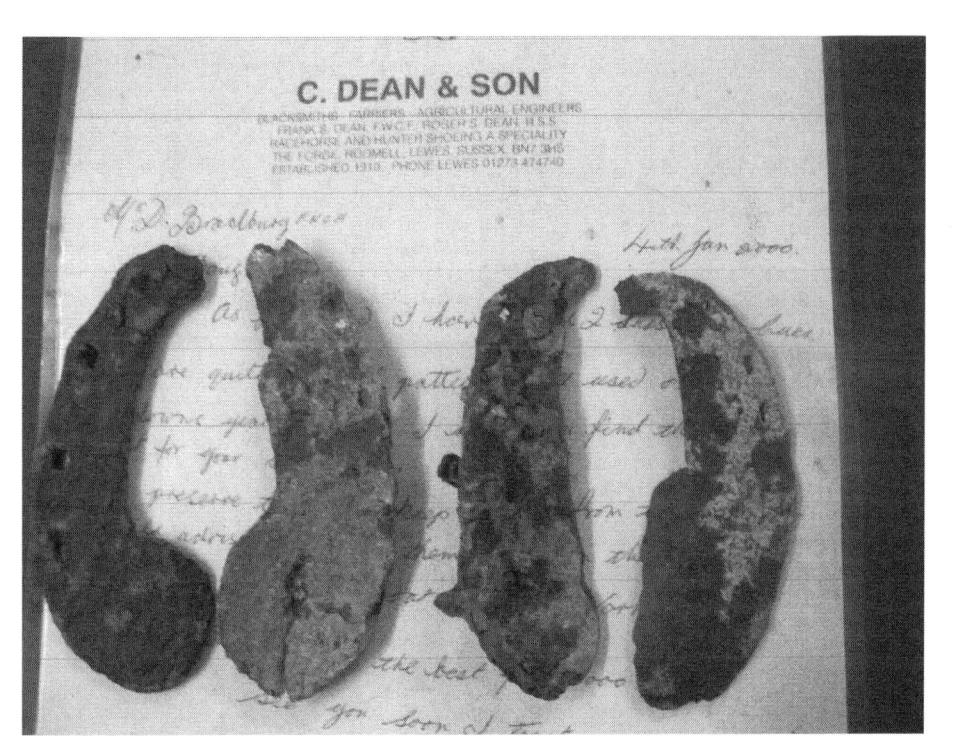

Ox shoes from Sussex

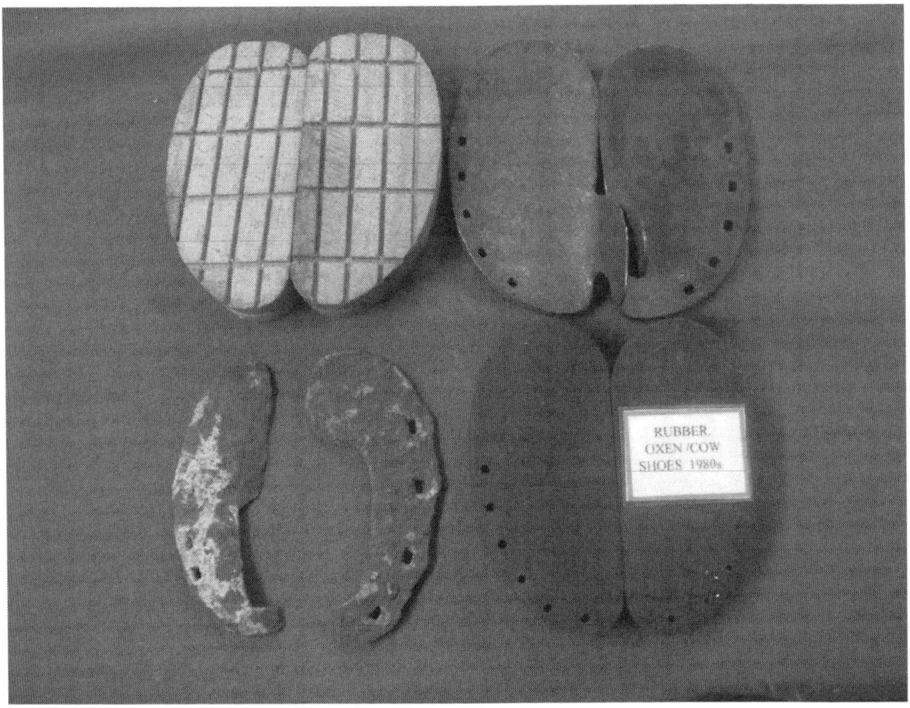
RUBBER
OXEN /COW
SHOES 1980s

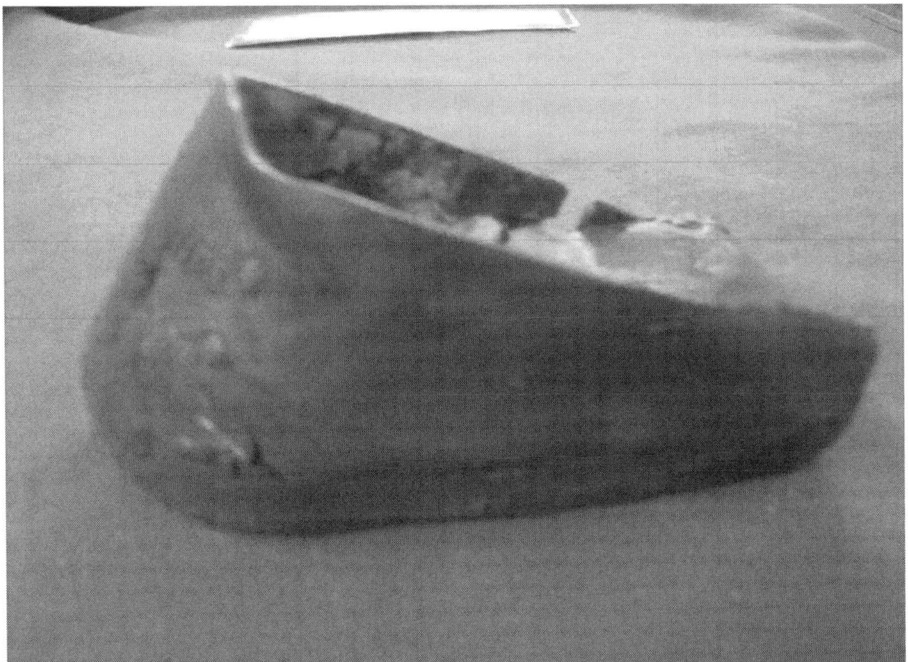

1. Wooden shoes that are stuck on using Tacnovite glue
2. A pair of factory-made shoes from a company in America
3. The ones Frank sent to me
4. Rubber shoes that can be nailed on or glued on
5. One half of the rubber stick-on shoe that encapsulates the hoof

In all my years as a farrier I only ever shod one cow, and that was up in Edale in Derbyshire when I first started up my business. Each individual hoof was shod in very light concave race-plate steel.

1963 Frank Dean FWCF shoeing a Hereford bull that had a hoof problem

1933 Mr. C. Dean AFCL (Frank's dad) outside the Abergavenny Arms in Rommel, Sussex, when the Atora Beef Suet Cart was on an advertising tour around the UK. Mr. Dean shod these bullocks before they moved on

1994 Working cattle fully shod in southern Spain

In 1994 my wife and I were on holiday with David and Judy Gulley in southern Spain. Whilst we were travelling down towards Gibraltar we saw bullocks ploughing a field. David stopped the car and asked the farmhands if he could have a go at driving the bullocks. They did not understand what he wanted until his wife came to the rescue by asking again in French. This time they agreed to let David drive the large animals a few yards. Satisfied with that, he then consented to get back in the car and we carried on our way.

Back to work

As I said, wonderful things had happened over the last few years. I had passed my fellowship exam and entered the livery company. I had been invited onto the examination board, and had been elected to serve a three-year term on the Farriers Registration Council. I was very much involved with running the East Midlands regional section of the National Association of Farriers, Blacksmiths and Agricultural Engineers, a role that was to culminate in the award of a commendation for outstanding services to the association. Now I had to get back to earning an ordinary living and travelling the highways and byways of Derbyshire and Nottinghamshire. But nothing stays ordinary for long in farriery.

"The WCF has given me your phone number"

In 1998 I took a call from a lady at the north side of Rotherham asking if I could take a look at her horse, as her vet had prescribed some remedial shoeing with special shoes and there was no one in her area that would do the work. She had phoned the Worshipful Company of Farriers in London for help and they in turn gave her my phone number as I was the nearest remedial farrier to where she stabled her horses. That was still a long way, and I told her it was too far for me to travel but if she could bring the horse to me then I would do the job the vet had requested. The lady agreed to do just that and arrived at my forge the following morning at 8am. The vet's prescription was for front bar shoes and hind egg-bar shoes. Neal and I completed the job and I asked the lady to bring the horse back in about four to five weeks for a refit.

"I will", she said, "and just before I go can I show you these photographs of a friend's horse?"

It was clear from the photos that the horse had suffered sheared heels. This occurs where the tissues of the digital cushion have been torn on the midline, and when the foot is placed on the ground one side lands first. It is this movement that causes the lameness through the soft tissue. I told the lady that unless this tearing of the tissues is stabilised straight away, then the foot may never heal properly and the animal will require special shoeing for the rest of its life. The treatment is a straight bar shoe to stabilise the heels. It is most important to keep the frog clean and free from grit at all times. The lady listened to what I told her and explained that the horse was a racehorse whose owners lived in Turkey and they would pay for me to go and have a look at their horse. I said "OK, sure I will," thinking she was just spinning me a yarn.

My son had done most of the work on the horse from Rotherham, and that afternoon he called to ask if the racehorse owner had phoned. They had not, but I told my son they had and that they wanted me and his mum and our two friends Stewart and June to go to Turkey for two weeks. Well I tell you he went ape shit on the phone, ranting about how he had shod this horse and it should be him that was going, and so on. After letting him go on like this for a while, I told him that in fact the owner had not phoned, and eventually Neal calmed down. That was on the Monday. Then on Thursday my phone rang and it was a voice speaking in broken English, "Mr. Bradburrry, this is Prince Bashir speaking."

Thinking it was my son trying to wind me up, I said "Oh yes? Give me your number and I will ring you back." Well, the number he gave me was a bloody mile long. Immediately I thought, *Bloody hell, what have I done?* I phoned back and apologised. The caller again said who he was and went on: "You have seen the photos of my horse. When you come and fix? Tomorrow?"

I said that I had a business to run here.

"OK, tell me when."

I said "Monday, and there are two of us" – expecting him to say "Don't bother then."

In fact, he said "OK, no problem. Turkish Airways will ring you ten minutes after I put down this phone."

And they did, asking whether I wished to fly in the morning, afternoon or evening, and would I prefer to have the tickets delivered to my hotel or to pick them up at the desk at Heathrow.

I said that I would like to fly first thing on Monday morning.

"Very good, sir."

When I said to Neal that we were going to Istanbul on Monday morning his reply was, "Piss off, you had me once before and you're not fooling me again."

A Turkish sultan

Earthquake photo

Earthquake news report

Postcard view of Istanbul

Entrance to Istanbul racecourse

Racecourse stables. The stable lads live above. There are no windows and the only water is a cold tap on each corner block

Our visit to the racecourse in Turkey in 1999

When it sank in that I was not joking, Neal went down to the local car boot sale and bought an old briefcase to put our tools in. It cost 50 pence. I then phoned the flight link bus service from Chesterfield to Heathrow and found there was a bus at midnight on the Sunday night arriving at Heathrow at 3am. That was just right as our flight left at 7am. We were told that we were not allowed to take the tools on the plane as hand luggage but they must go below in the hold. All went well until we disembarked at Istanbul. As our briefcase went through the customs hall every bell in the airport went off. There were men standing there with guns pointing at the case and at us. The only words we could understand were "Open now." Imagine trying to explain "Just coming to put some shoes on a racehorse" when you don't know a word of Turkish and are standing in a ring of armed security guards. Neal and I made a noise like a horse, saying "Clip clop" and "HippoDrome" (as that is what they call their racetracks). After about half an hour of this performance they beckoned for us to leave, thank the Lord.

Waiting in the reception hall was a man dressed in Arabic clothes carrying a board showing the words "Master Doug". This man walked as though he had suffered a stroke, dragging one leg and with his right arm across his chest. Nevertheless, he insisted on carrying everything: my case and Neal's too, and the briefcase in his teeth. As we left Istanbul Airport in the man's not-so-new car, there appeared to be thousands of people on the streets. They had hung bed sheets from the trees to get some shade as the temperature was in the top 80s. I said to the driver "Why are all these people in the streets?"

His reply was "No English."

Next question: "What do we call this man we are going to meet?"

"No English."

I thought, *He called me Doug on the phone so it's either Mustafa or Your Highness. I will play this by ear.*

When we arrived at the hotel a princely-looking man appeared in long flowing robes. He touched his forehead, chin and chest and offered me his hand and a kiss on each cheek and the words "Welcome, Doug", so I replied, "Thank you, Mustafa." When he kissed me, Neal muttered "Dad, I am not into that." I said, "Just follow me, you will be all right."

"Doug, do you want a drink?"

I said "No thanks, we have had a meal on the plane. But can you tell me why all the people are in the streets?"

"There was an earthquake this morning at 3am. The provinces affected are Sakarys, Izmit, Istanbul, Yalova, Bolu, Zonguldak, Teckirdag and Eskisehir. Many people are still buried in the rubble and 14,000 people are listed as injured. The number of deaths is expected to surpass 10,000."

"An earthquake? Then we must phone home and let them know we are safe." But all phone lines were dead.

"Not a problem, Doug. Use the phone in my car while we go to the racecourse." He clicked his fingers and a limo appeared. The driver who met us at the airport had to follow behind in the older car.

The racecourse was pristine. I have not seen a place so beautifully set out anywhere in England. There were two courses, one of grass and one of sand, and each was like a snooker table. The stables were set out in a military style to house 500 horses. All were stallions, as they do not race mares and do not castrate.

Jokingly I said to Neal, "You do the shoeing and I will translate." It was now midday and it was very, very hot. The horse was a seven-year-old by the name of Prince Achmed and the problem was just as we thought: sheared heels. Neal shod the animal in bar shoes and then we were driven back to the hotel. As we entered Mustafa clicked his fingers, and at once a large wooden platter of fresh fruit was placed before us. "Help yourselves. It is all fresh this morning." There was every type of fruit you could name. Although these people do not drink alcohol, Mustafa said we could have a beer if we so wished. He went on, "Do you like fish? Tonight, I will take you to dinner at a fish restaurant."

Well I tell you, we had everything barring a whale – they just kept on bringing all types of fish. During the meal Mustafa turned to me, said "Doug, thank you very much" and placed an envelope in my top shirt pocket. Straightaway Neal whispered "Dad, how much?"

I muttered back "Do not be rude. I am going to the toilet to see." There were four one-hundred-dollar bills. We had only done the front feet. Not bad, considering we had also had a first-class flight, a five-star hotel and that was not all. When I sat down again, Mustafa said "Tomorrow I will show you the city and the Blue Mosque."

Back view of Neal walking towards the Blue Mosque, Istanbul 1999

My boot with its three-inch raise

The Blue Mosque was very big and beautiful. A tour of the mosque was also a long way to walk, especially for me because, as I told you a while ago, that accident on my motor bike had left me with a short leg and I had to wear a special boot. Everyone had to take their shoes off at the entrance, so you can imagine how difficult I found it to walk all the way round the mosque. I tell people that it was so bad that tourists started giving me money. I was pleased to reach the end of this tour and stand level again.

As we were leaving on the Wednesday morning, Mustafa said, "You will come back in four to six weeks, will you Doug? Is it possible for you to bring a vet with you next time to look at my other horses and also look at some young stock that are for sale about 100 miles further inland? I will have interpreters on hand for you, and two limousines."

Neal and I had a WCF court dinner to attend in London soon after we got back from Turkey. I looked round the guests and thought, *Who better to look after royal Turkish racehorses than Roger Johnson MR.CVS, a past master of the WCF?*

Roger agreed, and it was arranged for all three of us to go out to Turkey in September. Roger lived in London so we met up at Heathrow for the Monday morning flight, collecting our tickets at the desk as before and returning on the Wednesday. A good time was had by all, including a grand tour of Turkey to look at young racehorses. It involved passing through some military establishments, where we were told not to use cameras at any time. Roger made his veterinary report to Mustafa, then we all had dinner and came back home the following day.

This is the horse we went to shoe: a seven-year-old stallion named Prince Achmed

Second visit – Roger Johnson MR.CVS observing Prince Achmed's progress; Neal looking on with an interpreter

Mustafa hoped to enter his horse Prince Achmed in a very big race in December and wanted to know if it would be possible. I told him the way things were going it might be. After our visit in September I said it would be OK to start training. The next time we heard anything was on New Year's Day when Mustafa phoned asking to speak to me. My wife told him that I had just gone out for a drink. "Please tell Doug that I have won the big race and took the track record. I won 50,000 dollars. Doug will come in January, please, but the horses will be in Adana as it is too cold in Istanbul. He will need to change planes in Istanbul and catch a flight to Adana. I look forward to seeing him."

The flight from Istanbul to Adana, which is in the south-east corner of Turkey on the Syrian border, took another one-and-a-half hours. We took a wrong turn in the airport and finished up with all the locals hustling for taxis and before we knew it we were being ushered into one of them. "Where to?" was all the English that the driver knew. After three circuits of the car park, I realised we were in the wrong car. By this time Neal was panicking. The driver stopped outside the entrance and we shot out and back to the arrivals lounge where Mustafa's chauffeur was waiting for us. He just smiled and took us to the hotel. We were told it was the month of Ramadan. That meant no smoking or drinking from sunrise to sunset. If you were caught, you were put in jail. If you wanted food, you had to buy it as none was provided. We managed fine as we could drink privately in our hotel room.

When we arrived at the racecourse next day, we were asked to take a look at the horse belonging to the owner of the course. This we did, and shod it for him. Whilst Neal was dealing with this horse, the owner said "Would you like a drink of orange?" We would. He told the groom to see to that and anything we wanted. We were each brought a large glass of freshly squeezed oranges. This area is a beautiful place where there are acres upon acres of orange groves and bags upon bags of fresh oranges on the roadside for sale.

Next time Mustafa's horse was ready for racing, he invited me to go and see it run. Neal said he was too busy to go this time so I said I would go on my own as I did not want to let the prince down. The arrangements were as before. I shod the horse in aluminum bar shoes and changed my clothes for the racing. Mustafa took me into the parade ring with him, where I noticed the parade track was made of rubber bricks. This day at the races was a wonderful experience for me. I thought the only danger to the prince's horse was a big English thoroughbred, which was quite a bit bigger than Achmed. I was right. Mustafa's horse finished second, but he was still very pleased.

That night back in town there was trouble and two bombs went off. It had nothing to do with the racing but there was political unrest, and reports blamed the disturbance on the Shi'ites. That made me realise that this was somewhere I did not want to be. I told Mustafa that now his horse was sound again, he should keep it shod in the same way and it should be OK; if not, he could give me a ring. We parted at that.

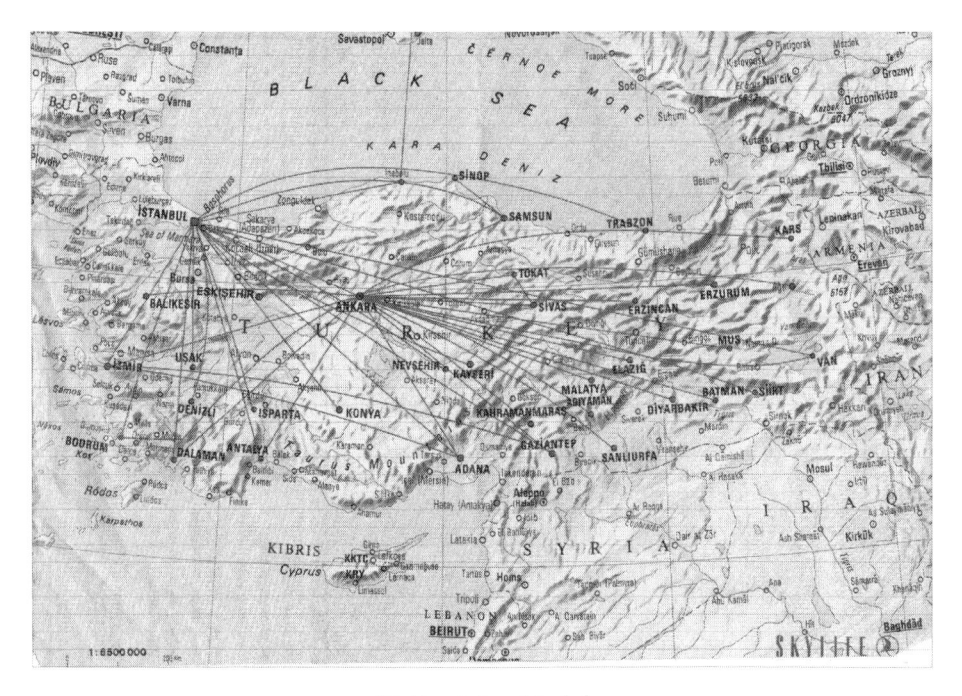

Flight map from Istanbul

My hotel in Adana

The English horse way in front, with Prince Achmed finishing in second place

Roger Johnson, Neal and I at the Blue Mosque, Istanbul

THE EXPRESS. TUESDAY, SEPTEMBER 14, 1999

New quake hits Turkey

AT LEAST seven people were killed yesterday in a new Turkish earthquake. Hundreds were injured and buildings crashed to the ground during the tremor, which measured 5.8 on the Richter scale.

The quake, centred on the city of Izmit, an area already decimated by last month's quake, was felt up to 50 miles away. It came as children returned to school after the earlier disaster.

News of a second quake

The stables in Adana for 500 horses

10

ORTHOPAEDICS AND HONOURS

1986 to 2004: my right leg gets worse

My leg had never fully recovered from the motorcycle accident some 30 years earlier, and pain kept flaring up. My GP referred me back to Chesterfield Royal Hospital, where I saw Mr. G.C. Baker, an orthopaedic surgeon. He suggested a revision of the triple arthrodesis that I had undergone twice already (an operation to fuse together three joints in the foot to form a solid mass). I agreed to this and asked if he would do the operation privately as I needed to get back to my work as soon as possible. Mr. Baker told me to turn up at the Park Hospital at Papplewick near Mansfield on the Friday morning of that week. I left hospital four days later with a plaster cast from my foot to my knee and two steel pins that went through the bone to keep it in line and protruded through the cast. I was told to put no weight on it at all for six weeks. This was the fifth operation on this leg and, like the other four, it did help for a time. But each time the leg became a little shorter.

I was still suffering a lot of discomfort in the leg but I carried on doing my job, until in 1994 the pain became so bad I returned to Chesterfield Hospital. By this time Mr. Baker had left and there was a new man in charge, Mr. A. G. Davies FRCS. Mr. Davies was a consultant orthopaedic surgeon and a very nice man, who tried several things to help but to no avail. On one occasion he asked me if I would attend a conference where he and his colleagues could discuss my case. I said I would be pleased to do so. And when Mr. Davies said there was nothing else he could do for me, I asked him to take my leg off. He said, "Let me refer you to two of my colleagues at the Northern General in Sheffield. One of them is Mr. Tom Smith, a specialist in ankle joints. You may have to wait a while to see him, but he is very good. If he can't help, the next choice is Mr. Datta, a consultant at the rehabilitation limb centre."

My first appointment came and it was for Mr. Datta. He said it would be a pity to take off my leg as it had a very good blood supply, but that I ought to see what Mr. Smith had to say. Two weeks later I saw Mr. Smith, who examined the leg and said he could put in a steel plate to straighten it for me. This came as good news, and I asked if he would do it for me privately. "Yes, come to the Claremont Hospital in Sheffield next Friday. Do not have anything to eat from midnight on the Thursday as I will do the operation first thing on the Friday morning." What a difference when you are paying for your healthcare.

At that time, the Claremont was a private hospital run by nuns. When I came round from the anaesthetic my leg looked unbelievably straight. The doctor said I could go home on

Sunday. When he arrived on the Sunday morning for the final check, I still had a rubber drain coming from the top of the plaster cast. While I was busy talking to the doctor, I did not see him grab the drain and pull it straight out. I yelled "F…… hell!" forgetting I had a nun standing by my side. That outburst must have ruined my chances of going to heaven.

Appointment letter

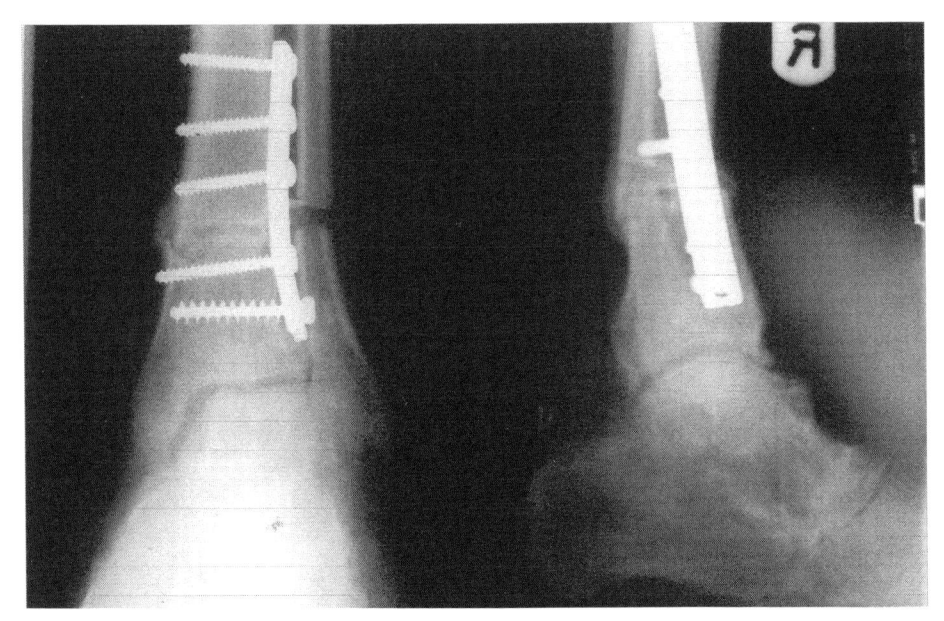

The medial and lateral x-ray of my right leg after Mr. Smith had broken my leg and removed a small wedge of bone and then fitted a steel plate. The area below the plate once consisted of many small bones but they were fused together in the previous operations and now it is just one mass of bone.

I was on crutches for several weeks. When I returned to the clinic to have the cast taken off, a male nurse cut down one side of the cast, pulled it partway open and forced my leg out. At this point I passed out and everybody started to run around. Mr. Smith was still bollocking the man when I came to. On all previous occasions when a cast had been removed, it had been cut down both sides and I can't think why this nurse did it differently.

My leg was not as good as it looked and I had difficulty in walking on it for two years. Mr. Smith said it would have been better to have put in a new ankle joint. I said, "Well why did you not do that?" He replied that it would have cost me over £10,000. I said I would have found the money from somewhere sooner than have to go through more operations. Mr. Smith said he had only done ten ankle joints, but would put me on the NHS list.

Time for a new ankle joint, 1997

My appointment arrived, and I was to go into the Huntsman Ward in the Northern General Hospital, Sheffield. After the operation I only stayed in hospital for about four days. The second day I was told to stand up and take a bit of weight on the leg and increase this every day. After a few weeks all seemed well and I went back to work. The pain eased off to a bearable level though it was not gone completely. On the next page is a diagram of what was done to my ankle. The part shaded in red is the new metal joint they put in place. This new joint worked well for a couple of years but then began to slip to one side and the pain started again.

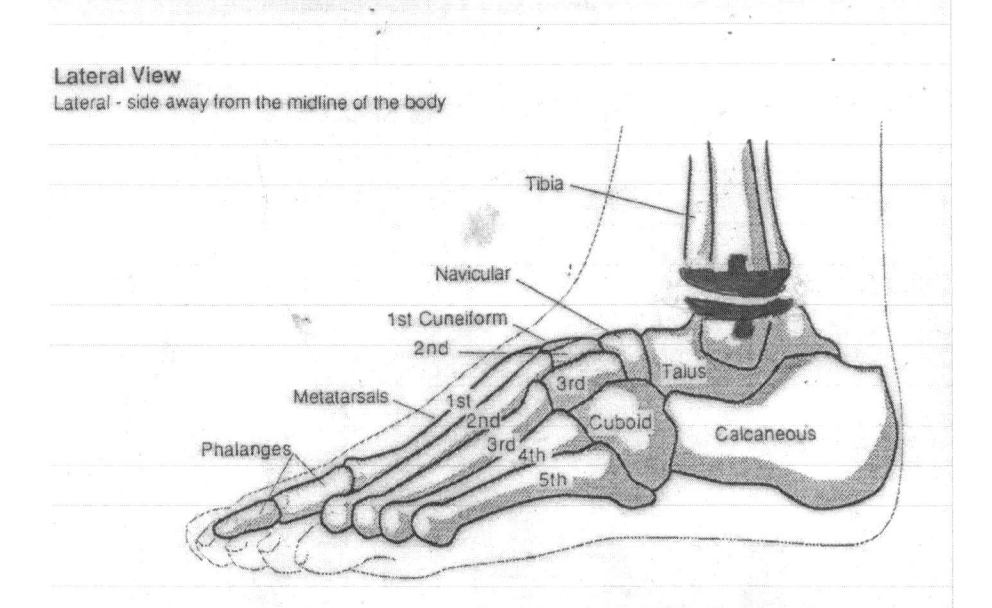

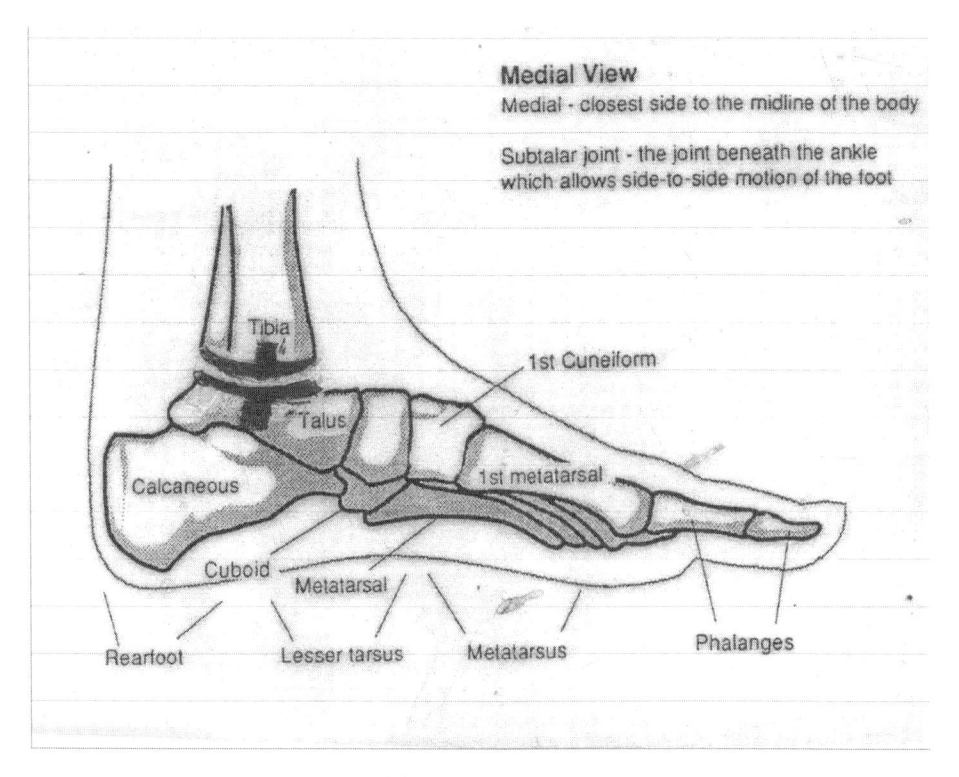

Lateral View
Lateral - side away from the midline of the body

Diagram of ankle joint

Medial View
Medial - closest side to the midline of the body

Subtalar joint - the joint beneath the ankle which allows side-to-side motion of the foot

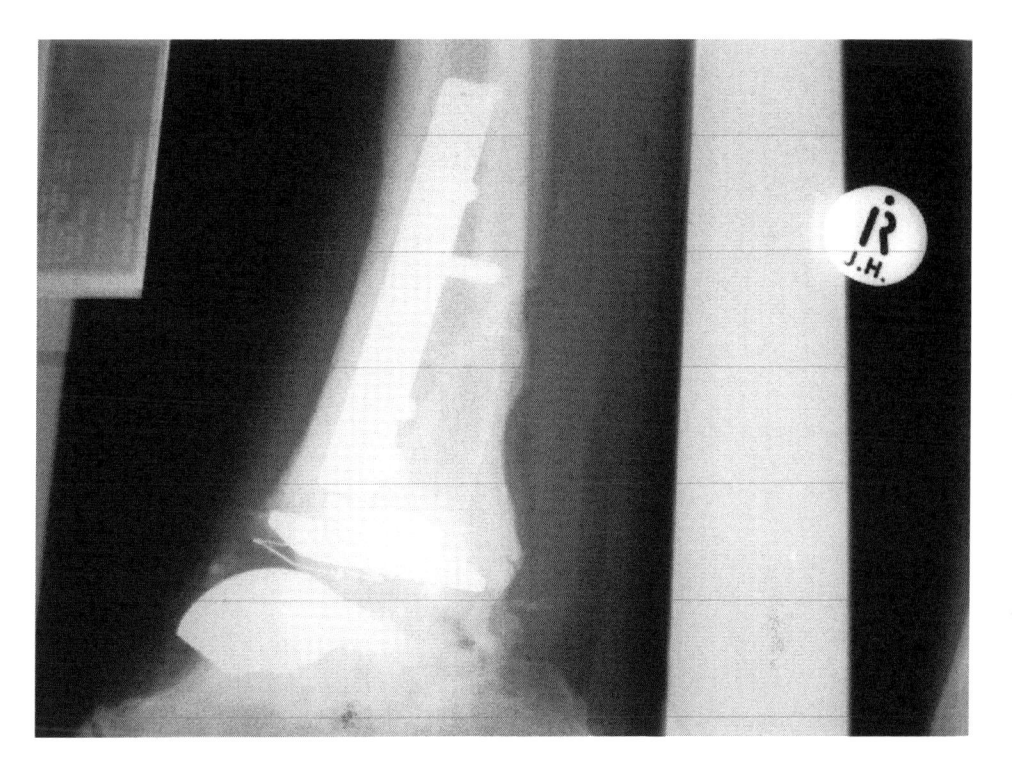

Medial and lateral x-ray of the new ankle joint in August 2001. It shows the bottom half has moved out of its position. I could feel it clearly

I went back to see Mr. Smith in 2002. This time he said the only option was to remove the ankle joint, put a steel rod from my heel up through the foot into my leg and fuse the complete area. This to me sounded horrific, but when you are in as much pain as I was you will try anything. So in 2004 I returned to the Huntsman Ward at the Northern General. At 7.30am on the morning of the operation a young lady doctor called Lois McGarth came to check if I was all right and if there was anything I wanted to ask her, as she would be assisting Mr. Smith that morning.

"Yes, there is. Can you tell me why surgeons never listen to their patients? I have asked them to remove the leg as this is now the ninth operation on it and I am still in pain."

"Well, I am listening to you," she said. "Would you like me

to cancel the operation for you and have a talk about it?"

This caught me by surprise. I told her that my wife and I always discuss things together first.

Dr. McGarth said "OK, have it done and then we will have a talk." And she kept her word. She came to see me the day after, and said "You have bloody hard bones, Douglas. The joint flew across the floor and just missed hitting Mr. Smith."

You can see the screws in the bone quite clearly from the x-ray. It did not show much change over the next few days, but after a week I was sent home from hospital. After another week the wound had still not healed and was seeping. The nurses at the outpatients' clinic had a look and called the doctors, but they told me to go home and let the district nurse do the dressings. I had been home for several days before the nurse came to change the dressing. By then I was feeling quite ill, and at lunchtime my wife and daughter-in-law took me back to the Northern General. I was admitted, treated with antibiotics intravenously and kept in for over a week. When they allowed me home the wound was still seeping a bit and not completely healed. The orthopaedic clinic prescribed me an array of different tablets: a selection of antibiotics, anti-inflammatories and painkillers totalling over twenty a day. The idea was to try and stabilise the infection in that area and stop it spreading further up my leg.

A week or two later my wife had to call out our local emergency doctor. He had a look at my leg and said it did not look good but I should try some different tablets. These seemed to work and all was well for about a month. Then my temperature went high and we noticed that the wound showed signs of redness around the area of the incision. My wife and our daughter-in-law did not mess about – they took me straight back to the Northern General. Dr. McGarth was not in work that day and I was seen by a young doctor who took one look and said, "Stay there, I will ask my boss to see you." This was Mr. Blundell, an orthopaedic surgeon. He showed great interest in my case and asked me to start at the beginning and tell him just what had happened over the years. He then said it was not good news, and he would recommend amputation. He consulted Mr. Smith, who did not agree with him and said the wound would heal. I had a further week on antibiotics before coming home.

When I saw Dr. McGarth the following week, she told me she was leaving the department to work with another surgeon, Mr. Getty, as part of her training, but she would refer me to her husband Dr. Simon Royston, who was a premier trauma surgeon, and would ask him to send me an appointment a.s.a.p. We heard nothing for a couple of weeks, so my wife phoned to find out why. This time we were told to go to Dr. Royston's clinic, and when we got there it was, "Sit down and wait, and the doctor will see you as soon as possible." All this time I was on crutches and in pain, so I was not in the most cheerful of moods. However, when he called me in, there was no white coat and no looking down at people from on high. His first words were, "Welcome to the basement. You can think of this hospital as a funnel. I get the patients that the ones in the white coats do not want so they fall to me at the bottom of the chute." He asked if I minded a young student doctor sitting in as he was learning the job. I had no objection to that.

Simon said he had looked at my case notes and could offer three choices. "The first one will kill you. The second is to take out two or three inches of the infected bone and after a year put the leg in a cage under tension and try to stretch the bone. But you are not an 18-year-old, are you? And the third is to put it in the bin."

I said I was ready to put it in the bin.

Simon said "You have made the right decision. The next question is, when do you want it done?"

I said as soon as possible please.

"Yes, they all say that. Go and see my secretary for a date. It is probably the best offer she will get today."

Simon's secretary told me I would need a pre-op assessment, which would take place the following Tuesday, and my operation would be done the week after. I would go straight to the trauma theatre at 7.30am and would be the first on the list because of being diabetic. The time passed very quickly and the day came for me to report to the trauma theatre.

Doug becomes legless

My wife and I set off at 6.15am, headed for junction 29 of the M1, found it closed and got diverted to junction 30 instead. At the hospital I was shown into a cubicle to get undressed and was told to wait in a room with four other patients and the doctor would be along shortly to see me. Joan left me to it with a kiss and "See you later." The nurse told her where she could get some coffee and said I would be back on the ward about 2pm, when she would be able to go and see me.

When I came round from the anaesthetic I could see my lower leg was no longer there and the stump was in a plaster-of-paris cast. I had a morphine pump in my hand for the pain and I was quite comfortable. The cast on my stump was to stop my leg contracting backwards. The only problem was a great deal of itching under the plaster and I asked Joan to bring me a knitting needle so that I could have a scratch. When the surgeon came round, I told him about the itching and he asked the nurse to have the cast removed and then call him. There was a mass of water blisters on the stump, apparently because I turned out to be allergic to the bright pink antiseptic wash they were using. Simon said, "I am deeply sorry for that, but it won't be a problem." The nurse took me to the shower and washed off as much as she could. At the first sight of my stump I thought, *Bloody hell – that stitching looks rough*. In fact, it looked like a mail bag, and I wondered if it would ever go right. That night I started to get phantom pains and the nurse gave me an amitriptyline tablet. Well, I tell you, after the first one I did not want any more of those. They gave me hallucinations. Since then I have been very lucky and only suffered the odd phantom pain now and then.

I had this operation on 9th September and vowed to the doctors that I would be walking by Christmas. I was in hospital for a week. Before I was discharged, two nurses brought me on a home visit by taxi to see if I was going to be able to manage around the house. They discussed with Joan what would need to be done before I could come home, such as having ramps fitted and the top of the stairs filled in. All of these jobs were done – at my own expense – thanks to my friend Mick Nightingale.

My main problem was going upstairs on my bottom backwards. When the lady from social services called to see how I was doing, I told her this and asked if I might be eligible to get a stair lift. She said, "Sorry, no, as the problem is not permanent."

I said, "I can assure you that the leg will not grow again."

She offered me a seat for the bath – a piece of wood that fitted across it. But she didn't notice that ours was a corner bath, and when the seat arrived it was useless. So, she came back and said the only thing possible was an electric bath lift, and she would ask someone to bring one for me to try. I might add that was the one and only thing I received from these people. I bought my own stair lift. Joan made up a bed downstairs for me, which did help a lot.

I had been home for a week when the district nurse came to change my dressings. When she removed the old dressing, she looked surprised and said "I did not expect this. I shall have to call the senior nurse, if you do not mind." This lady came, and turned out to be our friend Maddy, whom we knew well as I had shod her horses for years. Maddy took one look and said "I am calling the doctor. This does not look right." She placed a dry dressing over the stitches, but there were still a few water blisters left and patches of pink from the operation.

The local GP, Dr. Jackson, never moved the dressing to see the stitched area but noted the pinkness and the blisters and said "That is just cellulitis. It will clear up. Take these tablets and come and see me in a few days" time." Off he went. After he had gone, Maddy said "I do not like the look of that. If it were my husband, I would take him back to the hospital. But it is not my job to go against the doctor's advice, and I have not said what I have just said, right? It is up to you, Mrs. Bradbury."

Joan managed to get me in the car and back to the Northern General. I was admitted without delay, put straight on intravenous antibiotics and booked in for the operating theatre the following morning. Here the surgeons opened the stump up and washed it out, and told me afterwards it should now be OK. I spent yet another week in the hospital.

After that, things began to pick up, though there were still times when the going got tough. I attended the Chesterfield Royal for physiotherapy, and the Sheffield Artificial Limb and Appliance Centre made my prosthetic leg, and I must say what a wonderful job they did for me. Nothing was too much to trouble for them, no matter how big or small the problem.

By now it was December and I was doing well. One Sunday my daughter told me our grandson was to play for his football team that morning, and I decided to get my crutches out and go to watch. At the sports ground we discovered we had to cross three fields to get to the match. It was a good day out, but when I got home and took off my leg I discovered the friction on the stump had rubbed it until it bled, and the blood had soaked through three layers of the white socks you have to wear. No panic? I phoned the limb centre in Sheffield and was told to come in straight away. I expected a bollocking from the nurse on duty when I told her what I had been doing, but she was remarkably nice about it.

I was walking again before Christmas as I had said I would, and from then on everything got better and better. The consultant Simon Royston had made such a good job that I was even able to return to work. I had no more pain, which meant I could start to enjoy my life for the first time for many years. I must have become easier to live with too, as I could do just about all I wanted. In fact, there were things I could do without the leg that I could not do before I lost it.

A very special day: 23rd September 2010

On 23rd September 2010, the Worshipful Company of Farriers held an installation ceremony for their new master at the Vintners' Hall, Upper Thames Street, London EC4. Installing a new master is always a special day for the WCF, but this time it was also very special for the Bradbury family.

The WCF does not have its own hall in the city but hires different halls for its court meetings, dinners and lunches. On this occasion it chose the Vintners' Hall.

A historical note on the Vintners' Company

The Vintners' Company received its first charter in 1364 and is one of the twelve great livery companies of the City of London. It is ruled by a master, three wardens, and a court of assistants. It has employed a beadle since 1437 and a clerk since 1537, and about a third of the members belong to the wine trade.

A mediaeval tradition still upheld by the Vintners' Company, along with the Crown and the Worshipful Company of Dyers, is to own swans on the Thames. The Vintners were first paid to look after swans during the frost of 1509, and still hold a 'swan upping' week every July when the swans are counted and ringed. (Ringing replaced the nicking of beaks in 1997 – before then the Vintners' swans got two nicks in the beak, the Dyers' swans one nick and the royal swans went unmarked.) Organising the swan upping is the duty

Front entrance of Vintners' Hall, 68½ Upper Thames Street, London EC4

Rear view from Southwark Bridge

of the Vintners' junior warden and swan master. The company also holds a swan feast every November, though they have given up roasting swans for the occasion. The toast at Vintners' banquets is always "The Vintners' Company, may it flourish root and branch for ever with Five and the Master" – referring to the five kings of England, Scotland, France, Denmark and Cyprus, who were feasted by the wine trader Henry Picard in 1363 and are also commemorated in the adjoining Five Kings House. A notable swan feast in 1964 celebrated the 600th anniversary of the first charter in the presence of the Duke and Duchess of Gloucester, Prince Bernard of the Netherlands, the Princess Royal and Princess Alice, Countess of Athlone.

The site of the Vintners' Hall was vested by the will of Guy Shuldham in 1446. The hall was burnt down in the Great Fire of London but was rebuilt almost immediately and back in use by 1671. Its façade and entrance have been redesigned more than once, the present structure dating from 1910. The courtroom is one of the oldest chambers in London and contains carvings that date back to the refurbishment of the hall after the Great Fire, along with many fine pieces of furniture and a marquetry case clock given by the master John Canon in 1704. The master's chair was first mentioned in the archives in 1880 but may date to 1772/3. In this room hangs a fine painting of St Martin dividing his cloak with a beggar, which is attributed to Van Dyck or possibly Rubens. There are also portraits of Charles I; Charles II; Queen Mary II; Queen Anne's consort Prince George of Denmark; Robert Shaw, who was master in 1636; and Sir Thomas Rawlinson, who became master in 1687 and Lord Mayor in 1705.

The courtroom, one of the oldest rooms in the City of London

So, the Worshipful Company of Farriers had chosen a venerable site for a remarkable double event: the installation of Major Jeremy Fern TD DL as its new master, and a presentation to not one but three members of the Bradbury family.

The installation ceremony started with Common Hall, where the master from the previous year, Reg Howe, handed over the chain of office. The new master was sworn in and in his speech outlined his plans for the coming year before inviting questions from members of the livery. Then we all made our way in procession, led by a senior liveryman carrying the livery banner of a black-and-white flag with a horseshoe design, to the church of St Mary Aldermary in Watling Street. Following a short service and thanksgiving, it was back to the Vintners'

Hall, where 120 livery members and their guests sat down to dine in one of the splendid chambers of this ancient building.

What made it a particularly special day for our family was having three generations of Bradbury farriers there at once. I had previously received a silver medal from the WCF for outstanding services to the profession of farriery. Now my son and I were each to receive a master farrier's medal and certificate, an honour awarded only to farriers who had passed the higher examinations of the WCF to achieve associateship or fellowship. The mark of master farrier has been legally registered with the Company so that only those who hold it are allowed to use the term master and show the WCF coat of arms on their stationery. The main reason for legal registration is to uphold standards within the profession. It was brought in because the WCF was aware that too many young entrants who had just come out of their apprenticeship were travelling around the country calling themselves master farriers, remedial and therapeutic specialists, equinologists or the like. The Company was concerned that horse-owners were being misled by inexperienced farriers exaggerating their credentials.

I should have collected my medal on 24th June 2010, the date written on my certificate, but I had to cancel that occasion as I was in hospital having a new knee replacement. So, I was invited back for 23rd September, the same date as my son was due to receive his own award as master farrier. But not only that – my grandson Thomas was called forward to be sworn into the Worshipful Company of Farriers as a bonded apprentice to his father. This was indeed a rare occasion and I could not remember any farriers having done this for their apprentices in all my time as a liveryman. There have been young people sworn in, but to the livery rather than as apprentice farriers.

My son and I, along with five young men from Yorkshire, entered the court to receive our medals. After the presentation, the master expressed a wish to the court that I be allowed to remain in the room to witness the swearing of the following ancient oath, which dates back to 1356, by my grandson and son:

"I Thomas Ross Bradbury do sincerely declare that I will be good and true to our sovereign lady the Queen's Majesty that now is and to her lawful successors. I will be obedient to my livery master in all matters lawful and reasonable according my indenture, and will behave myself well and honestly during my term of apprenticeship."

This binding ceremony was carried out by master of the WCF Reg Howe and was one of the last duties he performed before mastership for the ensuing year passed in full to the new master, Jeremy Fern. This was most certainly a great day for our family and for the Worshipful Company too, a day that I am sure we shall all remember.

The room where we all had dinner 23rd September 2010

The master of the Worshipful Company of Farriers presenting Doug with his master's medal and certificate 23rd September 2010. My medal was no. 2; Neal's was no. 8

Three generations – Doug, Neal and Thomas. Tom was sworn in as a WCF apprentice on the same day.

At the Court meeting on September 24th, the Master was delighted to present certificates and silver medals to the following new Master Farriers:- **Mac Head, Sam Beeley, Doug Bradbury, Neal Bradbury, Stephen Hewitt, Craig McNeil and Chris Pedley.**

A line-up of master farriers

The Worshipful Company of Farriers

First established as a Fellowship by the Court of Mayor & Aldermen 1356
Incorporated by Charter of King Charles II 1674
Supplemental Charter granted by H.M. Queen Elizabeth II 1983

This is to Certify that

Douglas Bradbury

of   40 Thanet Street Clay Cross CHESTERFIELD

having passed one of the Company Higher Examinations, and met all of the requirements to use the Registered Mark was this day invested by the Court of

The Worshipful Company of Farriers

as a

Master Farrier

Dated the Twenty-fourth day of June 2010

The Seal of the Company was affixed Number *0002*
in the Presence of

Master _Reg Horne_

Chairman _James ____ F.W.C.F_
Examinations Board

Registrar _____

Douglas's certificate

And next...

One day in 2016 my grandson Tom was shoeing a horse for a couple called Lesley and Denis Orange. Mrs. Orange asked Tom if he happened to be related to a farrier called Doug Bradbury.

"I am. He's my grandad."

"Well, bless me. Your grandad used to shoe my horses over 30 years ago when my mother kept the post office in Riddings. After that I went to live in Canada. There I found people who could nail shoes onto a horse but didn't forge the shoes themselves as they were all factory made. The problem was, the factory shoes were never big enough for my horse. So I asked my mother to ask your grandad if he would make my horse some shoes, which Mum would then post out to Canada." She went on: "Thomas, it's time something was done for your grandad in recognition of all the young men he has trained and all the things he has done for farriery over the years, including making his museum. I wish I knew how to go about doing something for him. Any ideas? Or do you know anyone else that could help? Denis and I would support them in any way we could."

That night Tom told his dad what the lady had said. Neal could not think of anyone relevant, but had the sense to ask me discreetly if I knew an adviser who could help him with a legal matter. I didn't ask why and didn't want to, but suggested he get in touch with two dear friends of ours, Norman and Edwena Bird. Both were trained in legal matters and Edwena had been a JP for over 25 years.

That was all I heard of the matter until almost two years later, when I was 80. One morning in November 2017, a large brown envelope fell onto the doormat. It was marked "OHMS CABINET OFFICE – URGENT PERSONAL".

I thought "What the bloody hell is this? Surely not a tax demand at my age?"

The letter started "IN CONFIDENCE". I could not believe what I was reading.

> Dear Sir
>
> The Prime Minister has asked me to inform you in strict confidence that, having accepted the advice of the head of the Civil Service and the Main Honours Committee, she proposes to submit your name to the Queen. She is recommending that Her Majesty may be graciously pleased to approve that you be appointed a Member of the Most Excellent Order of the British Empire (MBE) in the New Year's Honours List.

It went on to say that if I accepted, there would be no further communication from the Cabinet Office but my name would be included in the list published in the London Gazette on 30th December 2017. The investiture would be at Buckingham Palace or St James Palace and recipients would be called forward within seven months.

Can you imagine trying to keep that news to myself until New Year's Day?

After a week of feeling shell-shocked, I got to thinking how it could have come about. I wondered if Edwena Bird might be able to give me a clue. When Edwena heard my voice on the phone, she gave a shout of laughter. "Congratulations! I knew you were being awarded something, as they phoned me three weeks ago to ask if you were still alive. But they didn't tell me it was going to be the MBE. I am so pleased for you and Joan. Get ready for a great day out. It will cost you an arm and a leg."

I thought, *Bloody hell, I only have one leg as it is. What else can they take off me?*

The *London Gazette* carried this notice under the list of those being awarded the MBE: "Douglas Bradbury, Master Farrier and Fellow of the Worshipful Company of Farriers. For services to the farriery profession and the community in the East Midlands."

After that announcement, letters of congratulation started to arrive. The first was from HRH the Princess Royal, past master of the Worshipful Company of Farriers, London: "Her Royal Highness is pleased to hear that you have been appointed a Member of the Most Excellent Order of the British Empire. Her Royal Highness considers your award well deserved recognition of your outstanding services to the farriery profession and the community in the East Midlands, and sends you her warm congratulations." Next came two marked 'House of Commons': one from the Rt Hon Michael Gove MP, Department for Environment, Food and Rural Affairs; and the other from our local MP Mr. Lee Rowley. And one from HM Lord Lieutenant of Derbyshire, William Tucker. From the WCF came letters signed by the clerk Mrs. Charlotte Clifford BA; the master for 2017/18 Brigadier Neill O'Connor; the assistant registrar for higher examinations Captain D.C. Goodall RN Retd; and one from a very dear friend of mine and a senior past master, Denis Oliver MR.CVS, who used to attend the college examination panels with me (and who sadly passed away in June 2018 aged 98). There were also hundreds of messages of congratulation on Facebook, all gratefully received. Now I just had to wait to be summoned to the palace.

I have to tell you I was having some health worries. I had been diagnosed with blood cancer in 2015, something for which there is ultimately no cure although the symptoms can be treated. The treatment left me in considerable pain in my lower back and pelvic area, so that I had trouble walking or standing and often had to use a wheelchair. I was also having trouble with my false leg. However, my invitation came through for 9th May 2018 at Buckingham Palace, and I told myself and everyone else that I was going to stand before the Queen at all costs. My pain consultant was a nice young lady called Dr. Smith, who understood where I was coming from. She arranged a spinal injection for me in January, which helped a little though not as well as I had hoped, and referred me on to a senior pain management specialist called Dr. Murray.

All the doctors and nurses made a huge effort to get me to the palace. The staff at the limb centre adjusted my prosthetic leg, and the orthotics team made me a support belt by order of Dr. Murray. Dr. Murray himself said he ought not to do what he was about to suggest, but he was willing to go ahead as it was such a special occasion and he could see how determined I was. So, he gave me two further injections in my spine. The whole team came together to get me to Buckingham Palace for my special day, and I thank you all.

9th May 2018

I was allowed to bring three guests: Joan, Gale and Neal. At first, we were told two only, and Gale said she would stand down and let her brother go, as he was the farrier now that I had retired. I said leaving her behind would be unthinkable, and I would not go myself if my daughter could not come too. In the end the palace officials agreed there would be room for us all, as several other guests had had to withdraw.

As there were four of us we decided to take a taxi all the way. We left Thanet Street at 4.30am, picking up Gale from her home on the way to the M1, and arrived at Buckingham Palace at 9.30am. The gates opened at 9.45am precisely, and after the guards had completed a thorough search of the taxi and ourselves we were allowed into the courtyard. In fact we were permitted to drive right up to the steps as I had been sent a disabled sticker on account of having to bring my wheelchair. Here a young man was waiting with a palace wheelchair. Neal and I rode up on the lift with him while Joan and Gale walked up the steps. The ladies were led into the ballroom where the presentation was to take place, and took their seats on chairs set out down the centre of the hall. Joan and Gale were three rows back on the left of the aisle. With Neal by my side, the attendant wheeled me into an adjoining picture gallery to line up with the other recipients. We were told that HRH the Princess Royal would be presenting the medals that day. The thought of meeting the Princess again was welcome news to me. She had been master of the WCF in 1984/85 and I had met her on various occasions. I instantly relaxed and felt able to look around and appreciate the rich and beautiful surroundings of the gallery.

The marshal gave us our instructions. Ladies had to curtsey "like this" before walking forward to greet the Princess Royal. Men must bow their head. We had to wait until spoken to, and then address the Princess as "Your Royal Highness". We were summoned into the ballroom in groups. My wife Joan said that as soon as my name was called, the Princess looked across and smiled.

I stood up out of my wheelchair and walked from the entrance on the left of the hall to where the Princess Royal waited on the centre step. Her first words to me were "Hello, haven't you retired yet?"

"Not yet, Your Royal Highness."

"What a wonderful achievement. Do you still attend the livery functions?"

"Yes, ma'am."

"That is wonderful. And how is your museum doing?"

"It is doing fine, thank you. I have members of the King's Troop of the Royal Horse Artillery coming to see it soon."

"Just what you always wanted." And after a little more banter she offered me her hand. I bowed, turned and walked with my stick across the red carpet to the exit on the right, where Neal was waiting with my wheelchair. A member of the royal household escorted us outside to wait for the other guests. Crossing the ballroom was the furthest I had walked for a long time, and I only just made it, but I want to thank all the doctors, nurses and technicians who helped me achieve this feat.

On the night of Saturday 12th May we held a dinner party at Bateman's Mill Hotel with some 26 friends to round off the celebrations. That night we had stars in our eyes.

Douglas' MBE medal

Presentation in the ballroom: Doug faces HRH the Princess Royal. Joan and Gale are three rows back on the left.

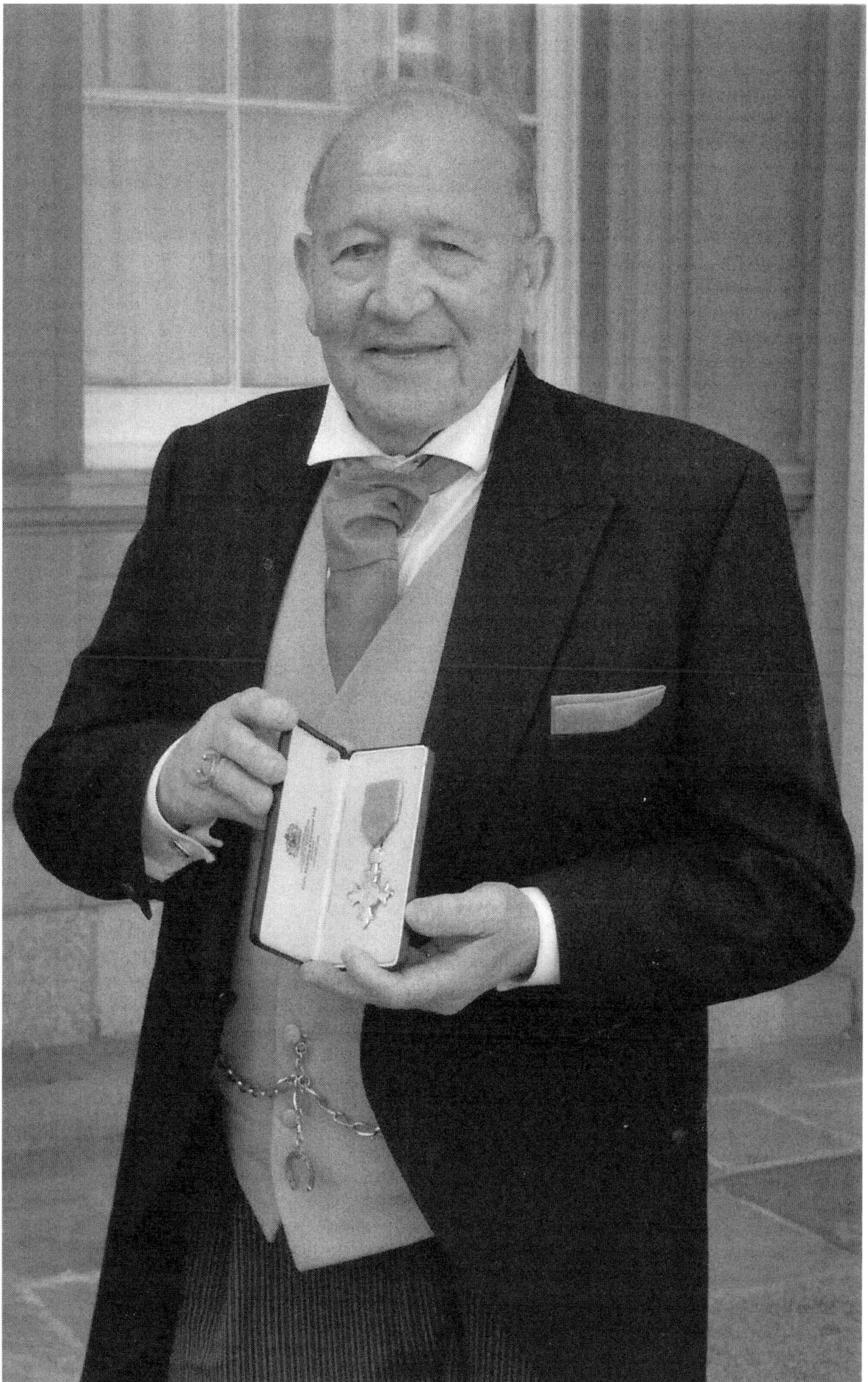

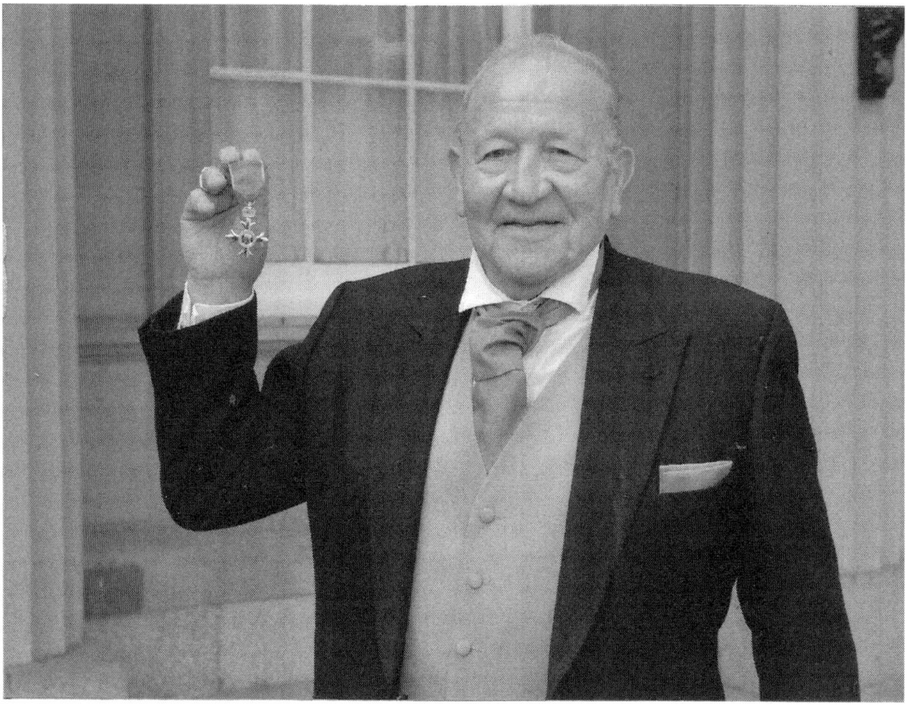

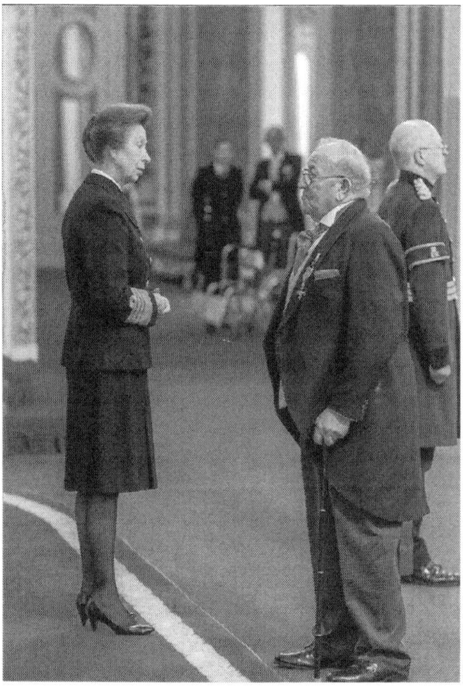

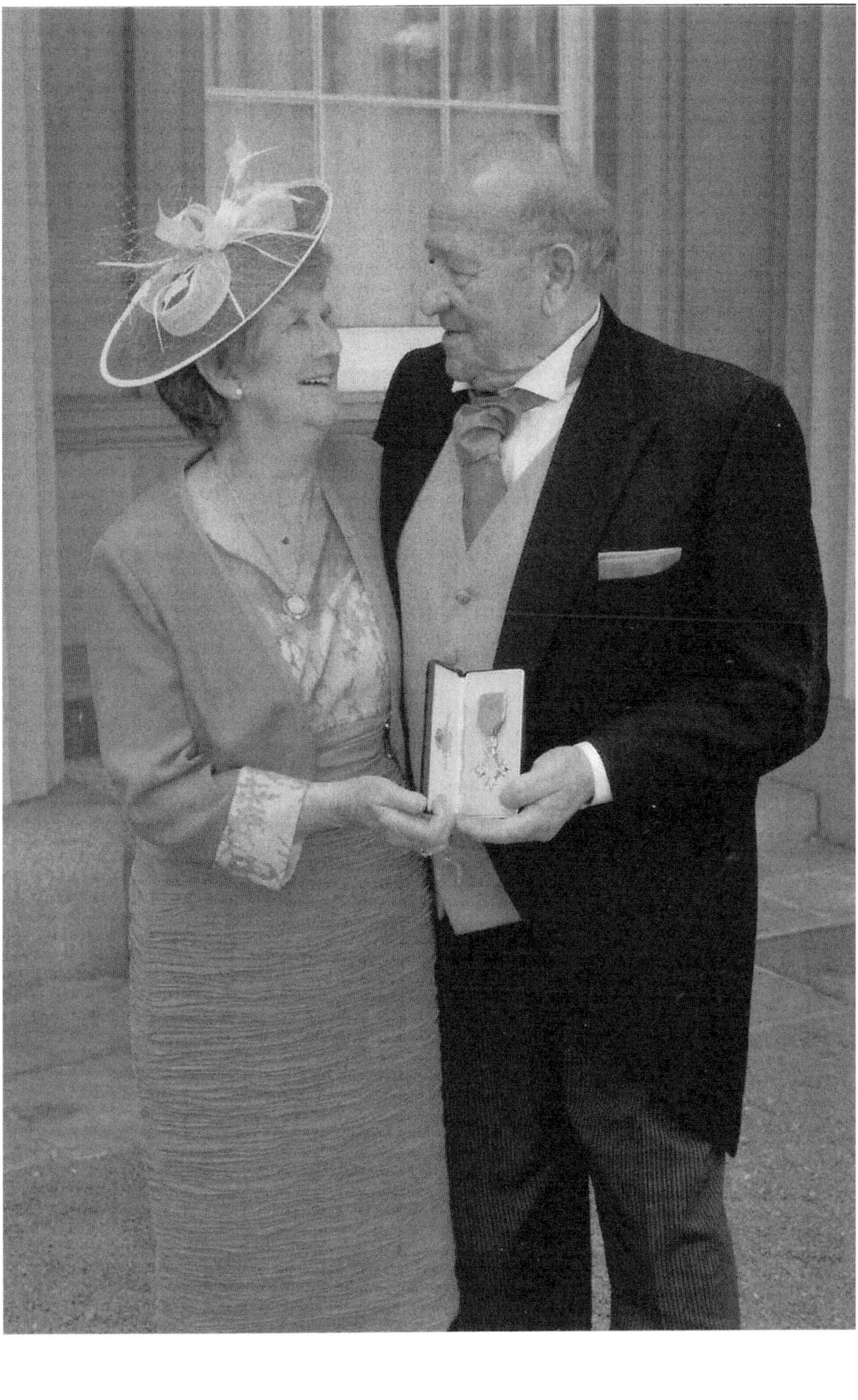

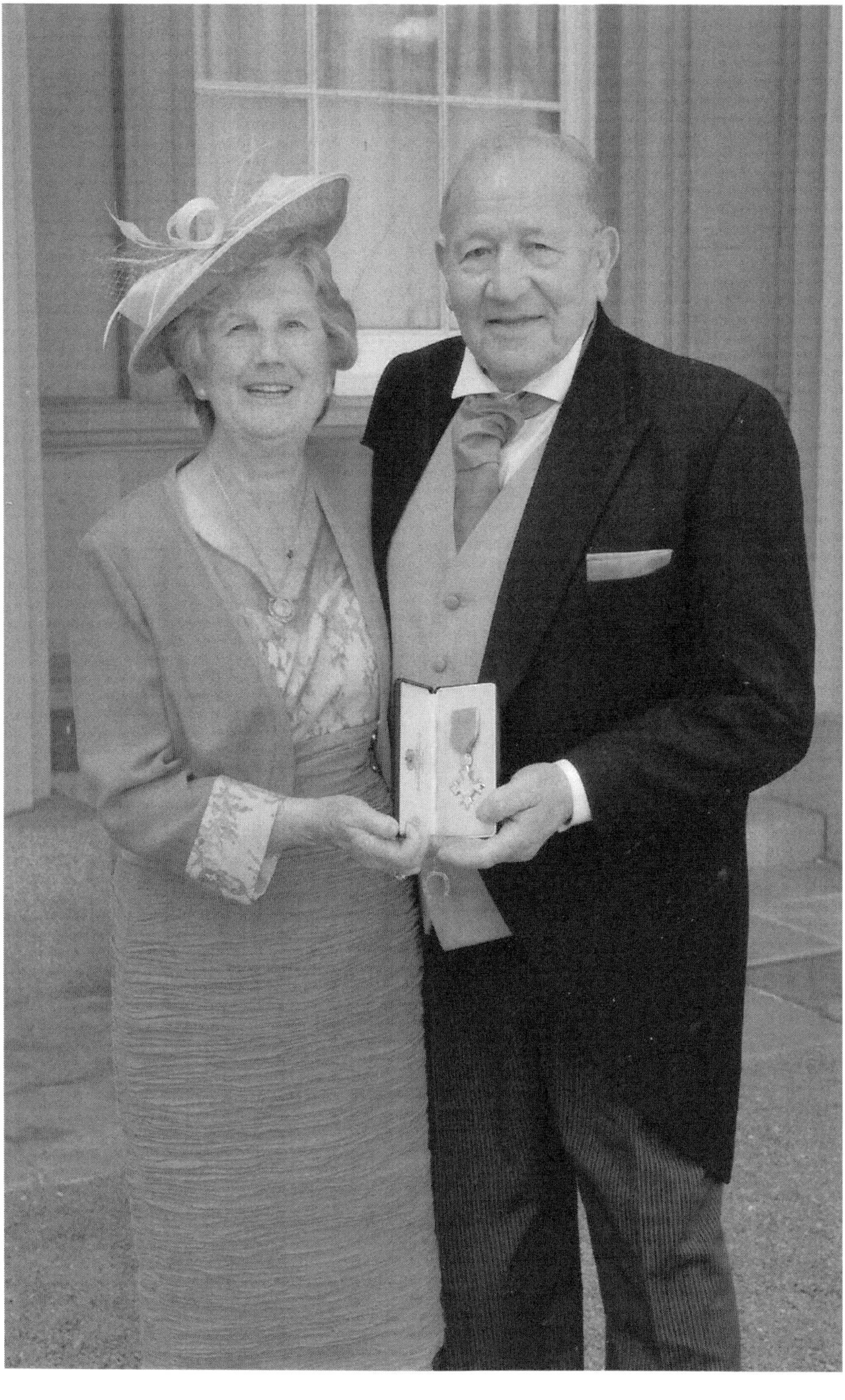

EPILOGUE

Doug finished writing his autobiography in 2019. As you have read, he was suffering with blood cancer. There must have been dark days, especially during this illness, when laughter did not come easily and he relied heavily on Joan and all his family to help him through. It took a combination of his final illness and Covid 19 to topple this "mighty man". He lost his final battle on 30th March 2020.

Doug's hammer and anvil are silent now, but it is Longfellow's words, echoing from another forge, that seem the appropriate ones to say farewell:

> "Thanks, thanks to thee, my worthy friend,
> For the lesson thou hast taught!
> Thus, at the flaming forge of life
> Our fortunes must be wrought."

E.B.
June 2020.

Printed in Great Britain
by Amazon